A Student Guide to **Play Analysis**

A Student Guide to
Play Analysis

David Rush

Southern Illinois University Press / Carbondale

Library of Congress Cataloging-in-Publication Data
Rush, David, 1940–
    A student guide to play analysis / David Rush.
        p. cm.
    Includes index.
    1. Drama—Explication. I. Title.
    PN1707.R77 2005
    808.2—dc22
    ISBN 0-8093-2608-6 (cloth : alk. paper)
    ISBN 0-8093-2609-4 (pbk. : alk. paper)
                                         2004029602

Printed on recycled paper. ♻

The paper used in this publication meets the minimum
requirements of American National Standard for
Information Sciences—Permanence of Paper for
Printed Library Materials, ANSI Z39.48-1992. ∞

To Wayne

Contents

Preface

This text has been developed from teaching play analysis in a variety of colleges and universities for more than twenty years. During that time, I experimented with different teaching techniques, approaches to dramaturgy, critical theories, and plays. The material in this book distills what seems to have proven most effective in the classroom.

The approach I take is predicated on the assumption that what students most welcome is an easy-to-understand and thorough set of definitions that they themselves can apply to any play in question and come up with their own conclusions. It would have often been easier for me to tell my students what, say, *Major Barbara* is all about or why *Death of a Salesman* is partly a realistic play and partly an expressionistic one; but whenever I did, I found my own opinions being fed back to me on quizzes, class discussions, or final exams. I learned that offering students a set of "tools" and allowing them to use those tools to build their own opinions was much more effective. It was more fun for them and more challenging for me.

Thus, each chapter of this book falls into two parts. First, there is a set of working definitions of relevant critical components of play analysis, and then, a set of questions that seek to apply those definitions to the play you are studying in class. The real learning comes in working with the questions—where students develop their own responses and interpretations based upon their respective answers. I stress over and over again that there are no right or wrong answers in play analysis—only well-formed opinions. The questions lead to the development of those opinions.

In choosing which plays to use as examples, I examined nearly a dozen classroom anthologies of world drama and used those plays that have been included most often. Nearly every text includes *Oedipus Rex*, *Miss Julie*, *The Cherry Orchard*, and other familiar titles. In those instances where I chose plays that were less ubiquitous, it was because they offered the strongest examples and are readily available.

I owe a debt of gratitude to the many students who have unknowingly served as field testers for me. Their reactions to my questions, their opinions on the plays in question, and their overall outspoken evaluation of my teaching has been immeasurably helpful.

I hope the book serves your needs and offers the beginnings of some wonderful classes.

A Student Guide to **Play Analysis**

Introduction: How to Look at a Play

Analyzing a play can be an intimidating task; there are so many different kinds of questions to ask: What does the play mean? What am I supposed to get out of it? What kind of people are in it? Who was the author? What was he or she like, and is that important? In the set I design for it, what color should the walls be?

These are all legitimate questions, but you'll notice that they all try to get at the play in a different way. Questions about the meaning, the characters, the author's life, how you might design it—these all begin from a different point of view. So, where you start depends a great deal on where you want to end up. If you're just reading for pleasure, you'll look at the play one way. If you're going to direct it, act in it, or design it, you'll look at it another. And if you're going to write a critical essay on its hidden symbols, there's another option.

However, to understand fully what a play is all about, there is still at bottom one basic question that permeates all the others: Why did the playwright write the play in this way and not in some other? Why, for instance, did she choose to tell Sally's story and not Steve's? Why did she make it a comedy and not a tragedy? Why is it set in the living room instead of the front porch? Why does the play begin at the end and work backward (and yes, there are plays that do that!)? It's only by providing yourself some legitimate answers for that fundamental question that you can begin to understand the play's meaning.

However, in order to do that—in order to guess why the writer chose one option over another—you first have to understand what the various options are. That is the ultimate purpose of this book: to help you understand the various elements that go into the creation of a play. Therefore, you'll find two basic kinds of materials in the chapters that follow: definitions and questions.

The definitions will explain for you what the various elements are: what we mean, for instance, when we talk about *plot*, *melodrama*, or *expressionism*. We'll explain what kinds of characteristic features are typically associated with those terms and how they are different from each other. Furthermore, we'll explain what the use of these elements typically implies—what they typically "mean"— and, therefore, why the writer might have used them.

Over the years, various conventions have developed around plays; it's part of the purpose of this book to teach you what these conventions are. For instance, a play we call a *tragedy* typically contains, say, a noble character, a bad decision, and the death of someone at the end; these characteristics form its definition. When we see a tragedy, we feel sad and understand that life is hard; these ideas are part of its meaning. Therefore, if the writer wants us to feel sad and to realize, once again, that life is hard, he'll use the conventions that have become associated with a tragedy; that is, he'll write a play that contains a noble character, a bad decision, and the death of someone at the end. It's like saying that a pizza sauce can have many flavors: for instance, spicy, sweet, or tangy. A spicy sauce might have, say, oregano, pepper, and garlic. Therefore, if I want to make my sauce spicy, I'll use oregano, pepper, and garlic. And when you taste oregano, pepper, and garlic—you'll get spicy!

Once we all understand these conventions, however, the real chore of analysis begins, and that involves asking simple questions: How has the writer used the established conventions? Does he use the typical elements in a typical way? Or has he altered them in some way? And if so, why?

For example, you might ask of a play: Does it have a noble character? Does it involve a bad decision? Does somebody die in the end? If your answers are all yes, then you can be pretty sure you have on your hands that which we call a tragedy, and—because you understand the conventions—you'll be able to see that this writer is also trying to say that we should feel sad and life is hard.

However, suppose your answer to that question is no, the writer has not used the expected conventions. This play is about a noble character, yes, and there's a bad decision, yes, but look here: It ends happily. Nobody dies; they all get married! What kind of tragedy is that? Why has the writer violated the conventions? What point might she be trying to make?

And that, of course, is where the real challenge and fun of play analysis begins—with a whole set of other questions: Why has the writer broken the conventions? What could she have had in mind? How does this skew the typical meaning of a play? These are much harder questions, and the answers to them are not always easy to come by.

They are harder because almost every play you read will be like this. You'll discover that the writer has used some conventional elements and not others. She's written a play that's a bit like tragedy, perhaps, and a bit like comedy, maybe a bit like melodrama, and maybe also a bit like something you may have never seen before. And she's done that because what she wants to say is not something as simplistic and easy to grasp as "life is hard and we should feel sad." She has something more subtle in mind, something perhaps more profound, and something that is uniquely her own. And it is this "something" that you as the reader of the play have to be able to decipher.

The Four Causes

In a way, play analysis is like learning to sing. To sing well, you have to know how to breathe, to relax, to use your vocal mechanisms, and to read music. And you pretty much have to know it all at the same time. The challenge is deciding where to start, realizing that in order to do any one step well, you have to take into consideration all the other steps at the same time.

We'll begin by restating an earlier point: There is more than one way to look at a play. We'll examine four aspects, which we'll call, for now, "windows," since they provide a way to look into the heart of a play:

- Its origins—where did it come from?
- Its purpose—what is it trying to accomplish?
- Its elements—what is it made of?
- Its content—what is it trying to express?

To illustrate, it might help to use a statue—say, Michelangelo's *David*—as an example.

Where did it come from? It was made by Michelangelo, who lived and worked in Renaissance Italy, when science and art were gradually coming out from under the power of the Church.

What is it trying to accomplish? To impress us and move us by its beauty.

What is it made of? Marble.

What is it trying to express? A strong, independent, virile young man, who stands proudly in defiance of whatever comes his way. A man who is not afraid of—what? Perhaps the Church itself?

This form of analysis was first described by Aristotle, the renowned Greek philosopher. His view of life was organic; he felt that all things in our universe—be they chairs, plants, or social institutions—were in a constant state of growth, gradually changing over time to achieve their perfect forms. That thing we call a rose didn't spring full-blown into being as a rose; it has developed through a slow and long period of evolution to become what it is now—and whether what it is now is its ultimate perfect form remains to be seen. Aristotle asked, "What would determine the perfect form for any object?" His answer came in the terms he labeled as the *four causes*—those "windows" listed above. Thus, in order to fully appreciate or understand any object—chair, plant, or social institution—he said that you first have to determine which of these four causes you are considering. In other words, which window are you looking through?

Since a play is an object too, it is also subject to the same laws of change and evolution as a rose. Therefore, the place to begin in play analysis is to understand what the four causes are, what they mean, and how they apply to the text at hand.

Its Origins: The Efficient Cause

The *efficient cause* can be considered the "whence" of the play; that is, where it came from. In this window, we are basically looking at history. The factors that make up the efficient cause include the life of the author, the times in which the author lived and wrote, the conventions of theatrical production, the kinds of people who made up its audience, and similar historical information. We can apply these facts to the play and ask whether or not they have influenced any of the other causes.

For instance, *Oedipus Rex* was first performed in ancient Athens, shortly after the end of the Peloponnesian Wars. It was a time of civil unrest and massive social change. People's faith in their gods was being shaken; traditions were coming into question. The play is about a man who has tried to disobey these gods and get away with it. If Sophocles had shown him succeeding, that would certainly have said something about how weak these gods were. Instead, Sophocles clearly shows him failing and therefore suggests that the gods are, in fact, as powerful as ever. This is why, at one point, the chorus declares:

> I shall not worship at the vent
> Where oracles of earth are breathed;
> . . . unless these oracles
> Are justified, writ large to man.
> Zeus, let this trespass not go hidden
> From you and your great eye undying.

Its Purpose: The Final Cause

The *final cause* is the "why" of the play: looking at what the author wants to accomplish. Is she trying only to entertain us and make us laugh? Is she intending to rouse our anger and make us go out and do something about a social injustice? Does she want to reveal some corruption, share some insight, make us aware of some revolutionary idea? In order to answer these questions, of course, you'll need to learn something about the play's origins (its efficient cause again) and then apply this information to the play.

Plays have many goals, serving a variety of purposes. Some of the more common ones are as follows.

Entertainment

Some plays seem to exist solely for the purpose of amusing us, giving us pleasure, and providing some escape. The plays of Christopher Durang are like this, as is Aristophanes' *Lysistrata* and many of the plays by Neil Simon. These are comedies or farces that center on love chases. The characters are greatly preoccupied with sex and come across as looking pretty silly most of the time. Therefore, the writers seem to be saying, "Look how foolish these people are. See how they become ridiculous slaves to sex! So just sit back, relax, and have a good time!"

On the other hand, could there be something underneath the surface of these plays that suggests the author wants not only to make us laugh but also to make us think?

Communication

Some plays are written because the author feels deeply about a certain issue and wants to share her ideas with us. She wants us to reevaluate our attitudes and to see things in a new light. Indeed, when you examine the plays we mentioned just above, you'll see that there is more going on than just people going bonkers with lust. The plays say something about how irresponsibly people go overboard for sex; about what a powerful weapon it can be if used in the right way; or about the obvious folly of war—if all it takes to stop one is a sex embargo! There's often a tinge of sadness under a comedy's surface, which clearly indicates that the writer has a serious point in mind.

Teaching

In some plays, the writer has a very specific message he wants to get across about a very specific subject. He doesn't just want us to think but rather to learn something. In the case of the medieval classic *Everyman*, the anonymous writer wants us to know about God's love, about the right way to live our lives, and about how to prepare for our dying. The writer is giving us a Bible lesson onstage. Émile Zola, writing in France around the end of the nineteenth century, wanted to show his middle-class audience the truth about poverty and deprivation; he wrote plays in which criminals, prostitutes, and suffering workers were seen onstage. In the twentieth century, Bertolt Brecht wrote plays that carried strong political agendas; he used his plays like the leader of a revolution would use a speech at a rally.

Motivating Action

In some plays, the writer actually wants us to go out of the theater and do something. Clifford Odets's play *Waiting for Lefty* is about a group of workers trying to decide whether or not to strike. It was written in the 1930s, when strikes were very much a part of the American labor movement's struggle to organize. At the end of the play, the characters decide in favor of the strike and begin to call out, "Strike! Strike!" Odets fully intended the audience to join in that call and go out of the theater supporting the labor movement.

Its Elements: The Material Cause

The *material cause* refers to the actual artistic tools the writer uses and is the "what" of the play. In our special spicy sauce, these ingredients included pepper, oregano, and garlic. For a painter, the material cause might include paint, water, and canvas, as well as line, shape, or mass. For a composer, the elements might include sound, rhythm, harmony, or tempo. You'll note that some of these elements are physical objects while others are concepts. Both are equally important.

The core of this book is an examination of the elements that make up a play. We'll be defining and examining many of them, but a few are mentioned here just to provide examples of the kinds of things that make up its material cause.

Plot

Plot is the sequence in which the story is told to us. Sometimes the sequence that we see is the same sequence as that in which the story took place; we call this a *linear structure*. However—as indicated above—there are plays that move backward in time, so that we see the events in an order different from that in which they actually occurred. We call this a *nonlinear structure*. Playwrights have clear and distinct reasons for choosing one kind of structure over another, and your task is to try to understand what those reasons are.

Characters

These are the people who inhabit the play and whose actions form the plot. Sometimes characters are very lifelike; that is, they seem to be like people we might know, as in Tennessee Williams's *The Glass Menagerie*. On the other hand, the characters might be nothing more than personifications of abstract qualities, with names such as Good Deeds, Fellowship, or Wealth, as they are in *Everyman*. Or again, they might look a little bit like real people but behave in oddly distorted ways, speaking mechanically and moving like robots, as they do in some scenes from Eugene O'Neill's *The Hairy Ape*.

Language

The ways in which characters communicate with each other might vary as greatly as the characters themselves. Some characters speak in a way that sounds like the language we ourselves might use, or the people next door, or the funky kid down the block. Other characters might use stilted, formal language, or even speak in regular lines of verse. Other characters might not use words at all, but speak in distorted ways that make them sound more like machines than like people.

Setting

A playwright is usually as careful about where she places her characters as she is about what kind of people they are. The environment in which the story takes place has a great influence on its meaning. This environment may be considered on many different levels. On the one hand, it might refer to the physical space in which the action takes place, such as a room that defines the nature of the people who live in it. It might be a poor shack or the drawing room of an elegant palace. It might be outdoors, on a plain or in a desert. Or it might vary from act to act. You'll notice in Anton Chekov's play *The Three Sisters* that the first act is in a drawing room, the second in a bed-sitting room, the third in a cubicle, and the last in the backyard. You'll also notice that each act shows how the fortunes of the Prozorov sisters grow lower and lower, as their increasingly narrow world is gradually taken away from them by the conniving woman who marries their brother. When you put these two ideas together, you can see that they are gradually moving away from the "heart" of their house, until they wind up being forced "outside" it.

The setting of a play, however, often means more than the physical location. It also often refers to the culture and society in which the play occurs. In the case of the Chekov play above, the three

sisters are living in a time when Russia was undergoing large social changes; when old ways were giving way to new, and newly
rich people were encroaching on the lives of the old wealthy. These
larger social forces determine how the characters behave as much
as, or more than, the actual rooms themselves.

A word of caution: A point that is relevant here concerns the
difference between the play *as written text* and the play *in performance*. Can they be separated? Plays, after all, are designed to be
performed; so, can we legitimately talk about them only on the
page? When a play is produced, other artists make contributions,
and other elements are introduced, such as costumes, lighting, scenery, sound effects, and music. Often these elements enhance our
understanding and clarify the meaning of the play. At other times,
these elements can skew a play's intent so that we aren't in the world
the playwright created but rather a world the designer grafted onto
the text. For instance, when a play such as *Julius Caesar* is set, not
in ancient Rome, as Shakespeare wrote it, but rather in Nazi Germany, as in the version Orson Welles produced in the 1930s, what
is it that we are actually seeing? What has the play become? Does
it carry the same meaning, and can it be analyzed the same way,
reaching the same results?

Let's agree on a basic assumption for the purpose of our study:
The play as a text does not really come to life until it is performed,
and so all these production elements are an important part of a play's
material cause. But in order to design the play, artists first have to
understand it. In order to decide whether Nazi Germany, Stalinist
Russia, or a Caribbean island is an effective location for a new look
at Shakespeare, we first have to know what is in Shakespeare. Thus,
we are going to be concerned solely in this study with the *written
text of the play*.

Its Content: The Formal Cause

The *formal cause*, the last of Aristotle's four, deals with the content of
the play, that thing that it's trying to show us. It's the meaning of the
play. These people, these conversations, these actions—what, collectively, are they supposed to represent? This is the window we look
through when we talk about "theme" or "message" or "subject

matter." But this cause also means more than just the "moral" of the play. Plays represent a wide variety of things; formal causes operate on at least four different levels.

The Intellectual Level

This level deals with what comes first to mind: that is, the theme or message of the play, that idea or bit of wisdom that is sometimes expressed as a sort of moral parable. As we watch events unfold, we're possibly meant to learn a basic truth that we carry away with us. We can't always reduce a complex play to a simple epigram, but there is some sort of concept or point underlying the events that we can discover. In *Romeo and Juliet*, Shakespeare creates a story about two kids who go against their families' wishes, get married, and suffer terribly because of their rash actions. Is there some point, perhaps, about moderation in all this? About relying on common sense? About the follies of blind obedience? About the power of hate over love?

The Metaphysical Level

This level deals with the nature of reality as the play shows it, giving us the author's vision of the world. When we examine our surroundings, what exactly are we really seeing?

Different writers have adopted a variety of views about the world; often these are a product of the social mores of their times or the influence of science on culture. Shakespeare lived in an age in which the universe was thought to be structured according to very fixed principles. Scientists such as Copernicus, Galileo, and Giordano Bruno had determined that the sun was the center of things, the universe was made of a series of concentric orbits in which the earth and stars and planets moved, and all things had their place in a proper order. God was at the top, the angels right below, kings next, noblemen below, and so on, down to the lowest living creature. Thus, when Shakespeare writes about the assassination of Julius Caesar, he depicts this act as disrupting the delicate balance of the very universe itself.

Many years later, scientific discoveries changed all that. Freud, Darwin, and others showed us that the world was fixed not by God but by natural laws. Reality could be seen as a sort of scientific laboratory ruled by principles of cause and effect. If you put into the mix such elements of human nature as passion, heredity, environment, the ego, or the libido, they suggested, you would see fairly predictable results, the same way that you could predict what would happen if you did a controlled experiment. Such writers as Henrik Ibsen (in *A Doll's House* and other plays), Émile Zola (in *Thérèse Raquin*), and Maxim Gorky (in *The Lower Depths*) saw the world as this clearly definable, observable, and predictable set of facts: What you see is what there is.

For writers such as Maurice Maeterlinck, however, the true world lies beneath what we can observe and control. In this view, what we see and hear on the surface are only symbols of deeper, abstract concepts. *Love* is such a concept, and the two title characters in Maeterlinck's *Pelleas and Melisande* (who are something like Romeo and Juliet) are only superficial symbols that let us glimpse how it works.

For other writers, such as Bertolt Brecht, the true world is a social organization, a way in which we organize our economic and political institutions to serve our needs. Unlike the worlds of Ibsen or Maeterlinck, Brecht's world is not fixed and permanent. Reality is created by power and wealth, and these influences can be altered. Money can be redistributed, power can be subverted. The central character in his play *The Goodperson of Setzuan* is a victim of a world in which greed and capitalism make her do some cruel things, but, as she tells us herself, these things can be changed.

For very contemporary writers such as Eugene Ionesco, the true world is nothing but a random, disconnected, fragmented place where chaos reigns. In *The Bald Soprano*, people live in a limbo state in which language is dead, so they can't communicate with each other; in which causality is dead, so numbers don't really add up to anything, geography is only a poor attempt to pin some sort of labels on vast unknown spaces, names have no validity because they are only arbitrary sounds we assign to stand in for people, and existence itself is questionable because most of the time we don't really know where we are or what we're doing. Sometimes, as in Edward Albee's *The Sandbox*, the only true existence is in the theater where the play is taking place.

How playwrights define their world is expressed in the *style* of plays they write: They might work in *realism, expressionism, absurdism,* or some other "ism." We'll explore these definitions in part three.

The Philosophical Level

While the metaphysical level tries to define what the nature of reality is, the philosophical level is a reflection of the author's attitude. The world may be a scientific laboratory, but does the writer think it's a good laboratory or a bad laboratory? Are we happy there or sad?

Some plays contain visions that are dark and brooding, expressing an extreme pessimism: The world of Shakespeare's *Macbeth* is not only a world of fixed hierarchies but also one that is futile and depressing: "a walking shadow filled with sound and fury / signifying nothing." Other plays contain opposite visions, showing worlds of frivolity and joy, as does Oscar Wilde's *The Importance of Being Earnest*, where everything always turns out for the good and marriage is a wonderful thing.

The playwright's attitude toward the world is expressed by the *genre* of the play: either *tragedy, comedy, melodrama, farce,* or some other. We'll explore these concepts more fully in part two.

The Structural Level

Whatever the intellectual, philosophical, or metaphysical nature of reality as the author sees it, a play is still a story about some people doing certain things that involve their interacting with other people. There is a series of events and scenes and exchanges of dialogue. There's a problem or a conflict, there are steps taken to overcome it, and there's some sort of resolution. In a word: When we see a play, we're looking at a *dramatic action*. We'll examine this concept of dramatic action in much greater detail in part one, but for now let's just understand that a play shows us, in addition to ideas and symbols and attitudes, a rollicking good story, and that what this story is makes up a part of the play's *formal cause*: the theme, message, or other content.

A Case in Point

Aristotle's four causes can be used to define all objects and identities. Let's see how they can be used to define *drama* itself. When Aristotle explained what a play was, he covered all four causes in his definition. His explanation appears in his work *Poetics*.

A word of caution, however: You'll note that he uses the words *poetry* and *tragedy* at different times; although they are really quite different from each other, for our purpose here, we'll consider both of them substitutes for the word *play*. Here is what he says:

> Tragedy, then, is an imitation of an action that is serious, complete, and of a certain magnitude; in language embellished with each kind of artistic ornament, the several kinds being found in separate parts of the play; in the form of action, not of narrative; through pity and fear effecting the proper purgation of these emotions. By "language embellished," I mean language into which rhythm, "harmony" and song enter. By "the several kinds in separate parts," I mean, that some parts are rendered through the medium of verse alone, others again with the aid of song.

Where are the *four causes* in this passage?

The Efficient Cause

Where does tragedy come from? What are its origins? The answer is in the phrase "Tragedy . . . is an imitation." Aristotle explains (elsewhere in the work) what he means by *imitation*: It is part of human nature to make copies of things and to take pleasure in doing so.

> Poetry in general seems to have sprung from two causes, each of them lying deep in our nature. First, the instinct of imitation is implanted in man from childhood, one difference between him and other animals being that he is the most imitative of living creatures, and through imitation learns his earliest lessons; and no less universal is the pleasure felt in things imitated. We have evidence of this in the facts of experience. Objects which in themselves we view with pain, we delight to contemplate when reproduced with minute fidelity: such as the forms of the most ignoble animals and of dead bodies.

Thus, the efficient cause is our own natural impulse to mirror our lives, to play "let's pretend," or to dramatize events that happened to us in order to impress or entertain our friends.

The Formal Cause

What does a tragedy show us? What are we seeing? The answer is in the phrase "an action that is serious, complete, and of a certain magnitude." In other words, we're seeing a kind of story that is about something: It contains an "action." When he uses the word *action*, however, he is not talking about the kind of action you see in the movies: a tense chase, or people fighting each other, or explosives going off when the bomb hits the factory. For him, the word has a distinct and different meaning.

In this context, *action* refers to an "event" or a "happening"; that is, anything that occurs. This occurrence, as we'll see in chapter 1, might be something we discover or learn; it might be something that we do symbolically as well as physically. Take the idea of becoming a more mature person; this might be the "action" of *growing up*, and we might do it physically as we age, or mentally as we learn, or psychologically as we take on more responsibilities in our lives.

However, no matter how we define the occurrence, it nevertheless has to be of a certain weight or significance ("serious"); it has to start somewhere and go somewhere, having essentially a beginning, a middle, and an ending ("complete"); and it has to be somehow "big" enough ("certain magnitude"). These terms seem relatively simple at first, but in truth they are rather complex and difficult; we'll spend the greater part of part two defining them.

The Material Cause

What are the building blocks of a play? The answer is given in two passages: "in language embellished with each kind of artistic ornament, the several kinds being found in separate parts of the play; in the form of action, not of narrative"; and "by 'language embellished,' I mean language into which rhythm, 'harmony' and song enter. By 'the several kinds in separate parts,' I mean, that some parts are rendered through the medium of verse alone, others again with the aid of song."

In other words, a play uses language, not abstract sounds like music would, nor colors and shapes like painting would. Furthermore, a play is presented before our eyes ("in the form of action"), rather than being told to us by a third person ("narrative"), as an epic poem or novel might be. In later chapters of *Poetics*, Aristotle goes into much greater depth about these component ingredients. In the chapters of part one, we'll define them in detail.

The Final Cause

What is a tragedy supposed to accomplish? As we watch it, what is supposed to be its effect on us? Does it have a useful purpose? The answer is in the phrase "through pity and fear effecting the proper purgation of these emotions." In other words, a play is supposed to have a certain emotional effect on us. We watch somebody who is like us ("pity") go through a traumatic experience that might likely happen to us ("fear"); as we watch, we become involved; we often say we're "caught up in the experience." We may laugh, we may cry, we may become shocked or scared or experience some other intense reaction. But when it's all over, we have a different attitude. We might feel satisfied that the bad guy was defeated; we might feel joy that the hero won the girl; we might feel uplifted when the underdog wins the race. The word *purgation* is often translated as "catharsis" and applies to any sort of emotional release. Thus, in its very simplest forms, a play, according to Aristotle, is supposed to make us feel better.

Thus, if we look at a play through our four windows, we see that, by definition, it is something

- that begins in our human nature;
- that tells a certain kind of story;
- that uses action and dialogue;
- that is supposed to make us feel better.

You're the Expert

As we go through this text, please keep the following in mind: Play analysis is largely a matter of opinion. Students often feel that there is some sort of secret hidden key to every play; that there is, buried down deep, the right answer to all these questions. This response often is the result of studying with teachers who have strong personal opinions, or who seem to speak with absolute authority just because they're teachers. My philosophy, which has guided me in my own teaching and studying and has been the prime motive for writing this book, is that there are no "right" or "wrong" answers to any question you ask of the play. After all, nobody really ever knows for certain what a writer intended, not even the writer. Despite what writers say in interviews or long essays or prefaces to their work, they write from a partly subconscious source: Inspiration often leads them down paths they only feel are right but aren't always sure why. We can only use as our guide into their minds what they say, when they say it, and why they are saying it; and then put that information into the mix with whatever we discover about the text itself.

Thus, if there are no right or wrong answers, what sort of answers are there? Simply: only well-informed answers. Answers that can be supported by evidence within the play, or from biographical sources, or from applying any of the principles in this book. You can't make mistakes, as such; but it is possible to make uninformed choices.

I hope you let that principle guide you as you work through this book and the course you're enrolled in. Go ahead: Prove that Sophocles' *Oedipus Rex* is a comedy, and that the main character of August Strindberg's *Miss Julie* is really a man in disguise. Just use lots of quotes.

Enjoy.

Questioning the Play

1. Which of the four causes are you applying to this play? Which "window" are you looking through? Why? Does more than one cause apply?

2. In regard to the efficient cause, what aspects of the author's life may have some bearing on this play? Is it to some extent autobiographical? Is it typical of the kinds of plays this person writes?

3. What was the society like in which the writer lived? To what extent does the play reflect the culture? To what extent might the play be a reaction or opposition to some aspect of that culture?

4. What were the conventions of theater at the time? To what extent do they influence the way the play is written? For instance, think of how a Greek tragedy was performed, and consider how those conventions dictated what Sophocles could or couldn't do in *Oedipus Rex*.

5. In regard to the final cause, what do you think the playwright was trying to accomplish with the play: How does he want us to respond? Are we to be merely entertained? Does he want us to perform some action as a result? Might there be more than one goal operative?

6. How does this goal impact the writing? If, for example, the playwright wants us to understand his view of life, how does that shape the way the story is told, the kind of characters he invents, or the kinds of things he has them say? Is he deliberately being clear, or does he have a reason for being unclear?

7. In regard to the material cause, how does the writer use the various structural elements of the play? Begin with plot: Is the plot linear or nonlinear? Why has the writer made that choice? How does that help her achieve her goal?

8. What kind of characters has the playwright drawn? What kind of language does she have them speak? How do these choices help her achieve her goal?

9. What influence does the setting (both physical and cultural) have on the characters in the play? Is there some deliberate correlation between what the story is and where it takes place? How do these elements affect each other?

10. In regard to the formal cause, what is the play trying to show us?

11. Does there seem to be an intellectual idea contained in the play? What do you think the writer's theme might be? What clues do you get from the play that lead you to this conclusion? (Note that the rest of this book will provide you with tips about what to look for.)

12. What is the world the writer seems to be dealing with? Is it the world as we see it, or some symbolic world that lies underneath what we see? How do you think the writer, in other words, is defining reality?

13. What seems to be the writer's attitude toward this world? Does he seem to think it's a good and pleasant place, or a hard and cruel place, or somewhere in between? What is there in the play that leads you to this conclusion?

14. What, ultimately, do you think of the play? How does it relate to your life, as you know and live it? Why do you think you've been asked to read it? How would you describe it to a friend?

Part One: **Structural Components**

1

What Is a Play?

Play Versus Story

If you were asked to define what a *play* is, you might begin by calling it "a story that's told on a stage." True, but then you might be asked: Well then, what's a story? And how is a story that's told in a novel, or one that you tell your roommate when you get home late, different from the story that's told by a play? As you struggle to answer that question, you realize that while a play may be like those "stories" in some ways, it is really not the same thing at all.

A *story*, as we understand it, is a series of events that we hear about, in which certain persons do certain kinds of things. They get involved with strangers, solve problems, make decisions, or handle unusual situations. And when it's all over and done with, they go back to where they were before. Usually they've been changed somehow by their experience, but perhaps not. Perhaps they look back and laugh at what happened and then forget it, or perhaps they are profoundly different for the rest of their lives.

To be precise, a story is a narrative that tells us what happened and is often composed of a series of incidents. Take the story of Little Red Riding Hood. All the things that happened to her along the way to Grandma's house make up the story: How she started off, how she stopped to pick the flowers, how she conversed with the wolf, how she got to Grandma's house, how she spotted the change in the old lady, how she was rescued by the huntsman, and how they got married and lived happily ever after. That's a good story.

But this does not necessarily mean that it's also a *play*. The difference between the two forms lies in two key factors.

1. A Play Shows a Very Specific Kind of Story

Stories tell what happened, in the sense that somebody had some interaction with another person or a thing, but a play requires that the story contain some special elements: If Red Riding Hood stayed at home and watched television, then got up to have a snack, brushed her teeth, and put out the cat, we certainly know that something happened, and we could, by definition, call it a story, but it wouldn't make a very good play. For that to happen, something about or within the narrative must provide an extra element; the thing that happened ought to be of a certain caliber, and we'll examine what that is in a moment.

2. A Play Tells a Story in a Certain Kind of Way

Some Parts Are Left Out

Does the narrative tell us everything that happened, or does it only include the highlights and leave out the boring or unnecessary material? Do we really need to know that Little Red Riding Hood stopped to sniff the flowers, that her shoes cramped, that she had a bagel for breakfast? No. All we need to know are the things that are most interesting and most relevant. (Relevant to what? you may ask; we'll deal with that question in chapter 2.)

The Events Begin and End at Particular Times

Does the storyteller start when Red Riding Hood first wakes up that fateful morning? Three years earlier, when she first moved with her mom to the forest? After she's already inside Grandma's cottage? Or years later, when she's an old grandma herself and is now remembering her childhood? The author makes very specific choices here for very good reasons.

Are you getting the difference? Essentially, it is this:

- story is content; play is form.
- story is meaning; play is structure.
- story tells what happened; play tells how it happened.

The rest of this chapter examines the first of the two key factors mentioned above and looks at what particular kind of story makes up a play. Chapters 2 and 3 deal with the second factor: how the story is told in a play.

What Kind of Story Makes a Play?

Aristotle told us that a play's formal cause was an "imitation of an action." Therefore, the place to begin is to explain what this means and define what we mean by *action*.

As we pointed out in the introduction, when you first hear the term *action*, you usually think of somebody running from place to place or doing some exciting deed. You might get this idea from action-adventure movies that you've seen. And, of course, there are plays like this: chases, narrow escapes, running in and out of bedrooms, murders, and sometimes even horse races. However, there are also plays in which everybody sits around and merely talks to each other. Nobody attacks anybody, kills anybody, or seduces anybody—and these plays can be just as compelling as the latest summer box-office smash. So the concept of action in plays must mean something more; it has to mean a certain kind of experience that has a certain kind of depth. To differentiate the sort of action that is unique to plays, a more accurate term for us to use would be *dramatic action*.

What Is a Dramatic Action?

First let's lay down a broad definition of the term and then take up one part of this definition at a time. A dramatic action is a specific event that occurs over a limited time in which a significant change occurs.

A Specific Event

As a play unfolds, we might be watching people do a variety of things, depending on the story, and a play could, in one sense, be considered a series of incidents. We listed a number of them that Little Red Riding Hood was engaged in. We can do the same for a classic play like Ibsen's *A Doll's House* and list the things that Nora does: She steals some candy. She cajoles some money from her husband. She meets with an old chum and offers to help her find a job. She flirts with her husband. She is threatened by a blackmailer and desperately tries to find a way out of her dilemma. Then even though Nora's blackmailer has a change of heart, she learns that her husband is unforgiving: He accuses her of being a dangerous influence on her children and blames her for all their troubles. As a result, she understands her situation in a new light and decides to leave. She slams the door behind her.

Taken separately, these incidents are interesting and compelling. But play analysis takes the larger view and asks us to look at the play as a whole; that is, to see what these events add up to collectively. Taken together, what's the whole that's larger than the sum of the parts?

In *A Doll's House*, we can see that all these various incidents collectively lead to Nora's making one large and important decision. She understands that her life has been a fraud and decides to abandon her home, husband, and family in order to discover who and what she really is. Nora leaves her old life behind her.

That's what really happens in the play: Nora leaves. It takes all the other incidents to bring it about. This, then, is the kind of dramatic action we're looking for.

Apply this concept to other stories, and see if you can't determine what single event overrides the details. Nursery rhymes and tales provide good examples. What one thing happens to Red Riding Hood? You might say, for example, that she is saved from danger. What one thing happens to Cinderella? She captures the prince. To Jack of beanstalk fame? He fights obstacles and becomes very rich.

A Limited Time

A dramatic action has borders; it takes place over a limited time— that period between the beginning of the play and the ending of the play. Certainly there is a world that exists before the curtain goes up: All of the people in the play had lives and experiences that happened to them. And certainly there is a world that exists after the curtain goes down: Those characters who are still alive will go on to have different lives and more experiences. But there is something significant in what these characters do in this particular time of their lives, between these two borders, and it is this significance that defines the dramatic action. Analysis begins, therefore, by asking:

- What are things like when the play starts?

- What are things like when the play ends?
- What is the nature of the difference?

When *A Doll's House* begins, Nora is happily married. She plays the role of a helpless little wife because her husband expects it. She obeys the laws of society. Because she harbors a guilty secret, she is at the mercy of others. She is, in a sense, like a doll in a house.

When the play ends, she is no longer married. She is an independent woman. She questions the laws of society. She is proud of her "secret," and she is out in the world.

What is the difference between the two? To answer that, we need to look at the next factor.

A Significant Change

This element has essentially two parts: the concept of *change* itself, and the qualifying idea of *significance*. Let's take the the idea of change first.

Change is the crucial element here: that which has altered during the course of time we've watched. When we carefully examine Nora's beginning situation and compare it to her ending situation, the nature of her change is clear. She's become single and self-reliant. She has, essentially, "left the doll's house." Or you might put it another way: She's "wised up," or she's "matured."

A dramatic action always involves an important change of this sort. It's this element that tells us that while watching television and then going to bed might be an okay story, it is by no means material for a play—unless, of course, watching television has somehow profoundly changed our lives in some significant way. Could that occur? Possibly, depending on who we are. Perhaps a young girl is undecided about her future and watches a documentary about nurses in third-world countries. How might her life be changed?

Now, what do we mean by *significance*?

Some changes that we see in plays can be very small, but others are quite large, and the question of significance is often relevant to the circumstances of the play. If, for instance, a character gets out of a chair, we can say the change is from sitting to standing. Usually this little action is so small we hardly notice it. But suppose that the character has been severely injured, undergone massive physical therapy for two years, overcomes a monumental depression, and now, finally, after great struggle, stands up—that can be a very significant change indeed. William Gibson's *The Miracle Worker* centers on the significant moment when Helen Keller—blind and deaf since birth—finally learns to speak one simple word, an act that opens the world for her.

The kinds of changes that turn story into play, therefore, are those that are vitally important to the lives of the characters and that, in one way or another, carry with them some deeper meaning. This doesn't mean the change has to be serious or tragic; it can be about something frivolous and silly, as it is in many comedies. What we're looking at is not the mood but the importance of the change in the life of the characters.

Since this concept of change is so crucial, let's examine it in greater detail.

The Nature of Change: Its Four Levels

Describe It with a Verb

As we look carefully at the specific nature of the change, we'll find that it's useful to describe it by using a verb. Actors do this all the time: They are instructed to "find the verb in the scene and play the verb." An active verb involves somebody *doing* something. As we've seen, for instance, Nora "leaves her house" (in both a literal and a symbolic sense), and Red Riding Hood "grows up." Even the girl watching television undergoes a change as she "decides the course of her life."

Again, the way to discover the relevant verb is to examine the difference between the ending of the play and its beginning. The verb labels the change.

Level 1: The Physical

Changes that take place on the physical level involve the state or condition that our bodies are in. A person might begin the play being very healthy and end it as an invalid, in which case the physical change from health to illness could be characterized as "growing sick." This is the sort of change that happens to Bessie in Scott

McPherson's *Marvin's Room* and to Oswald in Ibsen's *Ghosts*. A character might change from having sight to losing it; "becoming blind" is the change involved in *Oedipus Rex*. In the most extreme case, many plays move from life to death: Hamlet's physical change is "dying."

While physical changes often involve matters of health or of life and death, they can also involve other physical states such as geographic location. A person might begin the play living inside a house and end it by "moving out," and the character moves from being trapped to "becoming free." As we've noticed, this is the type of change that happens to Nora in *A Doll's House*, and we say that she is "leaving her old life." In Chekov's play *The Three Sisters*, the first act takes place in a drawing room, and the last in the backyard; the change moves from inside to outside and involves "being evicted."

Level 2: The Mental

Mental changes show how a character comes to think about things in a new way, such as "making a decision," "learning something new," "discovering a secret," or "solving a mystery." These changes occur in one of two ways.

The first kind of change appears when somebody who does not know something comes to know it: a change from ignorance to knowledge. A character "learns the truth" about what happened, who somebody is, what something means, what secret has been kept, or how the world operates. Liza Doolittle in *Pygmalion* (or *My Fair Lady*, depending on which incarnation you know) learns how to behave like a duchess; that she is as strong as any man; that the world can be tamed by a strong will.

A second kind of mental change occurs when somebody "makes a decision": A character moves from being uncertain to being certain about something or somebody. Nearly all romantic comedies use this kind of change, as the hero tries to get the heroine to agree to marry him. Trial dramas are of this type, as the opposing lawyers try to get the jury to acquit or to convict. But this kind of change appears in other types of drama as well; *A Doll's House* shows us Nora's mental action of "making up her mind" to leave home.

In some plays, both kinds of change appear. In David Mamet's *Speed-the-Plow*, Bobby Gould learns that Karen is a fake and thus is able "to decide" to reject her.

Level 3: The Social

On the social level, plays examine the ways in which characters' various kinds of relationships change.

The relationship might involve the way one character connects with another on an intimate, one-on-one level. In this case, the changes might include "falling in love," "falling out of love," "getting engaged," "breaking up," "getting married," "getting divorced," "cheating," or "forgiving." Romantic dramas, farces, dramas, even tragedies—all kinds of plays—deal with the relationships between people in an infinite variety of ways.

The relationship might also involve a broader sphere, showing how family connections change: Families "break apart," "become stronger," "grow to understand" each other, "forgive" miscreants, or "welcome" newcomers in. Eugene O'Neill's *A Long Day's Journey into Night*, Tennessee Williams's *Cat on a Hot Tin Roof*, and Arthur Miller's *Death of a Salesman* are all "family" dramas that show changes in the inner dynamics among relatives.

The relationship might be between an individual and society at large, involving changes in power, status, or connections. An individual might "fall" from a high place to a low one or "move" in the reverse direction; or start out as a member of the society and then "become cast out"; or be an outsider who comes in and "makes things better," or one who "destroys" what is already there. *Oedipus Rex* shows such a change, as do all the history plays of Shakespeare. In some respects, *A Doll's House* can also be said to be about Nora's changing relationship to her society.

Level 4: The Symbolic

When we first consider these various levels of change, we discover they all have a clear meaning at a surface level. However, we can examine all of them further to see if they also contain some additional, deeper levels of meaning. When we do, we find that they have symbolic connotations as well as literal. The play may move from one condition to another; from one idea to another; from one mood to another; from one metaphysical state to another. It is often on these deeper levels that we discover how truly significant a change can be.

Thus, a woman may leave her house physically as she walks out the door, but she may also "leave" it on other levels: She may be getting too grown-up to be treated as the child she once was, so that her leaving is a sign of her becoming mature. She may be asserting her independence from convention, so that her leaving is a revolution of sorts. She may be abandoning a family she took care of but that no longer needs her, so that her leaving might be considered an act of love. Thus, when Nora slams the door at the end of *A Doll's House*, that slam reverberates on many levels.

Other examples may help clarify this idea further: *Proof* by David Auburn moves from a world of doubt and uncertainty, in which there runs a question of madness, to a world of confidence, stability, and logical clarity. *The Cherry Orchard* moves from a world in which aristocracy is in charge to one in which peasants are now powerful; from a world filled with life, music, and purpose, to one of emptiness, death, and silence; from a world that people are entering to one that people are leaving.

The Levels All Work Together

The best play analysis examines how all these various levels of change work together. No play only shows change on one level; plays involve multiple levels of change. In *Oedipus Rex*, for instance, changes take many forms:

Physically. Oedipus puts out his eyes. So this is a play about a man who "becomes blind."

Mentally. Oedipus learns important things:

- Who he really is—this is a play about a man who "discovers" his self.
- Who really killed the former king—this is a play about a man who "solves" a great mystery.
- What power and influence fate and/or the gods have over his life—this is a play about a man who "experiences" a religious reaffirmation.

- What the nature of reality might be—this is a play about a man who "learns how to see" (even though he "becomes blind").

Socially. Oedipus's position in his community changes:

- He is no longer king—this is a play about a great man "falling."
- He is no longer a resident of Thebes—this is a play about a man "being cast out" as a scapegoat.
- He is no longer son or father, but a mixture of both—this is a play about a family "disintegrating."

Symbolically. The play moves in several directions:

- The city moves from being ridden with plague to being cured—this is a play about "cleansing."
- The people move from being frightened and desperate to being assured and calmed—this is a play about "restoring" confidence.
- The power/existence of the gods is in doubt at the beginning but demonstrated by the ending—this is a play about "affirming" and "redeeming."
- The world is like winter at the beginning but more like spring at the end—this is a play about "being born."

You can go as far as you want with this, depending on how you interpret the nature of the world at the beginning, how you compare it to the nature of the world at the ending, and how you identify and define the nature of the verb that describes the change.

A play tells a certain kind of story. The kind of story that appropriately makes a play is one that imitates an action. We use the term *dramatic action* to define the unique kind of action that we find in a play, and we define this term as the overall event that takes place from the beginning to the ending of the play and that involves a significant change. This change can be analyzed on many different levels and can often be expressed by a verb. The size, importance, and nature of this change is an important tool in play analysis.

Now that we know what kind of a story makes a play, let's begin to look at how a play tells its story.

The Six Elements of a Play

The next few chapters will examine the way in which a play is typically put together. We'll begin to examine its *material cause*.

To begin, we'll once again turn to Aristotle, author of *Poetics*. As he was the first to try to define a play in terms of its four causes, he also was the first to dissect a play to discover what elements made it work. He listed six of them. They are, in order of importance as he stressed them:

- plot: How is the story told?
- characters: Who are the people involved?
- language: How do they communicate with each other?
- thought: What sorts of ideas do they express?
- spectacle: What stage elements are brought to the play by its production?
- music: What sort of song and dance elements are added?

This book will examine in detail the first three. A few words, however, about the last three will help put play analysis in its proper context.

Thought

When Aristotle speaks of *thought*, he is referring to the intellectual content: those ideas that are contained within the speeches of the various characters. This is because the Greek drama that he knew was very closely related to what is now considered *rhetoric*, or "public speaking." The plays of Sophocles, Aeschylus, and Euripides often dealt with extremely controversial issues: Is it right or wrong to defy the gods? What should a man do if he is torn between duty to his family or duty to divine edict? Many scenes in these plays, therefore, are structured as debates. When you examine *Oedipus Rex*, for instance, you'll find debates between Oedipus and Creon on the role of leadership, between Oedipus and Jocasta on whether or not you must believe the gods, and between Oedipus and Tiresias on the dangers of pride. Thus, *thought* for Aristotle really means carefully organized arguments on one or the other side of these issues.

This makes sense when you examine the words *protagonist* and *antagonist* and realize that both are formed from the Greek word *agon*, which means "struggle." Thus, the protagonist is essentially *pro*, in the sense of "for," while the antagonist is essentially *anti*, in the sense of "against."

Over the years, however, this "debate" format became less and less pronounced in plays. Consequently, what Aristotle originally meant by *thought* has altered, so that now it is typically taken to mean something closer to "theme," "moral," or "message"—that central idea the play is trying to communicate. However, teaching you how to recognize and interpret this central idea is the subject of this book. Every other element in the play is working in tandem toward that end. The whole play can be considered an effort to communicate the central thought. None of the other elements can be examined without considering how they contribute to this overall meaning. Therefore, we won't devote a separate section to thought in this book.

Spectacle

Spectacle refers to how the play is presented; that is, the kind of stage, the look of the scenery, the style and form of costumes, the effects of stage lighting, the influence of sound, and to some extent the performance of the actors themselves. While these are important insofar as a play is most fully perceived by an audience in a live performance, we will keep these production considerations out of our discussion in order to focus our attention on the text. Therefore, we won't be examining this element in detail in this book.

Music

The last element, *music*, is another of these production considerations. Remember that Aristotle was drawing his conclusions about drama from watching the plays that were performed in his time. If you've studied theater history, you will recall that conventions of classical Greek drama included the use of a chorus: a group of characters that represented a collective crowd—such as townspeople, elders, or servants. Sometimes the main character would interact with this chorus, while at other times, the chorus would express itself in long passages that took place between the main scenes. These passages were musical in nature: The lines were delivered as singing or chanting and were accompanied by patterns of movement. In a sense, Aristotle was watching a sort of opera or musical; thus, when he lists music as one of his six key elements, he is speaking in this context.

After the Greeks, however, plays (as opposed to musical comedies or operas) were usually performed without this musical element. Thus, it is no longer one of the key elements in modern play analysis, although it can help us in looking at one of the other elements: language. We'll return to this point in greater detail in chapter 5, but just to complete the picture for now, understand that language does have an aural component: Just as music strikes our ears in pleasant or unpleasant ways, so does language. Some words sound soft and gentle, while others are harsh and guttural—say *kick*, and then say *moan*, and you'll get the point. Therefore, we will look at the musical elements in language but will not be discussing music per se in our approach to analysis.

These six elements have, for centuries, formed the starting point for any discussion of a plays's structure. And for most plays that you will study, they provide a good place to begin. However, in recent years, many writers have experimented with a wide variety of nontraditional ways of building plays. Contemporary writers, such as Suzan-Lori Parks, Mac Wellman, and Charles L. Mee, have been trying to redefine the very concept of a play itself. Thus, you may find that these six elements may only apply to a limited extent, or they may not apply at all. In that case, the questions to ask of the play involve the kinds of things the writers have used in their place. If there is no *plot*, what holds the pieces together? If there are no *characters*, who and/or what are we watching the actors pretend to be (if they're pretending at all)? We'll address these issues in detail in the last chapter of this book.

But at least to get us started and provide us with a solid foundation, let's stay with Aristotle for now and take a look in the next chapter at the first of his building blocks: plot.

Questioning the Play

1. What happens in the course of the play? How would you tell the story of the play to a friend?

2. Taken as a collective whole, what one single event does the play concern itself with? Can you describe this event in a short verb phrase, such as "leaving home," "getting married," "learning how to dance," or "preparing to die"?

3. What is the world like at the beginning of the play? List all the various ways that occur to you: what the characters are like, how they relate to each other, how they relate to their world. What is the mood: Happy or sad? Healthy or sick? Optimistic or pessimistic?

4. What is the world like at the end of the play? Consider all the same elements you did in question 3.

5. What kinds of changes occur in the play on each of the four levels: physical, mental, social, symbolic? What verbs describe these changes?

6. In what ways are those changes significant?

2

Plot: **The Beginning**

Aristotle considered *plot* the most important play element of them all and claimed that a person could get as much out of hearing just the plot—knowing nothing about the characters, nor hearing any of the dialogue—as he or she could from any production. You can see how. Look at any television movie guide, and consider how much you already know and how you react by just reading the blurbs: Two old friends get together to rekindle their high school romance, or an abandoned dog survives a cruel cross-country search to find its family, or a long-dead vampire awakens to avenge her brutal murder!

A Plot by Definition

By definition, *plot* refers to the deliberate selection and arrangement of the incidents that the playwright presents. The key concepts here are the terms *selection* and *arrangement*.

Selection

As we mentioned earlier, not everything that happens in a story can be, or needs to be, shown. We only see those incidents that the playwright feels are somehow connected to the dramatic action: those that tell the story in a compelling way and give the story meaning. The kinds of choices fall into several categories. As we look at them, we'll draw examples from Tennessee Williams's *The Glass Menagerie*.

The incidents all have something in common, which somehow contribute to the overall dramatic action; that is, they are related in some way to the significant change that takes place. For example, all the incidents in *The Glass Menagerie* contribute either directly or indirectly to Tom's decision to leave home and the feelings of guilt he has as a result. These include Laura's getting fired, Amanda's search for a Gentleman Caller and the burden it places on Tom, Amanda's preparations for the dinner, and the unfortunate consequences of the visit.

The incidents help us understand the characters better. In our example, each incident reveals important things about Tom's personality, his relation to Laura, the kind of family environment he lives in, his feelings toward Amanda, or his secret desires and dreams. Looking at them collectively, we can understand both why he chooses to leave and why he feels as guilty about it as he does.

The incidents are all related to each other. Either they are similar or they have key differences in four important ways.

Mood. Notice how many scenes in the play involve quarrels and recriminations, and then notice how they are contrasted with scenes of calm, connection, and affection. You'll find that one mood alternates with another on a fairly regular basis. What do you suppose is the reason for this?

Setting. Notice that, except for a few scenes on the fire escape, all the scenes take place in the house. Notice more carefully that the scenes that take place inside are confrontations or plans about the Gentleman Caller, while the ones that take place on the porch are those in which characters (specifically, Amanda and Tom) talk about dreams and longings. There is a reason why scenes about running away take place on the fire *escape.*

Characters. Only one scene brings in somebody from outside the family. What's different about this scene? For one thing, it puts Laura center stage, where she hasn't been before. For another, it shows us Laura's only real contact with the "outside" world. For a third, it's the scene in which the most important discovery is made and in which Laura learns how cruel the real world can be. In other words, of all three Wingfields, Laura is clearly the one most affected by the Gentleman Caller. Why do you think this is? What does this say about the other two?

Ideas. A close examination of the content of each incident reveals that they all deal with some aspect of truth versus illusion: Tom's opening monologue, Amanda's reminiscences at dinner, Amanda's discovering Laura's secret, Tom's escape to the movies and to the magic show, the frustrations over the plans for the Gentleman Caller, Amanda's pretense of richness and her plans to capture Jim, Tom's secret about the electric bill and the merchant marine, and finally, Jim's disclosure of his plans to marry Betty. All of them are about dreams of one sort or another.

Lastly, the incidents selected somehow make the story move forward. To explain what this involves, we must explore the second part of our definition of plot: the *arrangement* of the incidents.

Arrangement

How the incidents are arranged contributes greatly to the meaning of the play. The playwright has two options in this respect: to describe the events in the order in which they happened, or to describe them in some other sequence. We are most accustomed to the former; we are used to seeing things in a chronological order that usually suggests a specific cause-and-effect relationship: First, I goof off at work; then, I get fired; and then, I look for a new job. We call this kind of order *linear*.

However, even though the events are causally connected, we do not always see them chronologically. Scene 1 shows us the present condition; scene 2 is a flashback to the past and shows us how that condition came about; scene 3 brings us back to the present again. This jumping around in time gives us a *nonlinear* order.

However, as we said, the linear order is what you are most likely to meet in plays, especially the ones you study early on. Over the years, this linear structure has developed a unique and defining pattern; we have come to expect, and playwrights have commonly written, certain kinds of incidents to happen in a certain kind of order. You might say that a classic pattern has emerged and become more or less a standard. It was first described by a French critic named Gustav Freytag; thus, it's often called the Freytag Pyramid. (Why it's called a *pyramid* is something we'll get to later.) Late in the nineteenth century, plays that were written according to this formula were given a generic name; they were called *well-made plays*. Today, the term has lost its original, historic connection and is used to describe any realistic play that follows this basic order.

Dramatic Action: An Overview

Before we go into the detailed steps of dramatic action, let's note how it works as a whole.

The great seventeenth-century English mathematician Sir Isaac Newton tells us that a body at rest will remain at rest until something sets it in motion: A ball doesn't start rolling until somebody pushes it. Then the ball rolls, and after a while, it comes to rest again. All actions are like this and can be described as falling into three phases. The first phase is a state of rest, before something happens. The second is the period of time during which something happens. And the third is a new state of rest, after something has happened. For example, there is a period of time before you fix supper, a second period of time during which you fix supper, and a third period of time that goes on after you've fixed supper.

This three-step breakdown can be applied to all actions, large or small. Remember, the heart of a dramatic action is the series of events that lead to a significant change taking place in a specific situation. Thus, we have a period of time before that change starts to happen, a part that takes us through the process of change, and the part afterward. Since the meaning of the play is found by contrasting how the ending differs from the beginning, it's important to know exactly when these two states are presented to us.

Looking at *A Doll's House* and considering the large dramatic action as our unit, we find the three steps thus:

First, the world is (more or less) stable. Nora seems to have a normal and happy life. Along comes a man who wants to blackmail her, forcing her to do something about it.

Second, she goes through a series of events to get herself out of trouble. Somehow the danger passes.

Third, the world is (more or less) stable again, although in a *different way.* Nora leaves her house and starts a new life. It's not the same as the old life, of course, but she no longer has to deal with the blackmailer. She might have to deal with other things, but that would be another and different dramatic action, just like eating supper is different from fixing it.

Within these broad boundaries, a well-made play has seven parts:

1. State of equilibrium. This is when we are first introduced to the characters, the kind of world they inhabit, and some potential problems that seem to lie just below the surface.

2. Inciting incident. Something happens to disturb the characters and/or to upset their world, throwing it, as we often say, "out of balance." In this part of the play, one character begins to attract our interest; this person then typically becomes the center of interest and is often called the *protagonist.* We also learn some additional things about this person: what the specific problem she faces is, what she wants to do about it, where or how she is vulnerable, and how important this task is to her.

3. Point of attack of the major dramatic question. This is the central question that we wonder about as we watch the struggle emerge.

4. Rising action. Obstacles get in the way of the protagonist's goal; she has to react to these setbacks, make new choices, and deal with new situations.

5. Climax. This is the point at which the story turns in a major new direction, the protagonist faces a final obstacle, and final choices are made. This section often includes moments of what are called *reversal* and *recognition* and also helps define whether the plot is *simple* or *complex*, additional terms we'll define in chapter 3.

6. Resolution. The consequences of what has gone before take effect, and people make new adjustments to a new situation.

7. New state of equilibrium. The world is once again at rest but is now somehow very different from what it was before.

Take a look at figure 1 to see these steps laid out in a graph. You can see quite plainly why it's called the Freytag Pyramid.

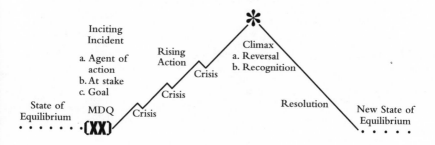

Fig. 1. The "Freytag Pyramid" depicting the key points that occur in the time line of a typical well-made play

The first three steps typically make up what we identify as the *beginning* of the play; the *middle* is what happens in steps four and five; and the last two steps define the *ending*. The rest of this chapter will examine the beginning, and the next chapter will look at the middle and the ending.

The Beginning

Step One: The State of Equilibrium

The *state of equilibrium* shows us what the world is like before something starts up. Traditionally, this world is often (but not always) revealed to us in the first scene or two. It's important to understand this world and to become familiar with this state for two reasons: First, the rest of the play will grow from it; here are the seeds for future incidents and the source from which conflict will emerge. Second, the ending of the play will stand in contrast to it; by noting how the beginning and ending states are different, we come to understand the action's change.

The important things to learn in this part include the characters, the world they inhabit, and the sources of potential problems that may emerge into conflict.

Who Are the Characters?

What are the basic facts: Who are these people, what are their names, how are they related to each other, what sort of personalities do they seem to have?

The playwright may choose a number of ways to reveal this information to us. One character might ask another a question. A character might bring up a fact or two in what looks like casual conversation. A character might step forward and actually tell us. Or we may have to find out in more indirect ways. The information that is thus delivered to us is called *exposition*.

What Is the Setting?

We define *setting* on several levels and derive important information from each level.

The historical framework of the event. The play may be set in a contemporary world, or in a historical past and a remote locale. If it's the latter, there may be unique characteristics of that time and place that are part of the meaning. The playwright may have set the play during this period for one of two reasons: either to show us how that time period is exactly like ours or, obviously, how it is very different. For instance, Arthur Miller sets *The Crucible* in nineteenth-century Salem, Massachusetts, where mass hysteria over suspected witchcraft results in the murder of many innocent women. But Miller wrote the play during a time in our country's history in which similar mass hysteria was emerging over suspected communist infiltrators in our midst. Thus, while the characters wear period clothes and speak in period dialects, they face problems similar to those faced by people in Miller's audience—so clearly Miller is trying to draw parallels between the two settings.

Another writer, Bertolt Brecht, on the other hand, has written many plays that also take place in the past: in ancient China, or during the Thirty Years War, or during the High Renaissance. But he wasn't trying to show parallels at all. For reasons of his own (which we'll discuss in chapter 15, on epic theater), he wanted us to be fully aware that those times were different from ours. His purpose was exactly the opposite of Miller's.

But what about a play such as *A Doll's House*? Clearly, Ibsen was writing about his own time. However, when we see the play today, it is, for all practical purposes, set in our past. How do we react to it? Do we see the similarities or the differences? Perhaps that's an open question that you can answer for yourself.

The physical environment for the action. How does the environment influence the story? A world that's indoors is very different from one outdoors. In the first instance, the characters lead sheltered, confined, "civilized" sorts of lives (one may assume), while those who live in the latter may be just the opposite.

You'll find important clues about the environment by noting what the author chooses to put in the stage directions. Ibsen was very careful to describe the room of *A Doll's House*. He calls it "a pleasant room, tastefully but not expensively furnished," which is intended to imply something important about the socioeconomic lives of the inhabitants, their standard of living, and their sense of values. Ibsen also tells us that there are just two doors: One goes to an entrance hall, and the other goes to an inner study, which we learn belongs to Nora's husband. In other words, a woman in this house has only two places to go—outside (the real world perhaps?) or where her husband works (his world perhaps?). Furthermore, when you see that, at the end of the play, Nora has to choose whether to stay here and live with a man who doesn't understand her, or leave him and take her chances in society, you can understand that these two doors have great symbolic resonance. When you also realize that the play starts with Nora opening a door and coming in from outside and ends with Nora closing the door behind her as she leaves her husband, this symbolic arrangement becomes even more important.

The tone of the world itself. We use the term *world* here in a larger frame of reference: the moral climate, or the overall tone or feeling of the universe in which the play exists. Does it seem a happy world or a depressed one? Is there a sense that the characters are safe, or are they in danger? Does it seem, as in *Oedipus Rex*, that the world is diseased, corrupt, and dangerous? Or, as in *The Glass Menagerie*, that the world is fragile, vulnerable, "lit by lightning"?

In *A Doll's House*, you'll notice that the very first word of the play is "Hide." As the play progresses, you'll see that nearly everybody in the play harbors some secret or other and goes to extreme ends to keep others in the dark—not a particularly happy or safe world to live in.

What Are Some Potential Problems That Seem to Lie under the Surface?

If you take another look at the three-part division of an action, you'll notice that we said the world is more or less stable at the beginning. Thus, while this first section of a play is supposed to show us a world that's in balance, a careful look often suggests that things aren't really as calm as they might seem. Tensions lie under the surface that can erupt later. We might see that some characters don't necessarily like others, or that money is short, war looks imminent, the weather seems unusual, or a love affair isn't going as smoothly as we'd like. In Sam Shepard's *True West*, we learn that the brothers haven't seen each other for a while, don't like each other, and are alone in their mother's house. In *Wit* by Margaret Edson, we learn immediately that the narrator is fatally ill. In Bertolt

Brecht's *Mother Courage*, we are plunged into the middle of a long war. In each instance, there is clearly something ripe for conflict.

What Conflicts Might Emerge?

If the problem faced by the protagonist is very small and easily solved, obviously there's no reason for the play; the whole dramatic action might be completed in ten minutes! But we like to see the protagonist struggle mightily with powerful obstacles. Indeed, the kind of obstacles the protagonist faces and the way in which she goes about overcoming them provide two very important indicators of what the play means.

Conventional well-made plays typically deal with four different kinds of conflicts. We begin to see what they are as we discover where the state of equilibrium is seriously unstable. In the world we meet, what seems to indicate difficulty ahead?

Do these difficulties come from some place inside the personality of one of the characters? If so, this might be a play examining psychological and emotional issues, dealing with some inner struggle. Shakespeare's *Hamlet* is an example: When we first meet the young prince, we learn that he is troubled by suspicions and doubts and doesn't know what to do about them, and he spends much of the play trying to make up his mind. In such cases, we often say that the essential conflict in the play is *man against himself*.

Do potential problems come from other people? If so, this might be a play that explores social and interpersonal relationships. Many of Chekov's plays are like this: People fall in love with the wrong people, are stuck in unhappy marriages, are being made miserable by other people, and find themselves unable to break away from these influences. In such cases, we can say that the essential conflict is *man against man*.

Do potential problems come from the culture in which the characters live? In the opening pages of *A Doll's House*, we learn very quickly that Nora is deceptive and manipulative; she hides the Christmas tree, she steals candy, and she lies to her husband. The man treats her with arrogant condescension, calling her his "little squirrel" and accusing her of "squandering money," so it's clear he neither respects nor understands her. The culture she lives in has predetermined how she should behave, but she finds ways to circumvent those conventions. Here, we identify the conflict as *man against society*.

Do potential problems come from some spiritual force? By this, we don't necessarily mean an organized religion, but rather that some deeper, more basic, and universal force is operative here. Oedipus, for example, has tried to thwart the prophecy of the gods: We know this is causing trouble because the first few lines tell us that Thebes is in the midst of a plague that has clearly been brought on by angry gods. Plays in which the divine, spiritual nature of the universe itself is opposing the protagonist are plays dealing with *man against God*.

Note that any one play can and often does use more than one of these kinds of conflict. A character may struggle with many different forces at the same time. In Arthur Miller's *The Crucible*, in which John Proctor's wife is accused of being a witch, Proctor at one time or another struggles with himself—as he tries to decide the right thing to do; with his wife—who suspects him of being unfaithful; with the court—a political body set up to investigate accusations; and with his sense of divine justice—which seems to be temporarily suspended during this time of madness.

Step Two: The Inciting Incident

The *inciting incident* is that event that throws the world out of balance, disturbing the original state of equilibrium and setting events in motion. Something happens that is so important that it requires somebody to do something about it. By definition, this concept seems relatively simple, but by asking some key questions, we can see how a closer look at this event also provides important clues to a play's meaning.

Where Does This Incident Come from?

Here, we can ask the same kind of questions we asked of the state of equilibrium: Where does trouble come from? Does it come from some place inside somebody? Does it come from one character's learning something about another character that makes a big difference? Does it come from a factor of society that makes itself felt? Or does it come from whatever the world of the play calls "God" taking an interest in human affairs?

In *A Doll's House*, the inciting incident arises when Krogstad appears and threatens to blackmail Nora. He knows that she's forged her father's signature to secure a loan. He knows that her husband so values his reputation that he would be devastated if it were revealed that his wife committed a crime. And he knows that Nora is so dependent on her husband for her support that she will do anything to keep her marriage intact.

So, the inciting incident actually has several origins: In part, it comes from another character (Krogstad), but it also comes from a character flaw in Torvald (his arrogance, his pride in appearances, his inability to understand the truth about his wife). It further comes from a society in which artificial and rigid conventions dictate how people live, forcing them to maintain lies. Putting all these threads together, we again come upon the idea of *hiding* and realize that the inciting incident reinforces what the setting of the play has already suggested.

Who Emerges as the Agent of Action?

The term *protagonist* is one of many terms in play analysis that seem to be self-evident. Most people would take this to mean "the central character," or "the hero" of a play, or "the character whom the story is about." But this is not necessarily the case. In order to better understand how plot gives meaning, we have to pause and redefine exactly what *protagonist* means.

When a problem appears, our attention is quickly drawn to two possible people: first, whoever the problem most affects, and second, whoever comes forward to do something about it. In most cases, these two are the same person. When Nora is threatened with blackmail, her marriage is on the line, and she starts taking steps to save it. We can say she begins to make something happen—or in a phrase more accurate for play analysis, *to drive the action forward.*

However, these two people are often not the same. The best way to explain this is to use a nursery fable: Humpty Dumpty. Yes, he had a great fall, and yes, he was very much directly affected by events. But he's not the one who starts taking steps to do something about it. It's the King's Men who come forward; they're the ones who try to "put Humpty Dumpty together again." Therefore, while the rhyme may be "about" our eggish hero, he is not the protagonist. He does not drive the action forward.

Look again at *The Glass Menagerie*. Laura's quitting typing school does most directly affect her: Her future is on the line. However, it's Amanda who starts taking steps to rescue Laura. Thus, Amanda is the protagonist.

Because of this split between the two ideas, the word *protagonist* is often confusing, and you run the danger of reading something into the play that may not necessarily be there. Therefore, a better and more accurate term for this character would be *agent of action*. This clearly indicates the person who makes something happen, who is active rather than passive, and who therefore becomes the driving force of the play.

What Is This Character's Goal?

Superficially, the agent of action's goal is easy to identify: She simply wants to solve her problem and get life back to where it was before. But this description doesn't go deep enough.

Characters in plays, like people in real life, are usually driven by one or more primary desires. They, like us, want to be happy, or safe, or successful, or loved. These, however, are inner goals. They are private, they live in the heart, mind, or soul of a character. Nobody can see them. The playwright's job is to find a way to bring that inner goal to the surface; that is, to create a story that will externalize it, so we can watch. The playwright often does this by asking, for instance, What does it mean for this character to "be happy"? The answer to this question becomes the outer goal and differs from person to person. For one person, *happiness* might mean having a daughter who's happily married. Here, you have Amanda. For another, it might mean getting to produce a major Hollywood movie. Here, you have Bobby Gould (in *Speed-the-Plow*). For a third, it might mean getting rid of a blackmailer. And here, you have Nora.

We see, therefore, that characters' goals operate on two levels. Playwrights sometimes use the term *character goal* to talk about the inner one and *story goal* to talk about the outer one. Another way to put it might be: The story goal is what the character wants to get, and the character goal is why he wants to get it. The first is all about play structure. The second is all about psychology.

So when we say that the inciting incident reveals the agent of action's goal, which "goal" are we referring to? Although the two might be very closely linked, we typically mean the story goal. Very often, this goal is best phrased as an infinitive verb; actors use this device all the time when they analyze their roles, and you'll notice that we've already started to do it in the description above. Thus, Amanda's goal would be to marry Laura off to some young man; Bobby Gould's, to get his name on a movie; Nora's, to buy Krogstad's silence.

It's important to understand and articulate this difference between story and psychological goals, and we'll explain why in a moment. But first, there's another important clue to be found at this point in the play.

What Seems to Lie at Stake for This Character?

The term *at stake* refers to that thing or condition or state that the agent of action holds most precious, how or where he is vulnerable. What is the one thing that he could not afford to lose? What would he fight hardest to maintain or restore? In some plays, a character will come out and tell us: "I would rather die than give up my freedom." In other plays, a character might reveal it by his actions, or the story might suggest it. Great playwrights raise the stakes as high as they can. Great plays are not about small issues.

Understanding what's at stake also provides additional clues about the nature of this play's conflict: What do we learn about the kind of person the agent of action is or the kind of play she's in? Amanda fights hardest to rescue Laura from being an old spinster. She's not fighting to find a man for herself nor to save her own life. Thus, she's brave and old-fashioned, and her play is about surviving, not about love or money. Bobby Gould fights hardest to get power and wealth; thus, he's ruthless and ambitious, and his play is about greed, not about art.

What, then, is at stake for Nora? She herself tells us at different times: her marriage, her children, her husband, her home. Not money itself or power or even romantic passion. This is a play about security. Or is it? As the events of the play unwind, a surprising thing happens to Nora. She finds that she does indeed end up with all these things, but she's learned that she really didn't want them at all. Instead, she wanted something much more valuable to her, something so important that she is willing to abandon marriage, children, husband, and home. Read the last scene carefully to find out what Nora really has "at stake."

Step Three: Point of Attack of the Major Dramatic Question

First, let's define the term *major dramatic question* (MDQ) and then discuss what we mean by *point of attack*.

The MDQ refers to that particular thread of action that forms the running core of the play. As the audience watches, they wonder about what is going to happen in the future, and that wondering can best be phrased and understood as a question: Will somebody get what they want? Will things turn out all right? Notice that this question is about incident; it is not about meaning. We are not asking what the play means, what the theme might be, or why the character might be so nasty. (Those kinds of questions might come up in other contexts, but they have no place in our discussion of plot.) In other words, the question begins with "will," not "what," or "why," or "how."

Furthermore, this wondering often focuses on the agent of agent, since this is the character who, as we've seen, captures our interest and drives the play forward. Therefore, the MDQ takes this character as its subject, and this character's story goal as its object. (This is why, as we saw above, it's important to identify this goal.)

Thus, because *The Glass Menagerie* uses Amanda as the agent of action and focuses on her goal, the MDQ would be: Will Amanda succeed in getting Laura married?

In *A Doll's House*—because it uses Nora as the agent of action and focuses on her goal—the MDQ would be: Will Nora get rid of Krogstad?

Point of attack is a term playwrights use to refer to that actual moment in the script when a specific thing happens or a specific line is said in which the MDQ is raised. It's the point at which the character's goal becomes clear, and we now begin watching to see whether or not he'll succeed. Another way of phrasing this is to say: This is the moment at which the play begins to move forward toward a specific future event; or the moment in which the *rising action* begins. This is the moment in the play that the director has to be absolutely certain the actor is in the right place, in the right light, performing the right business, and speaking as clearly as possible.

Often this moment appears when a character delivers a line that spells it out for us. For instance, Tom speaks to us at the beginning of scene 3 of *The Glass Menagerie*:

> After the fiasco at Rubicom's business college, the idea of getting a Gentleman Caller began to play an important part in Mother's calculations.

What could be clearer than that?

However, this moment might be subtle and require us to be more alert. In August Strindberg's *Miss Julie*, for instance, Julie never comes right out and says she intends to seduce Jean, but in the context of the scene, the following dialogue strongly implies it:

> JULIE: I do believe you're an aristocrat.
> JEAN: Yes, I am.
> JULIE: And I'm stepping down.
> JEAN: Don't step down, Miss Julie. Take my advice.

In other plays, a character other than the agent of action might say something that triggers the MDQ; the MDQ may have been raised before the curtain goes up and has to be recalled by somebody else, or the MDQ may be raised by some stage business at which there is no line at all—as when the title character of Ibsen's *Hedda Gabler* picks up and looks at her father's gun.

One more point to make about this key moment: Most often, the point of attack comes at the same moment as the inciting incident. Thus, as soon as trouble appears, we know where the play is going. The instant Krogstad makes his threat to Nora, we know she's going to have to take steps to defeat him. However, in many plays there is an extended period of time between the moment when trouble appears and the moment in which the agent of action begins to solve it. Often the character doesn't know what to do and takes a little time to learn more about the situation and figure out which of many options to pursue. Perhaps the character doesn't fully understand the nature or importance of the inciting incident, and it takes time to process the difficulty. These are the reasons for all of scene 2 in *The Glass Menagerie*.

In other words, when the inciting incident appears, we learn that the agent of action has to do something. The point of attack of the major dramatic question is that point at which we know precisely what he's going to try to do.

But we've now reached a bridge. We've spent time getting to know the world of the play and its characters. We've seen a disturbance come in and force at least one of the characters to begin to take some action. And since we've been told exactly what that action is going to be, we're poised and anxious to see how it all turns out. We've left the beginning, and it's time to move into the *middle*.

Questioning the Play

1. If you were writing a newspaper blurb for this play, like a one-sentence movie description, how would you describe it? What's the verb of the dramatic action?

2. Why has the playwright selected the particular events you find in the play? What element do they all have in common? In what important ways do they contrast with each other?

3. What information does the state of equilibrium provide about the characters? Who are they? How are they related? What sort of people do they seem to be?

4. What information does the state of equilibrium provide about the setting? If the play is historical, why do you think that particular period of history was chosen over another? Does the playwright seem to be drawing comparisons with our time or stressing differences? What does the physical environment suggest about the world of the play? Are there descriptions in the stage setting that seem to be of large importance?

5. What is the tone or mood of the world itself? Why?

6. What potential problems are hinted at in this first part of the play? Does the play look like it's a struggle between man and himself, or another person, or society, or nature, or God?

7. What is the inciting incident? From what source does it come? What might this say about the world of the play?

8. Who emerges as the agent of action? Is this person the same as or different from the central character? Why?

9. What is the agent of action's character goal? The story goal? What clue to the character's personality do you get by examining which story goal the playwright chooses to represent the character goal?

10. What lies at stake for the agent of action? What does that tell you about her personality? What clue might it provide about the meaning of the play?

11. How would you phrase the major dramatic question? At what specific line or stage direction does it emerge clearly? Does it emerge at the moment the inciting incident appears, or is there some scene in between? If the latter, what does that scene accomplish?

3

Plot: The Middle, the Ending, and Other Matters

The Middle

Step Four: The Rising Action

As the agent of action struggles to achieve her goal, she meets various kinds of resistance and has moments of success and failure as events move us closer and closer to a moment of ultimate victory or defeat. The events that make up the middle section of the play are collectively called the *rising action* because we in the audience are supposed to feel a sense of mounting tension and increasing suspense as we watch them unfold.

Three important concepts now need to be defined and examined: *strategies*, *obstacles*, and *crises*. It's difficult to discuss them separately, however, because they are very tightly linked to each other. So, in this chapter, we'll define them one at a time and then examine how they are used in *A Doll's House*.

What Strategies Does the Agent of Action Use?

Once we know what the agent of action is trying to accomplish, our interest immediately shifts to wondering how she will get it. The plans she uses are called *strategies*. A character typically might have several options to choose from; the choices she makes both tell us about her character and, again, the kind of play we're in.

For instance: If you're a college student, one of your aims might be to become a success. This is a character goal, which we'll dramatize as a story goal: to receive your graduation diploma. How will you get it? You might study hard for four years. You might take very easy classes and coast. You might decide to go online and find some company that will sell you a fake diploma. Which will you choose? If you choose the first, we know you are conscientious and honest. If the second, you're honest but a little lazy. If the third, well: I wouldn't want to hire you.

The first thing to understand, therefore, is that strategies help you analyze a play because they reveal character.

A second thing to understand about strategies is that more than one may appear in a play. Indeed, the rising action often consists of several of them, closely interconnected. Sometimes a character needs to generate one strategy in order to complete another one, so that the rising action becomes a connected string, and you can see the various steps as an "in order to" list. Let's use a familiar film to illustrate.

In *The Wizard of Oz*, we find that Dorothy's goal is to get back home:

IN ORDER TO DO THAT, she has to get help from the Wizard;
IN ORDER TO DO THAT, she has to get to the Wizard;
IN ORDER TO DO THAT, she has to travel to Emerald City;
IN ORDER TO DO THAT, she has to get help;
IN ORDER TO DO THAT, she has to enlist the aid and friendship of Scarecrow, Tin Man, and Lion.

Sometimes a string of strategies is interrupted. Something comes along that takes the agent of action on a side trip, to accomplish perhaps a new, temporary goal. Thus, once Dorothy gets to the Wizard, he throws her a challenge: "Bring me the broom of the Wicked Witch of the West." Dorothy has been presented with what we might call a "side goal"; something she has to stop and take care of before she can proceed with her main goal. She now has to do what the Wizard wants:

IN ORDER TO DO THAT, she has to kill the witch;
IN ORDER TO DO THAT, she has to get to the witch;
IN ORDER TO DO THAT, she has to travel.

These side strategies make up a large section of the film. You'll also note that this side strategy is itself interrupted by others: Once Dorothy has been captured, she has to find a way to get out; our interest shifts to her friends, who now have as their goals and strategies whatever it takes to rescue Dorothy. As you can see, this can get a bit complex, with goals mixing up with other goals. But at any given point in the play, some strategy or other is directly or indirectly related to that overall important goal. And as soon as we've navigated these side channels, we get back to the main current—Dorothy getting home—and pick up in the string above where we left off.

At other times, a string of strategies comes to a dead end, or the character decides not to pursue the goal after all. In Chekov's play *The Cherry Orchard*, the family is faced with bankruptcy unless they do something to raise money. But they never try. Instead, they generate strategies that are designed to avoid the issue.

What Obstacles Appear to Block the Way?

Obstacles are those forces or events that make it difficult for the agent of action to achieve her goal.

Where do the obstacles come from? Some are already hinted at in the initial state of equilibrium, so we aren't surprised when these buried issues surface and become major problems. Other troubles come into the play later on and surprise both the agent of action and the audience. In either case, some possible sources are as follows:

- A new character appears who was or wasn't expected.
- Somebody whom the agent of action might have been depending on doesn't come through.
- Some act of nature (snowstorm, flood) surprises the agent of action.
- Something happens that forces the agent of action to act faster or sooner than planned.
- Some new information comes along that sheds new light on a situation, either for good or for bad.
- Some secret that's long been buried is suddenly exposed.
- The agent of action discovers a feature of his personality that he didn't know about: Perhaps he's stronger than he thought he was, or weaker, or could tap dance after all.

A few pages below, we'll go in detail through the structure of *A Doll's House* and see examples of nearly all of these.

How do the obstacles help you understand the play? Our discussion of the state of equilibrium pointed out that where the inciting incident comes from (inside the character, another character, or a force of nature) helps us understand the play's meaning. If you consider it, you'll see that the inciting incident is really the first of several obstacles in the life of our character. Therefore, the same principle applies to the other obstacles: Their sources provide meaning. In *A Glass Menagerie*, most of the obstacles come from some failing within the key characters: Amanda's inability to think pragmatically; Laura's inability to enter society; Tom's inability to adjust to his life. On the other hand, most of Nora's problems stem from various conventions or laws within her society: It's against the law for her to forge a signature; her husband is too concerned with appearances to tolerate Krogstad; she can't get money from Dr. Rank because it could cause a scandal.

What Crises Develop?

A *crisis* is any moment in the play in which a character is faced with a new development or an unexpected problem and must undertake a new strategy. (See the discussion above about side strategies.) You can also think of the moment as a turning point. Some find it useful to use an Aristotelian term: *reversal*.

Think of the moment the inciting incident appears as a crisis—just the first of many. Skipping ahead, the moment that we'll come to learn is called the *climax* is also a crisis—probably the last of many. During the middle section of the play, crises occur whenever something comes along to thwart the efforts of the agent of action. And as we said before, the three elements, *strategy*, *obstacle*, and *crisis*, are inextricably linked. An obstacle presents a crisis, forcing a new strategy.

You may have noticed we've been discussing these elements as though they were bad things. However, a turning point can also be a good thing. This new character can be a friend. This secret we've uncovered can be a treasure. And identifying the moments when crises appear shows you which lines in the play are more important than others. As a director, designer, or performer, you can identify which ones need to be emphasized by blocking, design elements, or acting.

How About an Extended Example?

Trying to sort out the difference among these three concepts might be difficult at first, because they are so tightly interconnected. Think of it this way:

- A strategy is the *plan*—a method of getting the job done.
- An obstacle is a *force*—something that makes the job harder.
- A crisis is a *moment*—a point in the story at which obstacle collides with strategy.

To see how this works, let's closely examine how Ibsen uses them in *A Doll's House*.

1. The rising action begins with the inciting incident about two-thirds of the way through act 1, when Krogstad comes to Nora. He tells her he's being fired from his job at the bank where Torvald (Nora's husband) is manager. He also reveals he has proof of a crime she committed years ago: She forged her father's name on a bank-note in order to get a loan. It is important to note that the loan was to pay for a trip abroad that was intended to help her husband recover from an illness, and that the reason Nora felt she had to forge the signature was because she knew her husband would have been too proud to take money from his father-in-law. Since Krogstad knows how important appearances are, to both Nora and her husband, he warns her: Unless she convinces her husband not to fire him, he will expose her.

- obstacle(s): Krogstad is *another character*. The threat he holds over Nora comes from her fear of what people will think: that is, *the conventions of society*.
- crisis: Nora must do something about this. This is the inciting incident. It provides the point of attack of the major dramatic question: *Will Nora be able to stop Krogstad? How will she do it?*
- first strategy: Nora appeals to Torvald, talking to him about Krogstad, thinking she can influence him not to fire the man.

2. Torvald expresses his intense dislike for Krogstad and asks Nora not to speak up for the man. He doesn't approve of Krogstad's character and shady past and thinks he is a bad influence.

- obstacle(s): Torvald is *another character*. Torvald's *attitude toward the conventions of society* is inflexible. Nora is unable to confess to her husband because she knows he will be angry: *her fears and attitudes toward society's conventions* constrain her.
- crisis: Nora has to think of another way around Krogstad.
- new strategy: She gives up trying to reason with her husband and instead begins to flirt with and tease him, trying to soften him up by playing her usual game of cute and helpless wife.

3. Nora returns to the subject a few minutes later. This time, Torvald's reaction is even stronger. As her husband, he forbids her to try to defend Krogstad ever again.

- obstacle: Torvald is not just another character now, but a representative of a *social institution*, namely marriage.
- crisis: Nora now knows her problem is more serious than she thought, because her obstacles are bigger.
- new strategy: Nora is at a loss for a while, not quite sure what to do. The act ends with both Nora and the audience in suspense.

4. At the beginning of act 2, Nora seems to be toying with several possible strategies. She wonders aloud to the nursemaid what the children would do if she "weren't around" and suggests that she might be going away. She hints to Mrs. Linde that she might have to ask help from her friend, Dr. Rank. Later on, we get some clues that she might even be contemplating suicide. But Nora doesn't actually begin to pursue any of these; she takes no active steps to make any of these things happen. What she does, however, is resume an earlier strategy: She once again asks her husband about Krogstad. Because she is such a creature of habit and social convention, she assumes that this normal, polite, discreet approach is still the best.

- obstacle: Torvald tells her he's already given the job to Mrs. Linde. This is *new information that makes a difference*.
- crisis: Nora has to change gears almost immediately.
- new strategy: She tries another approach, warning Torvald

that he must give Krogstad the job for his (Torvald's) own protection and hinting that this is more serious than he realizes.

5. It doesn't work. Torvald grows angry.

Work through the rest of the play yourself, and notice the pattern: A strategy is set up; when it is blocked, a crisis appears, and a new strategy is initiated. Bit by bit, Nora's options run out. The last third of act 2 and the first part of act 3 draw us closer and closer to a showdown. Krogstad is determined to destroy Nora. Nora is unable to stop him. She finally does what she should have done all along: tell the truth to Torvald, only to find a last, surprising, and devastating obstacle that changes the course, not just of her strategies, but of her whole life. We'll get to that in a moment.

What has this analysis revealed? Have you noticed how much deception there is? How many of the strategies involve Nora trying to play her constant role of helpless, conventional housewife, obeying the rules spelled out by society and her husband? And how many of the obstacles come from those same rules? How do these insights reveal the play's overall meaning?

Now the action has indeed risen, and it's time to move to the showdown itself.

Step Five: The Climax

The term *climax* has been defined in many ways: the moment of highest tension, the moment when the outcome is settled once and for all, the moment when the events turn for the last time, the moment in which the final and most important crisis appears, and finally, the moment when we know it's all over. In one way or another, all these definitions are useful. Something major happens, and the outcome is now unavoidable. I like to think of the climax as the moment in which, one way or another, the MDQ is about to be answered once and for all.

As hard as it might be to define it, it's sometimes equally as hard to spot where this moment occurs. Sometimes it happens in one line, and other times, over a period of minutes. Once again, Aristotle's *Poetics* provides some guidelines. He tells us there are two important moments to look for in the plot: *reversal* and *recognition*. He goes on to say that a play in which both of these moments occur can be called a *complex* plot, while a play in which only one or neither appears is called a *simple* plot.

Reversal refers to that moment in which, as Aristotle says, the action turns in a different or opposite direction. This should sound familiar: When we defined *play*, we noted that it is an event in which a significant change occurs, and you'll recall we looked at possible ways to interpret the kinds of change that are involved. We also met this concept above, when we used it to define a moment of crisis. Another way, therefore, of understanding climax is to see that it is the moment at which this major, overall change either actually takes place before our eyes or becomes completely inevitable.

The Greek word for this concept is *peripeteia*. You may find this term used in many critical studies of plays. Aristotle cites *Oedipus Rex* as his classic example and describes how Oedipus's life suddenly changes as he goes from being a powerful, confident ruler, to becoming a helpless, weak outcast.

The second term, *recognition*, refers to a moment in which, as the term implies, a character "recognizes" something important, that is, achieves some understanding, changing from being ignorant about something to having information about it. A character might learn something about another character, the truth about a secret long hidden, or a truth about himself. Finally, he might learn something about the nature of the universe. You'll recall this is how we defined a mental action.

The Greek work for this concept is *anagnorisis*, and often what the character learns is part of the play's message. The playwright typically wants the audience to come to the understanding along with the character. Drawing his example again from *Oedipus Rex*, Aristotle points out that Oedipus learns several important things:

- He himself is the murderer whom he's been looking for all this while.
- He is not the son of the people he thought were his parents, but of another couple entirely.
- The prophecies of the gods turn out to be true after all, so

it would be wise in the future to believe in them and do what they say.

- Life is very cruel indeed, and sometimes it would be better to have not been born in the first place.

That's an awful lot of insight for one play.

A moment of reversal, therefore, and an important recognition are the two elements that appear at a play's climax. Aristotle makes one more important point about them: They often happen at the exact same time. When the shepherd tells Oedipus the secret of his true identity, that is the moment his life suddenly turns around. The news destroys him. The recognition has caused the reversal and turned his life from happy to miserable.

It can work the other way as well: A reversal can happen to cause somebody to recognize something. In Shakespeare's *King Lear*, for instance, the pompous, arrogant ruler is turned out of his house by a cruel daughter and sent, nearly naked, into a storm. Suddenly, and for the first time in his life, he is helpless and outcast: He's not impervious to wind and rain, as he thought he was. This recognition of his humanity is so powerful and frightening that it drives him mad.

What about the moment of climax in *A Doll's House*? When does it occur, and what happens?

The moment occurs around the middle of act 3. Torvald has read Krogstad's letter and, as Nora expected, is not happy. He accuses Nora of having ruined him and his happiness, calling her an evil woman who ought not even to be around the children. And then Ibsen pulls a surprise: Another letter arrives from Krogstad. It seems that he's had a change of heart. He's fallen in love with Mrs. Linde, and they are to be married. He will have his chance at respectability after all. He gives up the blackmail, setting Nora free.

This moment is certainly of the highest tension. The MDQ is clearly answered. The agent of action has had a sort of indirect showdown with the villain, and we know it's all over from here. Furthermore, the moment also provides us with what Aristotle termed a complex plot because it clearly contains an important recognition (a bit of news) that reverses Nora's fortune from bad to what looks like good.

However, then something even more important happens. Torvald reads the new letter and realizes the pressure's off. He shouts out, "Nora, I am saved!" Nora looks at him quietly and asks, "And me?" This one exchange is really the core of the play and might be the true climax. Nora's fate takes another turn, even more profound than the first. She also learns something. On the one hand, she sees her husband for the fraud he is. But more significantly, she sees the control social conventions have placed on her life; it has forced her into a series of hypocrisies and lies.

And how does it now change her life? Does it make her better or worse to know this? Ibsen devotes the rest of act 3 to a discussion between Nora and Torvald, in which she explains that she can no longer live in a household dominated by social hypocrisies. She must find out who she is and what her own true life is meant to be. And the only way she can to that is to leave. Thus, she walks out of the house, a direct contrast to the first moment in the play when we saw her walking into the house. Is this a reversal that goes up or down? You decide.

Simple or Complex?

According to Aristotle's guidelines, therefore, *A Doll's House* is clearly a complex plot, because it contains both reversal and recognition. Are there plays that do not contain these elements, in which the agent of action's life does not change, but just continues to go further in one direction? Or plays in which the agent of action never understands anything of importance, but comes to the end just as deceived, ignorant, or foolish as he was at the beginning?

Many people think *Death of a Salesman* by Arthur Miller is such a play: They argue that Willy's life doesn't really change (it just continues to fall), and that he never comes to any insight (dying in the grip of the same delusional dreams that have always controlled his life). On the other hand, they say that the real agent of action of the play is not Willy, but Biff—who does understand the truth about his life and is able to change. It's a matter of interpretation.

We've now passed through the *middle* of our plot. Let's turn to the kinds of scenes that make up the *ending*.

The Ending

Step Six: The Resolution

What comes after the climax is a winding-up of the story. The major dramatic question has been answered either yes or no. A reversal of some sort has or has not taken place, and the agent of action has learned or not learned something very important. In this section, therefore, the characters adjust to the new situation. They may make important decisions; they may sit down and discuss what has just happened; they may prepare to start another series of strategies to do something else. The clue to understanding the play lies in noticing how they adjust.

Do the characters form new alliances? Do the lovers get together? Does the father start to like the new son-in-law? Does the wrong-doer get forgiven?

Do the characters make new decisions? Will the people accept the new government? Will the ambitious son leave for America after all?

Have any characters gone through personality changes? Has the arrogant king lost his pride and become humbled? Does the young man have a better understanding of the way of the world?

Who has left for good? Who has come to stay? Who has died? And how do these new changes affect the main characters?

Step Seven: The New State of Equilibrium

As the play ends, the world has reached a new *state of equilibrium*. The force that had disturbed it has been taken care of, the problem has been solved, and the world is different.

But how is the world different? In what specific ways does the situation at the end differ from that at the beginning, and what does that change tell us? Use the four kinds of changes we discussed in chapter 1.

Physically. Have we gone from somebody being alive to being dead? From somebody being inside something or someplace to being outside? From somebody being sick to being healthy, or the reverse?

Mentally. Have we gone from somebody not knowing something to now fully knowing it? Has somebody made an important decision?

Socially. How have relationships changed? How have social alliances been altered? Has a political structure been changed?

Symbolically. And what does it all suggest on a larger, thematic level? If we've gone from somebody being alive to somebody being dead, what does that individual's death possibly stand for: The death of a dream? An ideal? Evil? What does a marriage symbolize, besides just two people getting married?

What about Other Kinds of Structures?

The well-made play structure we've just dissected is only one of many possible ways in which plays are arranged. The writer may choose to show the action in this normal, chronological sequence in which cause and effect are clearly visible. Or he may choose to vary this form in a number of ways.

Starting in the Middle

It's useful to visualize the well-made play structure we've just examined as a visual graph and label the steps we've identified. Now would be a good time to take a second look at figure 1 and examine the steps of the Freytag Pyramid.

Let's use an up arrow to show when the curtain rises (that is, when we come into the play) and a down arrow to show when it falls. Depending on the play we have in mind, we might put these arrows almost anywhere. For instance, we might come into the play very early in the plot and leave at the very end, as we do in figure 2.

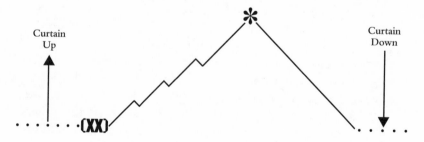

Fig. 2. A Freytag Pyramid depicting the curtain going up and coming down outside the parameters of the action in the play

Or, as in figure 3, we might come in later, say, after the inciting incident has already taken place, and leave before the *resolution* is complete. As audience members, we'll need to discover what the *antecedent action* is; the term refers to those events that happened beforehand. The way in which we'll learn about these events is through *exposition*; this term refers to any lines of dialogue or stage activity that provide us with necessary information.

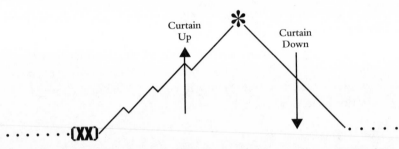

Fig. 3. A Freytag Pyramid depicting the curtain going up well into the action of the play and coming down before the action is resolved

Why would a writer begin her play at this late stage? Does she think it will be a more exciting way to get the audience's attention? Or is she showing us a world in which balance and leisure just don't exist at all? Many classical Greek tragedies are of this sort, taking place on the very last day of the agent of action's life, in which her ultimate fate will be decided. All the events of her past have to somehow be reported to us, so that the first part of the play is often taken up by extensive exposition. Modern writers, too, often use this convention of a "fatal day." Eugene O'Neill does it most vividly in *Long Day's Journey into Night*.

We've also noted, in figure 3, that we might leave the play at almost any spot on this chart. The curtain could come down before the climax: There may be no visible resolution at all, and we are left wondering how it all turns out, in which case the writer may be saying something about the uncertainty of the world or wanting the audience to make up their own minds. The curtain may come down at the moment of climax, in which case the writer might be letting us know that what happens afterward is really not important at all, or that it is up to us, the audience, to complete the story. Or the curtain may come down some time after the climax; this is indeed the case in *A Doll's House*: The play concludes with the discussion between Nora and her husband and does not show us what Nora's life is going to be like after she shuts the door behind her. Ibsen does this because, for him, this discussion—and the points it raises—are the very reason he wrote the play.

Working Backward

Several interesting plays have been written in which the events unfold backward. The curtain goes up at the end of the action, and each successive scene that we watch takes place earlier and earlier, so that the curtain goes down at the beginning of the story. *Betrayed* by Harold Pinter does this. The play begins as a couple meets to end their love affair. We work backward in time to see how this affair has evolved and end up at the moment it began. Why does a playwright do this? Perhaps he's drawing a contrast between the way things begin and the way they end and wants to say something ironic about expectations. Or perhaps he sees the world as a mysterious place, in which we can't ever make right assumptions about people because we don't always know their secret origins.

Using a Flashback

A play can begin in the present and then jump back in time to show us what happened in the past. In *The Glass Menagerie*, Tom remembers out loud for us and describes the events that led to his present rootless life, so that scenes of *now* alternate with scenes of *then*. In David Auburn's *Proof*, an important scene in act 2 is set several years before the rest of the play, in which we see the father's lunacy just beginning.

Works like these are essentially two plays in one, and you'll note that each, in its own way, could very well be a conventional well-made play. The story in the present (called the *frame story*) is about somebody trying to do something by remembering (clear his conscience? solve the mystery?). The story in the past (called *past action*, or in film-talk, *back story*) is about somebody (the same person?) also trying to do his own something. The meaning is often found in how the two levels contrast with, or shed light upon, each other.

Montage Sequences

Many plays skip freely around in time and space. Scene *B* may take place after, before, or at the same time as scene *A*. It may use the same characters or completely new ones. It may be in the same place or elsewhere. It may be a point earlier or later in the story or may even be another story altogether. We have to pay close attention to the road signs the writer provides that tell us where and when we are. This variation is illustrated by Thornton Wilder's *Our Town*, which skips freely between a series of events and a series of characters that constitute life in a whole community.

A great many contemporary plays, often collectively labeled *postmodern*, are like this. For writers of such plays, the point lies in the relationship among the events. If they aren't connected by chronology, they may be related in mood: Does each scene grow progressively darker or lighter or more suspenseful? Do the scenes share or contrast ideas, similar or different characters, like or unlike events?

Random Illogic

Some plays contain scenes that don't seem to have any logical connection at all; they skip around at random, as though the writer had thrown a handful of note cards in the air and just wrote the scenes in whatever order he picked them up. We'll examine plays of this sort in our discussions of theater of the absurd (chapter 14) and postmodernism (chapter 16), where we'll see how writers such as Samuel Beckett, Eugene Ionesco, and Mac Wellman portray worlds without logic or coherence.

Questioning the Play

1. What is the story goal of the agent of action?
2. What strategies does she generate in order to reach this goal? Can you work out a strategy string and track how one strategy leads to or from another? Are there side strategies as well?
3. How do these strategies relate to each other? What, if anything, do the strategies all have in common? How are they different? What is significant about this?
4. Where do the major obstacles come from? How are they re-

lated? That is, compare and contrast them as you did the strategies in order to find any meaningful pattern.

5. What important lines, stage directions, or incidents stand out in which obstacles and strategies come into the play? In other words, highlight the key crises that appear.

6. What definition of *climax* is most useful to you?

7. Where does the single most important reversal take place? What direction does that reversal take: Does the hero's fate get worse or better?

8. What key recognition comes to the agent of action? What new knowledge is gained? How does this insight provide clues to the meaning of the play?

9. Does the play have a simple or complex plot? Why? Why is it important to know?

10. What important changes are made clear during the resolution?

11. In what ways does the state of equilibrium at the end of the play differ from that at the beginning physically, mentally, socially, and/or symbolically?

12. Has the writer used the well-made play pattern or chosen some variation on it? Why? What possible meaning is communicated by the arrangement of the incidents?

4

Characters

For the same reason the playwright carefully selects and arranges the events that make up the story in order to express a particular attitude or idea, so he carefully creates particular kinds of people to fully help him clarify his theme and has them do and say certain kinds of things. What kinds of choices does the writer make and why, and how do we use the *characters* to understand the play?

We analyze characters in three different aspects, and each aspect provides us with different clues. These three include:

- The *literal aspect*—what kind of people are they?
- The *functional aspect*—what roles do they perform in the structure of the play?
- The *connotative aspect*—what ideas or concepts might they symbolize?

The Literal Aspect

We usually begin by looking at and talking about characters as though they were real people. They have personalities, dreams, and fears we recognize because we share them. But remember that these characters are deliberately conceived by a working intelligence with a conscious purpose in mind. The playwright gives her characters specific backgrounds and personalities because she uses them to express a particular vision. Out of an infinite range of possibilities, she deliberately picks only certain traits. Perhaps all the characters share one particular feature (they're all afraid, though in different ways). On the other hand, perhaps one character deliberately contrasts with another (one is greedy, another is charitable; one comes from the city, another from the country).

What specific clues are useful in understanding the *literal aspect* of a character? You'll recall in our discussion of plot in chapter 2 that one of the important things that emerged at the inciting incident is that one character becomes the agent of action of the play, perhaps because he seemed the most interesting or because he seemed to be the active force in solving the problem. You'll also recall that we examined this agent of action with three questions. These same questions apply to all characters:

What Is the Character's Goal?

Keep in mind two things: First, every character has both an inner (psychological, or *character*) goal as well as a visible and active (*story*) goal, which represents for the character that condition that must be met before the inner goal can be satisfied.

Second, the way in which the character translates the inner goal to the story goal determines to a great extent what kind of person he is. One man may find "love" by marrying the girl of his dreams, while another may find it by seducing every woman he can.

What Strategies Does the Character Generate to Achieve That Goal?

As with goals, the kind of strategies a character uses is an indicator of the kind of person she is and of what the playwright is trying to say.

If we define Amanda's goal in *The Glass Menagerie* as "trying to provide for Laura's financial security," we can see that she goes about it in a romantic way: She sets about trying to find her a husband by getting Tom to bring home a gentleman caller. What she does not do is any number of very practical things: get Laura into therapy, help her study the typewriter at home, or help her learn some craft that might provide income. But no, Amanda is a dreamer trapped in her own illusory past, and so her strategies for Laura are as doomed as she herself is.

Where Is the Character Vulnerable? What's at Stake?

A father defends his children; a hero defends his country; a woman protects her social reputation. Identifying what's at stake tells you not only what sort of person this character is but also what values the playwright might hold as important.

There are, of course, any number of other ways to analyze the character's personality. You might, as actors do when they study a role, consider the character's background, his manner of speaking, his fashion of dress, his relationships with other characters in the play, or what kinds of things he does when he is "offstage." Determining what kind of person you're dealing with reveals meaning in several ways.

Consider which part of the character is most dominant throughout the play. One crucial trait may take precedence over any number of others, and the play is driven by that trait. In tragedies, as we'll see, this overriding character trait is often pride, arrogance, or willfulness. In comedies, this overriding trait often gets a character into trouble because he's tunnel-visioned and out of control.

Consider whether other characters in the play have traits that are very much like this one or ones that are very different. Compare and contrast, and see whether the playwright is using these relationships to make her point. (We'll come back to this idea when we discuss *foils* below.)

Consider whether and how the character's personality changes at the end of the play. Is it a change for the better, for the worse, or no change at all?

The Functional Aspect

The plot has to be set up and moved along, information has to be revealed, the vision of the author has to be clarified, and above all, the audience has to be engaged. To those ends, characters often have different "jobs" to do. This is their *functional aspect.* There are seven of these functions.

- protagonist, or as we're naming it, the agent of action
- antagonist
- confidant(e)
- foil
- *raisonneur*
- utilitarian
- comic relief

The Protagonist, or Agent of Action

We've discussed how to identify this character when we defined those things that emerged from the inciting incident. This character's function is to make the events of the play happen. It's the passion behind this character's goal and the power behind the strategies she generates that drive the play forward.

Remember, a play may be about a particular individual, but that individual may not be the person who makes something happen; rather, that individual might have things happen to him. He might be a passive character, not an active one. The poem is about Humpty Dumpty, but it's Harry, the king's man, who drives the action. Similarly, while Shakespeare's *Othello* is about the Moor, the character who makes things happen is Iago.

The Antagonist

The *antagonist* is any person who stands in the way of the agent of action achieving her goal. In some cases, this person may be deliberately trying to prevent her success, taking an active role in generating opposition; thus Krogstad becomes an antagonist to Nora. In other cases, this person might be a passive stumbling block: somebody whose presence or unconcern or attitude simply makes the protagonist's goal harder. Nora's husband, Torvald, functions in this way: His arrogance in not being willing to consider letting Krogstad keep his job, his insistence that his wife not meddle in his affairs, and his fear of being made a public scandal—all these attitudes work against Nora.

The Confidant

A *confidant* (the feminine form of the word is *confidante*) is any character whom another character confides in or delivers information to. This may be a friend of another character, a servant in the household, a messenger, or even a stranger passing by. At one point or another, the agent of action may serve as a confidant to another character by being a good listener, or the antagonist may even be a confidant to the agent of action.

What are some reasons one character needs to reveal information to another?

Delivering exposition. One character will tell another a series of facts that the audience essentially needs to have in order to understand what happens later—where we are, who some of the characters are, what's been happening in the past, and so forth. The long scene between Nora and Mrs. Linde in the first act of *A Doll's House* is of this sort, and Mrs. Linde serves as Nora's confidante there. (Note that while the major bulk of exposition often appears early in the play, new information and a new exposition may appear at any point.)

Revealing inner secrets. One character will express his feelings to another, revealing part of his personality. Nora tells things about her fears and dreams to Dr. Rank that she could never share with her husband.

Making plans. When the agent of action is putting together a scheme, she often will tell a friend what her intentions are. Sometimes the audience learns what the agent of action's goal is because she shares her dream with another. In this way, Amanda in *The Glass Menagerie* enlists Tom as her confidant in regard to getting Laura married.

Expressing a philosophy or idea. When the character holds deeply to a particular belief, acts out of an inner moral compulsion, or is committed to a political cause, he will often explain himself to a good listener. In the long discussion that ends *A Doll's House*, Nora speaks of her beliefs to Torvald.

The Foil

A *foil* is any character who in some way compares and contrasts with another. Playwrights create foil characters to help illuminate the personality of other characters as well as to help dramatize the meaning of the play.

We learn much about people by seeing how much they are like or different from someone else. Because, for instance, one character is gloomy, the cheerfulness of the other becomes more noticeable. Because one is clever, the stupidity of the other stands out.

Compare and contrast Nora and Mrs. Linde. We see that Nora has been sheltered and "protected" by the men in her life; she doesn't fully understand how the world works. On the other hand,

Mrs. Linde has had to go out into this world, find her way, earn her living. Nora's weak and naive; Mrs. Linde is strong and experienced. Indeed, some critics say that when Nora leaves at the end of the play, she has almost become Mrs. Linde, or certainly will in the near future.

How many foils might there be in a play? While they often come in pairs, they sometimes come in multiples. Consider the characters in Chekov's *The Cherry Orchard*: Lopakhin is the former serf who is taking steps to save the old estate, while the members of the family do nothing. He is competent, while the family's matriarch, Ranevskaya, is unable to make a decision. He is uneducated but smart, while Petya, the tutor, is a perpetual student who knows very little. He is an outsider who wins, while the others are insiders who lose. But at the same time, he is afraid of relationships because he knows what they entail, while Varya (a lovesick young girl) is ready to jump into marriage with him, not knowing what a mistake it would be.

The Raisonneur

It might help you understand what this term means by knowing that it has its roots in the French word *raison*, which means "reason"— in the sense of "idea." Plays are intended to communicate to the audience some idea, some theme or inner meaning. A *raisonneur* character, therefore, is any person who, at some point in the play, utters a line or delivers a speech that sums up or expresses the central idea of the play. Putting it another way, a *raisonneur* character acts as a spokesperson for the author.

Any character may be a *raisonneur* at any given point in the play. Sometimes you can't miss it: A character may deliver a long monologue on the topic of the play. In many plays by George Bernard Shaw, characters deliver fully developed arguments about the issue at the heart of the play. In acts 2 and 3 of *Major Barbara*, there are speeches about economics, about religion, about class structure, and about poetry, all of which are major ideas Shaw felt strongly about. In classical Greek plays, the chorus often serves as a collective *raisonneur*; it does this, for instance, at the end of *Oedipus Rex*, when it comments how wise one is to be afraid of the gods.

More frequently, a *raisonneur* may simply say in one brief, almost throwaway line what the play is about; and it might pass so quickly that you won't catch it unless you're paying close attention. For example, in *A Doll's House*, Nora says to her husband, "Society has done me a great wrong." And in August Wilson's *Fences*, Bono says to Troy, "Some people build fences to keep people in and others build fences to keep people out."

The Utilitarian

The job of a *utilitarian* character is to help move the plot forward when there is no other or better way. If an important letter has to come into the play, somebody has to bring it onstage. If an important crisis needs to be developed, an important twist of the plot needs to be started, or a new character has to be introduced, the playwright may bring into the play a servant, a messenger, a friend, or some outsider to do this job. This role might be relatively small, such as any number of maids and butlers who appear in nineteenth-century dramas. Or it may be somewhat more important and actually serve other functions as well.

To turn again to *A Doll's House*, we've seen how Mrs. Linde functions as both a confidante and a foil to Nora. However, at one point in the play, she decides to try to do something about revealing the hidden secrets of the household and urges Nora to confront her husband. This urging helps Nora come to her final decision, so that Mrs. Linde here fills a utilitarian role. Furthermore, she is also the person who saves the day. By deciding to marry Krogstad (the man blackmailing Nora), she rescues Nora from his clutches, thus leaving her to go out into the world as she does. By providing this important plot twist, she is being utilitarian again.

Comic Relief

Very often, and for a number of reasons, the playwright will insert a scene or a moment of comedy that temporarily halts the forward action of the plot. This moment often occurs after a particularly tense or frightful situation, or within a long scene that might otherwise become tedious. The moment is intended to lighten the mood and to provide an important contrast to the surrounding situation, making the dark material all the darker by comparison. A famous example appears in Shakespeare. In act 4 of *Hamlet*, Hamlet comes upon a gravedigger preparing a new grave. The two of them exchange awful puns, making us laugh for a moment and taking our minds off the danger and corruption we've been seeing. But when we suddenly learn that the grave being dug is for Ophelia, Hamlet's innocent love, we are thrust even more horribly back into the play's darkness.

Furthermore, while comic relief is most often provided by the characters who do nothing else, playwrights will also create characters who have major roles in the play but who, as foils to other characters, are foolish and silly throughout and who, whenever they appear, bring comedy into the play. In *The Cherry Orchard*, the family is joined by a neighbor who is always asking for money and who is mocked by others.

As you may have noted, one common thread appears in the definitions above, which is important enough to be stressed once again. At any given point in any play, any character may fulfill one or more of these functions. A confidant is not only a confidant but may also be a foil, a *raisonneur*, and occasionally a comic relief. Watch for what a character does, not who he or she is.

The Connotative (or Symbolic) Aspect

Characters and their relationships seldom exist in plays on only a surface level; they often represent larger thematic ideas. While a story may be compelling and interesting, a dramatist is rarely just telling it for its own sake. He wants to express his attitude or vision about these larger ideas: a social problem, a moral issue, a philosophical question. But since he's writing a play, not an essay, his first job is to involve the audience in the suspense of the story and only secondarily to communicate his larger message. Therefore, he'll create characters who in one way or another represent different sides of the issue or different values within his construct. The characters, in a word, are to be seen as *symbols* of something larger, and this is what we call their *connotative aspect*. Our job in play analysis is to probe beneath the surface to determine what these larger "somethings" might be.

What kind of clues do you look for? Look through either or both the character aspects we've mentioned so far—the *literal* and the *functional*—and while keeping in mind how they change over the course of the play, see what relationships and contrasts emerge among them. What do the characters have in common, or how are they different? Identify the various goals and concerns: Do all the characters want the same thing, or do some stand out by wanting something very different? What is the nature of that difference? What elements make them foils? What kinds of *raisonneur* statements do they deliver? And after having identified these, ask yourself what possible meaning or ideas you can extrapolate from them.

Then look at the overall dramatic action: What things happen to these "ideas"? How are things changed? Does something win over something else? Does something transform something else into a new identity? How is the end of the play different from the beginning in this symbolic dimension? Take a two-character play; for example, August Strindberg's *Miss Julie*. In this play, the agent of action and the antagonist serve as foils to each other in many ways, some on the surface and some only suggested underneath. What possible connotations do they present? Here are some of my observations; what might you add to them?

Julie is an aristocrat; Jean is a servant.
Julie is passionate; Jean is intellectual.
Julie wants to fall (into the arms of a servant); Jean wants to
    climb (on the money of his mistress).
Julie is female; Jean is male.
Julie loses; Jean wins.
Julie dies; Jean survives.

Symbolically, therefore, Strindberg might be saying that men are stronger than women; the lower classes are healthier than the upper classes; sex is stronger than intellect; and so forth. Furthermore, notice how, in many ways, both of the characters somehow transform into a part of the other:

Julie commands at the beginning but takes commands at
    the end.

Jean is strong at the beginning but becomes weak at the
very end.

Julie grows and changes in her self-awareness; Jean comes
back to where he was at the beginning.

You can carry this as far as you like, finding deeper levels of
meaning as you go. Can you ever be wrong? Can you ever go too
far? No, not as long as you are prepared to justify your ideas by
specific moments or lines that you find in the play, nor as long as
your ideas have consistency and logic behind them.

Consider very carefully this third aspect. Once you've examined the other two, this one is where the real play analysis takes
place. This is where you find the most interesting interpretations
of the play and from which you can draw the most sophisticated
conclusions. In part 2, when we examine *genres* and talk about
characters in various other kinds of functions, we'll return time
and again to this same point. It's one thing to see how the characters work within the structure of the play, but a much better
thing to determine how they work on the intellectual and thematic plane.

Questioning the Play

1. Begin first with the literal aspect of the characters: What kind
of people are they? Examine their goals, their strategies, and their
vulnerabilities to see what they have in common or how they are
different. Does one general similarity develop among them all? Are
they contrasted in some unique way? What conclusions about the
play's meaning can you draw from these relationships?

2. Which characters perform which functions in the play? Does
one character perform different functions at different times?

3. Which is the agent of action? Is this the same person whom
you might also call the *central character*? Which character acts, and
which character is, in contrast, acted upon? If they are different,
what significance does this difference have? Why is the central
character unable to act?

4. Who is the antagonist character? Where does this force come
from?

5. How are the foils related to each other? What comparisons and contrasts can you make? In what ways, if any, are the agent of action and the antagonist foils for each other? How do these conclusions contribute to the meaning of the play?

6. Where do you find, if you do, *raisonneur* moments? What speeches seem to express the larger idea of the play? Who makes them? Why?

7. How do these speeches reinforce the other conclusions you've drawn about the play? Does the overall dramatic action (that is, *change*) illustrate the same idea that the speeches do?

8. How do the characters function on the connotative level? What forces or metaphysical concepts might the relationship of the characters suggest? How do these conclusions contribute to the meaning of the play?

5

Language

Language as a Set of Codes

Language is the element through which a play's events are communicated; hearing the characters talk to each other lets the audience perceive and understand the play's meaning. In a basic sense, any language is a set of signs that we use to send messages to other people. Some of these signs are visual: We all know that a red traffic light that faces us means we are to stop, while a green one means we can go. We all know that when we smile at somebody, we are pleased about something; when we take a step back from them, we are a little afraid. These physiologic signals form what's called *body language*. When the house lights dim in the auditorium, we know that the play is about to start; these signs form a language of *theatrical convention*.

While playwrights may use a particular visual sign in their plays (such as insisting that a character wear a white dress or carry a purple robe), the most common set of signals is, of course, verbal. This chapter, therefore, is concerned with how words reveal the ideas within a play. This is done in two different ways:

- using words as *symbols of meaning*
- using words as *euphonics*, that is, words as sounds and rhythms

Words as Symbols of Meaning

Words form the basic building blocks of our spoken and written language; we have all learned that certain visual scribbles arranged in a certain sequence and that certain sounds we make with our face and throat muscles (also arranged in a certain sequence) refer to particular things or ideas. When we see scribbles and hear noises, our brains translate them into concepts, so that when we see five particular squiggly lines in a particular arrangement (like this: <c h a i r>) or hear the sounds that are associated with those scribbles, we all know we are making reference to something that we use to sit down on. Words are merely stand-ins (symbols, if you will) for the actual thing.

However, symbols can often be deceptive. We may think we all know what the speaker is referring to when he says "chair," but in truth, we may not. That's because words have different levels of meaning, and playwrights are careful to take these different levels into account when choosing them; and we must be equally careful when we try to understand them. These different levels of meaning involve *denotation* and *connotation*.

Denotation

The *denotation* of a word is its prescribed, dictionary-type definition. For example, the sentence you just read gives you the denotation of the word *denotation*, because it told you its definition. This level is scientific and objective; it supposedly means the same thing to all of us who use it. Thus, we all agree that *chair*—at least when it's used as a noun—means a thing we use to sit on. (When it's used as a verb, what does it denote?)

However, there are many types of "things we use to sit on," and each is slightly different from the others. Is this sittable object plain or fancy—a toilet or a throne? Does this sittable object have four supports or three—a kitchen chair or a stool? Is this sittable object valuable or not—an antique or a piece of junk? And is this sittable object safe and cozy or quite lethal—a means of relaxation or an instrument of execution? Thus, while the word *chair* has a denotation that is supposedly objective, it still encompasses a wide range of possibilities. The playwright is careful to use words that have precise meanings. Clearly, he won't have a character say, "I'm going to get you a rocker" when he really means, "I'm going to execute you."

The question of denotation is made even more complicated when you realize that cultures vary, times change, and history often makes a difference. What, for instance, is a *boot*? To an American, it might be a kind of footwear. To a British citizen, it's the part of a car where you store luggage. Furthermore, in some situations, *boot* isn't a noun at all, but a verb. You can "boot" up your computer, or you can "boot" somebody out of your office. However, to Shakespeare, it's a verb that means almost the opposite; it's something you do for a good reason. Therefore, when the queen in *Richard II* says in act 3, scene 4, "It boots me not to complain," she's not talking about starting herself up or kicking herself in the pants.

Connotation

Connotation refers to a whole layer of associations, ideas, or attitudes that are often attached to a word. This is a highly subjective meaning and often varies from person to person. The most obvious examples of connotative meanings can be found in abstract terms, but they apply to concrete terms just as well.

For instance, consider the word *patriotic*. Its denotation states that it's a characteristic of a particular kind of person who will stand up and defend his country against danger, and that ought to be simple enough. However, for Americans, the word also brings to mind perhaps a member of a band of stalwart colonists in 1776 who stood proudly against British tyranny, or someone who was played in a movie by Mel Gibson, or something that makes you feel warm and fuzzy and that is, overall, a good thing. Thus, the army names one of its most lethal missiles the "Patriot," intending you to see a weapon of destruction as a "good thing." On the other hand, suppose you were King George in 1776 and were told that the colonists were fomenting revolution in the name of *patriotism*; you might easily bring to the word a connotation of gun-toting, lawbreaking, disobedient traitors. Or the word *patriotic* might conjure up in somebody's mind a person who gets up on a soapbox and preaches endlessly about why this land is better than any other, and how we should hate, suspect, and eliminate anybody who doesn't vote for his party. Such a person clearly means to "defend his country against danger," but because there is something harsh and hateful about his bigotry, he gives to the word *patriotic* a negative and ugly connotation.

Using Denotation and Connotation

With all this possible confusion about meaning, how does a playwright decide exactly which word to use? She asks herself several questions:

1. What would the denotation and connotation be to the character who is speaking? In *The Glass Menagerie*, for instance, when Amanda refers to the men who used to come visiting her, she uses the phrase "entertaining gentlemen callers." She doesn't say, "spending time with young men" or "having dates." There is something about the word *entertaining* that means more than just having a conversation or passing the time—something, perhaps, that connotes being responsible for them, or putting on an act. Likewise, there is something in the phrase *gentlemen callers* that means more than just visitors—something, perhaps, that suggests formality, manners, a bit of antebellum chivalry. The kind of woman who would use these words is a person who perhaps still lives in the past, still has old-fashioned ideas about courtship, and is a little bit lost to reality. And this is the kind of woman Amanda proves to be.

2. How do the denotation and connotation contribute to the sense of the world the play is creating? How do they help convey a time, a place, and a mood? We've seen how Amanda's word choices suggest that she's an old-fashioned woman living in the past. The words used by Laura often convey a similar idea. When Laura tries to describe a look on Amanda's face, she says, "you get that awful suffering look on your face. Like the picture of Jesus' mother in the museum" (act 1, scene 2). She doesn't call the look "disappointing" or "unhappy" but gives it a formal, almost antiquated tone. Likewise, she refers not to "Mary," but to "Jesus' mother," which also suggests something formal and perhaps old-fashioned. It seems, therefore, that Laura lives in a world very much like her mother's. Tom and the gentleman caller, however, both live in a world of harsh necessities and cold realities. Tom calls his mother an "ugly babbling old witch"—nothing formal about that. He thinks "dead people are lucky"—nothing antiquated about that. Jim, the gentleman caller, refers to Laura's limp as a "clump" (whereas Amanda insists on referring to it as a "slight defect"). This is how he describes the world he lives in: "Knowledge—Zzzzzp! Money—Zzzzzp! Power! That's the cycle democracy is built on!" Clearly, a different world from one that involves *gentlemen callers*.

3. How do the denotations and connotations of words help convey the meaning of the play? Take a look at the last lines of the play, when

Tom says he reaches for "anything that can blow your candles out—for nowadays the world is lit by lightning! Blow out your candles, Laura" (act 2, scene 7). He contrasts two opposing sources of light, *candlelight* and *lightning*, in terms of softness versus hardness, romance versus reality, beauty versus ugliness, gentility versus power. Notice how Williams has brought those two different values into conflict. Which of those two win? What does it mean for Laura to "blow out" her candles: Give up the past? Face the world? Or live in darkness? Has the symbolic action of the play been all about "blowing out candles"?

Words as Euphonics

Euphonics refers to the sounds words make when you speak them. It's an important consideration in play analysis because plays are meant to be performed, and so words usually reach the audience through their ears, rather than through their eyes. Words are meant to provide an aural experience rather than a visual one, and how they sound often carries as much meaning as what they symbolize. In this sense, language is very much like music or spoken poetry, in that it helps create mood by

- the sounds of the vowels and consonants;
- the use of assonance, dissonance, and alliteration;
- the emotional quality of rhythm.

Moods in the Vowels and Consonants

Writers who work with spoken words, such as poets, song writers, speech makers, and playwrights, are very much aware that vowel sounds in themselves carry subtle emotional values. They use comparative terms like *bright* or *dark*, *open* or *closed*, and *advancing* or *retreating* to try to categorize these values. You'll have to talk aloud to yourself as you read this section to fully appreciate them.

The Sounds of Vowels

Some vowel sounds are made with the lips and throat open and relatively relaxed and are typically held in the air for a brief length of time. When you say *above* or *mount* or *high*, you are making these kinds of sounds. They typically convey an idea of freedom, expansiveness, optimism, and so on—whatever emotion or idea you might think of as open or bright or advancing.

Other vowel sounds are made with the throat somewhat constricted and tense, and you don't hold them very long but cut them short with a consonant: the sounds in *hatred, anger*, or *depressed* are these kinds of sounds. They typically convey, as you would expect, tense and harsh emotions, such as those that are associated with—well—hatred, anger, and depression.

Some vowel sounds are made with the lips somewhat pursed and constricted, and they may be held a bit longer, as in *moon, beautiful*, or *push*. Moods that come to mind from sounds like these are somewhat darker and perhaps romantic, pleasant, mysterious, and so forth. Think of a *beautiful tomb* under the *moon* at *midnight*, and you'll get the idea.

The Sounds of Consonants

Like vowel sounds, consonants also have certain emotional undertones.

- *Plosives* such as *b* or *p* convey power, firmness, coldness.
- *Labials* such as *m* or *n* convey something softer, more leisurely, warmer.
- *Sibilants* such as *s* or *z* convey something soft as well, but perhaps a little colder and snakelike.
- *Gutturals* such as *ng, k*, and to some extent *r*, convey quickness, harshness, perhaps aggression.
- *Labiodentals* such as *t* and *d* convey something sharp, clipped, a bit abrupt.

Please keep in mind that all of these descriptions are extremely oversimplified and general, and you can no doubt find words that prove the exception. Also, it is true that sometimes a playwright has to use a word because of its meaning and has no choice about its euphonics. If a character, for instance, says, "I will murder you" rather than "I will kill you," it might be because the connotation of *murder* is more important than the sound of *kill*.

Example

Here are some lines from *The Glass Menagerie*. Speak them aloud to yourself, and see if you can analyze the feelings or emotions the sounds suggest. Amanda is reminiscing to Laura and Tom about the summer she met the man who was to be their father and is talking about the dress she wore.

> I wore it on Sundays for my gentlemen callers! I had it on the day I met your father—I had malarial fever all that Spring. The change of climate from East Tennessee to the Delta—weakened resistance—I had a little temperature all the time—not enough to be serious—just enough to make me restless and giddy. (act 2, scene 7)

Notice how the sounds support the emotional values of the ideas. The earlier words are largely open: *SunDAAYs, gENtleMEN cAWllers, DAAY, FATHerr,* and especially *maLAArial.* Then notice how, as the ideas and memories grow darker, the sounds turn colder and darker as well: *EEst TenneSEE* and *dELLta,* particularly in *wEEkund reSIStuNS* and *teMPraCHUR.* And notice how the sounds of the last two words are very much opposite in feeling and provide a rather abrupt contrast in feeling: *RESluss* and *GIdee*—sounds that once again are lighter and looser—the way you might feel if you were "restless and giddy."

Assonance, Dissonance, and Alliteration

These terms all relate to how the sounds in one word relate to the sounds in another word.

Assonance. This refers to vowel sounds that are similar to each other but aren't related in the sense that rhymes are. Words *rhyme* when their last accented syllables contain the same vowels prefaced by different consonants. In other words, the sound and the stress are the same, but the consonant is different. Thus, *cable* rhymes with *unstable.* In the same way, *ride, bride, unsatisfied,* and *denied* are words that rhyme.

When the vowel sounds are similar but *not* connected in this way, we are talking about *assonance.* Thus *cable* is assonant with such words as *stay, maybe, neighbor, relate, vacation*, and so forth—words in which the long *a* vowel sound is repeated but not in the final stressed syllables.

Words that are related to each other through assonance tend to reinforce in the listener's mind whatever that vowel sound is. Notice in Amanda's speech above how often an open *a* sound appears: *callers, had, father, malarial*, and *that*—all contributing to the languid mood we noted earlier.

Furthermore, words that are related through assonance also tend to convey to the listener a subtle sense that things are connected and belong together; like is with like—in other words, there's a subtle sense of harmony.

Dissonance. The opposite effect appears when the vowel sounds of words are different. A subtle sense of disharmony, tension, or imbalance is conveyed to the listener as *dissonance.* If you think of the harsh sounds of city traffic during rush hour, or loud and grating chords in rock music, you understand what dissonance is. Look again at Amanda's speech above and notice that right after that long string of open *a* sounds there suddenly appear the words *change of climate.* Notice how this new phrase clashes with the others: In the first place, we are suddenly hearing a more closed, stressed sound in the *i* in *climate*, and in the second place, that long string of fairly relaxed, almost languid open *a*'s are cut short by the abrupt, harsh, almost hammerlike stop of the final *t*—a definite discord in the music of the moment.

Furthermore, notice that there are more harsh consonants following this moment: more hard *t*'s, *p*'s, and *f*'s. Thus, while the first part of the example flows, the second half clumps. This dissonance subtly enhances the emotional ideas themselves: a languid summer suddenly gives way to tension and trouble.

Alliteration. While words are related to each other through their vowels, they are also related through their consonants; the term used to describe the repetition of similar consonants is *alliteration.* For example, a famous alliterative phrase begins with "Peter Piper."

Notice how often *m*'s appear in Amanda's speech: *gentleman, met, malarial, climate, temperature, time*, and *make me.* All these *m*'s help convey a sense of harmony, balance, and unity, and—because they are soft, almost "humming" sounds—a sense of grace, gentility, and softness throughout the whole section.

Connective Techniques

These three devices (assonance, dissonance, and alliteration) connect words within a particular speech. But they are also used to connect one speech with another, often appearing in exchanges between different characters. The playwright will use these devices when she wants to suggest how one character might be very close to, or very much like, or in the same world as another character—or, on the other hand, how these characters might be separated or different. Here's a short exchange between Amanda and Laura, which occurs just after Amanda has discovered that Laura has not been attending school. As you read it aloud, notice how many similar sounds are shared between the two speakers and where important differences appear:

AMANDA: Laura, where have you been going when you've gone out pretending that you were going to business college?
LAURA: I've just been out walking.
AMANDA: That's not true.
LAURA: It is; I just went walking
AMANDA: Walking? Walking? In winter? Deliberately courting pneumonia in that light coat? Where did you walk to, Laura?
LAURA: It was the lesser of two evils, Mother. I couldn't go back there. I—threw up—on the floor! (act 1, scene 2)

Have you noticed:

- how the repetition of *w* sounds relates the two women, especially in how they each say *walking* several times, but also in Amanda's *where*, *when*, and *winter*?
- how few *w* sounds appear in Laura's last speech, which begins to move the two women apart?
- how both characters use soft consonant sounds for the most part, and how often they each use *b*'s?
- how many times they each use words with a long *o* in them?

- what a sharp contrast there is between nearly all of their exchanges and Laura's last phrase? All the previous softness is brought to abrupt dissonance when Laura says "threw up"—a harsh close to the passage, which subtly suggests how the two women see the world in very different ways.

Rhythm

Very much like music, spoken language falls into patterns of stressed and nonstressed sounds. Some syllables—like some notes—receive greater emphasis than others; our ears perceive these patterns, and our minds give meaning to them. For instance, you see the following six letters on the page: *desert*. How do you know what they symbolize? You can only know for sure when you remember how they sound when they are spoken. If you put emphasis on the first syllable, you get a sandy place; if you stress the second syllable, you get a traitorous action.

By choosing words so that their stress patterns combine to form a larger unit, playwrights create sentences that have an overall sense of *rhythm* to them. Poets make very deliberate use of these patterns and arrange their words into lines that have specific rhythms. It's beyond the scope of this book to go into all the details of *prosody* (a word meaning "the science of verbal rhythms used in poetry"), but no doubt you've already had exposure to this study when you learned, for instance, that lines of poetry fall into short units called *feet* and are described by how many feet each line has.

Thus, a foot might be one of several kinds:

- two syllables, one unstressed followed by one stressed, as in "be-YOND"; this foot is called *iambic*
- two syllables, one stressed followed by one unstressed, as in "GO-ing"; this foot is called *trochaic*
- three syllables, two unstressed followed by one stressed, as in "i am GO-ing to FOL-low you HOME"; this foot is called *anapestic*
- three syllables, one stressed followed by two unstressed, as in "SLOW-ly i MOVED to the O-pen-ing DOOR"; this foot is called *dactyl*

An individual line of poetry consists of a specific number of these feet and is named accordingly. A line that has three feet of iambs is called *iambic trimeter*, as in

a-WAY, a-WAY we GO
be-YOND the DIS-tant SNOW

An iambic line that has four feet is called *iambic tetrameter*, as in

i THINK that I shall NE-ver SEE
a PO-em LOVE-ly AS a TREE.

And no doubt you are already familiar with *iambic pentameter*, the five-footed line that Shakespeare and other writers of blank verse use:

when TO the SES-sions OF sweet SI-lent THOUGHT
i SUM-mon UP re-MEM-brance OF things PAST.

It's one thing to discuss rhythm in poetry, where these rhythmic devices are used most often, where lines are laid out on a page in very specific lengths, and where the rhythm often falls into these very specific and recognizable patterns; but it's quite a different matter to observe how rhythm appears in the dialogue of a play. Unless that play is specifically written in verse (like those of Shakespeare and some modern writers like Maxwell Anderson or Jean Giraudoux), the rhythm is likely to be much less regular and much less noticeable.

But playwrights still use rhythmic patterns when it suits their purposes. Rhythm helps contribute to the emotional quality of a speech or moment, helps relate one character to another, and some-times adds beauty or comedy to the scene.

Rhythm can appear within an individual line. Returning to *The Glass Menagerie*, notice in act 1, scene 3, that Tom is exploding in anger at his mother. He has a fairly long speech that gradually grows more intense (it's the speech that ends with his calling her a "babbling old witch"). Around the middle of the speech, Tom speaks the sen-tences below. If you examine them closely and say them aloud, you'll discover that they are a series of iambic pentameters:

oh I could TELL you THINGS to MAKE you SLEEP-less.
My EN-emies PLAN to DY-na-MITE this PLACE.

They're GO-ing to BLOW us ALL sky-HIGH some
NIGHT.

Certainly, the actor playing Tom wouldn't speak these sentences in such a forced rhythmic pattern, but even speaking them "naturally" gives you a sense of something heavy, almost martial, and rapid.

Rhythm can appear within a speech. When a character delivers a fairly long speech, the playwright will often vary his sentence rhythms, sometimes alternating longer ones with shorter and sometimes building a series of sentences that have similar rhythms, only to contrast them with a different rhythm at the climax. In the same speech of Amanda's that we examined earlier, when she is reminiscing about her "gentlemen callers," notice how Williams uses rhythm to build a mood: He has Amanda begin to remember hunting for jonquils. Over the course of several long sentences, Amanda speaks about the flowers:

> It was a joke, Amanda and her jonquils! Finally there were no more vases to hold them, every available space was filled with jonquils. No vases to hold them? All right, I'll hold them myself. (act 2, scene 6)

Now, notice how the rhythm abruptly changes to something less languid and dreamy and more harsh and choppy:

> And then I—met your father. Malarial fever and jonquils and— then—this—boy.

And then she abruptly changes the subject with a line that's another iambic pentameter, with the same martial-like beat we've met before:

> i HOPE they GET HERE beFORE it STARTS to RAIN.

Rhythm can appear between speeches. A series of individual lines can share a common rhythm. When this happens, the characters are somehow connected to each other emotionally; at the same time, the moment of the scene has an emotional quality of its own. In the following exchange, Tom has brought home good news to Amanda: He has found a gentleman caller for Laura. Notice how the two bounce short, springy, and quick-paced lines back and forth, almost as though they were playing a happy game of Ping-Pong with each other:

AMANDA: It's definite them?
TOM: Very definite.
AMANDA: Soon?
TOM: Very soon.
AMANDA: For heaven's sake, stop putting on and tell me some things, will you?
TOM: What kind of things do you want me to tell you?
AMANDA: Naturally I would like to know when he's coming.
TOM: He's coming tomorrow.
AMANDA: Tomorrow?
TOM: Yep. Tomorrow.
AMANDA: But Tom!
TOM: Yes, Mother?
AMANDA: Tomorrow gives me no time! (act 1, scene 4)

When you read it aloud, you may find yourself laughing at the silliness of this banter; Williams gave it this sprightly rhythm for that very reason.

Here are some other passages from plays in which the rhythm shared by two characters is an important part of the emotion as well as the meaning of the scene. The first is from *Waiting for Godot* by Samuel Beckett. Two tramps are trapped in an existential void, waiting forever for someone named Godot to show up. In this passage, they compare themselves to the dead, realizing why they talk so much to each other:

ESTRAGON: It's so we won't think
VLADIMIR: We have that excuse.
ESTRAGON: It's so we won't hear.
VLADIMIR: We have our reasons.
ESTRAGON: All the dead voices.
VLADIMIR: They make a noise like wings.
ESTRAGON: Like leaves.
VLADIMIR: Like sand.
ESTRAGON: Like leaves. (act 1)

The passage goes on like this for another page, but you get the idea.

In sharp contrast, here's an exchange from Noel Coward's *Private Lives*. Amanda and Elyot, two sophisticated comedy-of-manners types, are having yet another of their petty quarrels:

ELYOT: It's a pity you didn't have any more brandy; it might have made you a little less disagreeable.

AMANDA: It doesn't seem to have worked such wonders with you.

ELYOT: Snap, snap, snap, like a little adder.

AMANDA: Adders don't snap, they sting.

ELYOT: Nonsense. They have a little bag of venom behind their fangs and they snap.

AMANDA: They sting.

ELYOT: They snap.

AMANDA: I don't care, do you understand? I don't care. I don't mind if they bark, and roll about like hoops. (act 2)

The language playwrights use to convey their ideas is a multilayered set of symbols. The first level is the denotative meaning of the word: What exactly does the writer want the character to say? The second level is the connotative meaning: the unspoken attitudes, ideas, and/or associations that the word suggests. The third level is emotional: the subtle way that the sounds and rhythms of both words and speeches make us feel when we hear them spoken.

Questioning the Play

1. What is the native language of the playwright? Are you reading the play in its original language or are you reading a translation? This is important to note because you may or may not be "hearing" the language as the author wanted you to, but rather filtered through a translator's choice of words. This could have an effect on the ultimate meaning of the play, and it might be more or less important, depending on why you're examining the language.

2. What words in the text might have ambiguous denotations? What effect does this have on the meaning of the line, the scene, or the play?

3. How do the connotations of important words contribute to your interpretation of the character who speaks them? Of the world the playwright is trying to create? Of the mood or emotional quality of the scene or the entire play?

4. What key passages have unique euphonic qualities? Are certain vowel sounds used in such ways that they contribute to the mood or meaning of the scene or play? The same with consonants: Where do assonance, dissonance, or alliteration contribute to the meaning of the scene or the play? To the relationships between the characters speaking these lines?

5. What key passages are given additional meaning by the use of rhythmic patterns, either within single lines, within single speeches, or in extended passages between speakers?

Part Two: **Genres**

Plays are often grouped into categories, such as *tragedy*, *comedy*, *melodrama, farce*, and a small variety of others. These categories are called, collectively, *genres*. Thus, *genre* refers to the particular category a play falls into depending upon the author's attitude toward the life it portrays.

Traditionally, plays have fallen into two broad categories: those that are upbeat, funny, supposedly optimistic, and that end happily; or those that are sad, seemingly pessimistic, and that end sadly. The first is thought of, naturally, as *comedy*, while the second is *tragedy*. Variations on these provide us with *melodrama* and *farce*, giving us four primary genres.

Of course, these broad generalizations are extremely superficial and simplistic. No one play is ever all one genre or all the other. However, we can define what we call "pure" or "classic" genres, according to four basic areas:

- the overall mood of the play
- the sort of world or society in which the play is set and the typical kind of conflict that might be dramatized
- typical plot patterns that are used
- typical characters who appear

Your job is to apply these characteristics to the play in question. Your process should involve the following activities:

- Understand what the genre typically looks like, in its "classical" state.

- Notice to what extent the play under consideration has some, none, or all of these elements.
- Draw what conclusions seem appropriate, given what you know of all four causes.

In other words, if it quacks, swims, has white feathers, a yellow beak, big paddle feet, and is named Donald—is it a duck? Or something else?

The following charts lay out for you how the four basic genres relate to each other according to a number of factors. Take a look at them now, as you begin your study, to get a broad overview of the kinds of things we'll be defining. After you've finished this unit, use the charts to review and fix the material in your mind.

But now let's look at a tragic duck.

Tragedy	Comedy
Deals with man and God (or the Universe): what should our lives be like?	Deals with man and society: what should our cultures be like?
Begins and ends with an assumed moral code	Begins with a flawed society and ends with an open one
Contains a mood of solemnity	Contains a mood of ridicule: sources of laughter verbal wit, jokes, etc.
Deals with characters "better than us"	Deals with characters "lower than us"
Tragic hero: elevated, responsible makes tragic error/*hamartia* commits act of shame falls	*Alazon* ("blocker"): in a position of authority has "false/blocked" ideals inhibits "love" needs to be "educated"
Nemesis: seeks vengeance	*Eiron* ("teacher"): eliminates blocks
Innocent victim	Buffoon
Plot concerns: the fall of a man his redemption	Plot concerns: a marriage an education a trick interface with "green world"
Scene of suffering/scapegoating	Climax/confrontation
Insight	*Cognitio*
Restoration of universal moral code; sense of redemption	New, open, free society established; marriage

Melodrama	Farce
Deals with man against man: how do we experience and resolve interpersonal conflicts?	Deals with man against chaos: how do we navigate through extreme complications?
Begins with sense of threat and danger; ends with security possibly restored	Begins with a deceit; ends with forgiveness
Contains a mood of suspense	Contains a mood of urgency, desperation, danger
Deals with characters very much on a par with us	Deals with characters who might be said to represent "our secret selves"
The "good guy" represents values of author, serves as a sort of *raisonneur*	The "sane person" represents more normal/rational behavior
The "bad guy" serves as major complication	A varied collection of fools, false lovers, etc.
A character in distress	Knave, buffoon, etc.
Plot consists of a series of reversals that cause increasing danger	Plot consists of a series of ever more complicated twists of fortune, coincidences, disguises, etc.
A culminating "big scene" or a major confrontation	A scene of chaos
Sudden rescue	*Cognitio*
Victory of the "good"	Forgiveness and reconciliation

6

Classic Tragedy

The word *tragedy* has changed its meaning drastically over the centuries. Today, we use the term to identify almost any sad situation in which somebody typically dies. Thus, when a famous humanitarian is killed in a plane accident, the media calls her death "tragic." When a young man dies from accidentally drinking too much alcohol, his parents take comfort by calling his death a "shocking tragedy." The word seems to imply that there is some quality to the event that makes it unusual and perhaps important, that gives it some meaning, and that hopefully provides mourners a measure of comfort.

However, in its truest sense, the word has a different meaning. It began as a term used to define a particular kind of play written and performed by classical Greeks such as Sophocles and Euripides. Indeed, the word is composed of two Greek roots: *tragos*, which means "goat," and *odos*, which means "song." This is because these plays were first performed in ancient Greece as entries in annual contests, and scholars think the first prize may have been a goat. Thus, *tragedy* really means "goat song."

The features of these early plays provide a model for what we call *classic tragedy*. We'll look at the typical "pure" form, setting up a standard against which you can analyze the play you're studying.

What Is the Mood of a Classic Tragedy?

Because somebody usually dies, we assume that the mood of a classic tragedy is serious, and our attitude toward the people and events is dignified and respectful. We are often moved by the sight of somebody suffering, especially if we feel that this suffering is undeserved. And yet, somehow we don't feel too sad; we feel that something good has come out of the experience. We understand a little bit more about what life means. Something has been affirmed; even though somebody has died, we admire that person for his hero-ism or self-sacrifice and see something noble in his death. We feel a sense of hope and redemption. In this way, we might even af-firm that classic tragedy has a sort of happy ending after all.

What Sort of World or Society Forms the Setting?

Classic tragedies may be set in a variety of locations: the courtyard of a palace, the back porch of a house, or some other public gath-ering place. However, these are only the superficial settings; on a symbolic level, the underlying action of the play takes place on a much larger scale. The issues at stake go beyond the personal ex-perience of one character or his relations with his family or com-munity and reflect deep moral values: How should a man live his life? What moral codes should guide him, or is he above any such restrictions? What do we consider *right*, and how do we define *wrong*? What is man's relation to a Supreme Being?

When Oedipus, for example, sets out to find the cause of the plague attacking his city, he at first seems to be simply trying to solve an ancient mystery. However, as the plot unfolds, we learn that Oedipus is somehow intimately connected to the gods; be-cause he has tried to defy their edict, his fate is tied up with theirs. Therefore, the play is not merely about a king helping his city but rather about a man coming to understand how the gods work. In a sense, therefore, the true setting of a classic tragedy might be considered the universe itself. Not the physical universe, as in a science fiction movie, but the spiritual, religious, metaphysical universe that underlies the physical world we see and that forms the basis for our belief structure.

If you recall the discussion in chapter 2 of the various kinds of conflicts in plays, you can see that the conflict in *Oedipus Rex* lies between *man and God*.

What Typical Plot Pattern Does a Classic Tragedy Follow?

A classic tragedy typically follows a five-step pattern:

- The state of equilibrium establishes a *universal moral code*.
- The inciting incident occurs when a character commits an *act of shame*.

- As the plot develops, this character undergoes *suffering*.
- At the climax, the character achieves some *insight*.
- As part of the resolution, the *universal moral code* is restored by some act of *redemption*.

The State of Equilibrium Establishes a Universal Moral Code

The term *universal moral code* refers to that particular set of values or ideals that permeate the culture of the play. A society always lays down some moral laws to govern itself; these may be written or only assumed, but they always function to answer the question of what is right and what is wrong. In Judeo-Christian culture, the Ten Commandments form part of its universal moral code: People generally agree it's bad to commit murder or dishonor one's parents. For the ancient Greeks of Sophocles' day, the universal moral code involved paying respect to the dictates and power of the various gods.

What are some other rules that might make up a universal moral code? Some seem to be present in all societies: For example, most people believe that it's wrong to steal. Some codes might be unique to one particular culture: It might be bad to work on Sunday to you but perfectly all right for your neighbor. Codes might be large or small: It's wrong to assassinate a president, and it's also wrong to cheat on your algebra homework. Codes might be inflexible and powerful: We might agree that, yes, it's always wrong to steal, but circumstances might call the code into question. Suppose I have to steal in order to keep my children alive? Is one "wrong" made "right" by a set of circumstances?

How do you discover the universal moral code of a particular play? What, in this world, qualifies as right or wrong? Typically, you'll get clues during the initial state of equilibrium. A *raisonneur* character might articulate what it is, as does the chorus in *Oedipus Rex*, when they say (in the first Choral Ode):

What is God singing in his profound
Delphi of gold and shadow?
What oracle for Thebes, the sunwhipped city.
Fear unjoints me, the roots of my heart tremble.
Now I remember, Oh Healer, your power and wonder.

At other times, a character will allude to the universal moral code indirectly; this happens several times in August Wilson's *Fences*. In the very first line of the play, Bono says, "Troy, you got to stop that lying!" Later, Rose echoes this attitude: "Troy, you ought not to talk like that; Troy ain't doing nothing but telling a lie." A few moments later, Troy begins talking about death and how he has no fear of it; Rose admonishes him with, "I don't know why you want to get on talking about death. . . . I don't like to talk about it" (act 1, scene 1). At another point, Rose again expresses her beliefs about life, when she tells Troy, "God's the one you gonna have to answer to. He's the one gonna be at the Judgement" (act 2, scene 3). Time and again, similar references appear in the play to questions of lying, respecting God and death, and behaving in a good way. As the play progresses, we see how deeply and terribly Troy has lied (about his past, about his mistress, about his brother's money); and we see how Troy defies death and disrespects God, setting himself above both of them.

In other plays, the universal moral code is implied in the choices a character makes and how she feels about it; when Nora tells Mrs. Linde that she feels no guilt at all about forging her father's signature (lying) in order to get money (fraud) to save her husband's life, she's obeying a moral code that, in her universe, puts human life above strict honesty and banking rules.

The Inciting Incident Occurs When a Character Commits an Act of Shame

An *act of shame* is any deed that violates an important part of the universal moral code. If the code defines right from wrong, clearly an act of shame involves doing what's considered wrong. The word *shame* is used to indicate the gravity and seriousness of the deed.

Typically, the character who commits this act of shame is the play's agent of action. For the purposes of our discussion, we'll call this person the *tragic hero*. He or she drives the action of the play forward and forms the center of our attention. As with any agent of action, the tragic hero's goals, at-stake elements, and strategies are important clues to the play's meaning. We note two essential characteristics of this act.

An Act of Shame May Be Relative

Oedipus Rex illustrates how an act of shame can be subject to interpretation. We have already identified what constitutes the universal moral code in that world: obedience to the gods. We know they foretold that Oedipus's fate involved killing his father and wedding his mother. However, we saw that Oedipus decided to defy the gods' forewarnings and to leave the country of his birth. Now, in one way, this decision of his might be regarded as completely sensible: After all, patricide and incest are taboo almost anywhere. We might think him a wise man and call his decision an act of courage instead.

Later, Oedipus meets an old man on the road and, in a fit of anger, kills him. As if defying the gods weren't bad enough, now he's committed an act of murder. But, as we said before, sometimes an act of killing can be considered a *good* thing. Is that the case here? Might self-defense be involved? We don't have the whole picture, you know, just the reports of unreliable witnesses.

And still later, when his city suffers under the plague, Oedipus sets out to solve the mystery he thinks caused this plague. Is that such a bad thing to do, or would he have done better to let things stand as they were and leave the past undisturbed? But then the city would have perished. What's a guy to do? The issue's not so cut-and-dried after all.

The answer lies in the setting. Clearly in *his* world, the act of killing the old man might find some justification; the decision to dig up the past might be considered a wise one; but what remains at the core is still true: He disobeyed the gods by taking his fate into his own hands and trying to be stronger than they. Thus, we might say this defiance would be his act of shame.

While many acts of shame are relative, is there some element that is universal? Yes.

An Act of Shame Involves a Public Dimension

The committing of this crime affects a significant group of people, not just the perpetrator. It's like throwing a stone in a pond and making ripples: In one way or another, the act threatens the security of a larger population. When Oedipus defies the gods, he puts the power of the gods in jeopardy, which indirectly affects the status of the whole known world. When Troy (in *Fences*) lies and behaves as arrogantly as he does, his actions affect his wife, his son, his brother, his illegitimate baby, and who knows how many successive generations.

This, therefore, is why classic tragedies often are set in public locations, or locations that representatives of the public have access to.

As the Plot Develops, This Character Undergoes Suffering

Just as you knew when you were a child that if you broke certain rules in your house you would be punished, and just as any civilization dictates that criminals who break laws will be punished, classic tragedy demands that the tragic hero who commits an act of shame must suffer punishment for it. Not only that, but the suffering needs to be severe—almost total. He might even have to die, as Troy does. He might cause the death of loved ones, as Creon does in Sophocles' *Antigone*. Or he might need to be banished: set adrift to live in another city, as Oedipus banishes himself.

In this way, classic tragedies typically involve *exclusion*. The tragic hero is cast away and separated, so that something is lost. But something is also gained.

At the Climax, the Character Achieves Some Insight

You'll recall, in our discussion of the well-made play structure, we noticed that two important things happen at the climax: a moment of *reversal* (wherein the story takes a sharp turn up or down), and a moment of *recognition* (wherein the agent of action often learns something of importance). Recognition appears in classic tragedy in several ways. The tragic hero may realize what it is that he has done wrong, as Oedipus learns of his mistake. He may realize the gravity of his act of shame—just how many people he may have inadvertently harmed or how deeply he may have harmed them, as Troy Maxson does in *Fences*. Or he may realize an important truth about the universe and the universal moral code itself. At the end of John Millington Synge's short play *Riders to the Sea*, Maurya, a strong Irish woman who has just buried the fifth of her sons to die at sea, now realizes a simple but profound truth:

Michael has a clean burial in the far north, by the grace of the Almighty God. Bartley will have a fine coffin out of the white boards and a deep grave surely. What more can we want than that? No man at all can be living forever and we must be satisfied.

At these moments, when characters articulate their insights, they often become *raisonneurs*, expressing the philosophy of the writer.

As Part of the Resolution, the Universal Moral Code Is Restored by Some Act of Redemption

Because he has committed some act of sin, the tragic hero is punished and cast out of the world he tainted by his crime. And because he has been cast out, the world is in some way a cleaner, better, purer place. In this sense, he becomes a sort of symbolic sacrifice, or what's referred to as a *scapegoat*. The word has a biblical origin, stemming from a dictate in Leviticus, in which the citizens are ordered to choose a goat, place all their sins symbolically in that goat, and then drive the goat out into the desert to die. Thus, in tragic parlance, a scapegoat is any person who suffers in the place of others. In Christian doctrine, Jesus became a scapegoat for all humanity.

In the beginning of *Oedipus Rex*, the city of Thebes is ridden with plague and sickness; once the cause of the gods' anger has been found and cast out, the city is cured again. In *Fences*, Troy's death somehow improves his family: His sons have found themselves, his wife is bringing up his illegitimate daughter, and his brother is able to "dance" him into heaven. The tragic hero has redeemed himself by bringing good after all.

Furthermore, the universal moral code is restored, and the new state of equilibrium is a positive, hopeful one. We are left with a universe that once again knows what is right and wrong, in which good does exist, and in which we can once again have faith. It is because we have this sort of "happy ending" that we can say classic tragedy is uplifting.

What Characters Appear in a Classic Tragedy?

There are three main categories of characters: the *tragic hero*, the *nemesis*, and the *innocent victim*.

The Tragic Hero

As we have seen, the *tragic hero* is most often the agent of action of the play: Because he wants something bad enough (his *goal*), he will do the worst possible things in order to get it (the *act of shame*). However, not every agent of action who commits a crime qualifies as a tragic hero. Two key characteristics must appear.

The Tragic Hero Must Be Elevated, either in Spirit or in Position

The idea of *elevation* comes from Aristotle. In a long discussion in *Poetics*, he remarks that "tragedy deals with characters above us, and comedy with characters below us." In another passage, he indicates that tragic heroes (at least those in the plays he knew) were typically of royal families, like the House of Thebes or House of Atreus. From this, critics have drawn the idea that a tragic hero should have a high social status, and indeed, most classic tragedies are about kings or princes. However, as times changed, critics began to question this interpretation, and many words have been written on just what that means and whether it's true; that is, can Willy Loman actually be a tragic hero although he is just a middle-class guy and not a king? Can there, indeed, be a tragedy of the lower classes?

We might safely answer yes, if we take *elevation* to have more than just a sociopolitical meaning and use the term to mean "better than us" in other ways; that is, someone who is braver, nobler, morally stronger; who works harder, feels more deeply, suffers more keenly, and lives life more passionately. Thus, while Willy Loman may not have the status or income of a king, the passion of his life, his dreams, and his experiences are somehow a bit larger than our own. It might be on this level of meaning we can call Troy Maxson (in *Fences*) or Maurya (in *Riders to the Sea*) tragic heroes: small people with large souls.

This accounts for being elevated in spirit. However, the tragic hero must also be in a position of some authority. He holds some status in his community; he is responsible for the welfare of others so that what he does affects people who depend on him. In this respect, a king certainly qualifies, but so does the president of the United States. So does the mayor of a town. So does the chairman of the Committee on Public Safety. So does the professor who teaches this course, and so do the father or mother of even a small family. This is why his act of shame is so bad; his crime draws others into its vortex. Again, it is on this level that the two examples in the preceding paragraph work: Both Troy and Maurya are "elevated" in being heads of their respective households.

The Tragic Hero Must Be Guilty of *Hamartia*

The concept of *hamartia* also comes from Aristotle. When he discusses what might "change" in plays, he lists four various possibilities and considers how they might or might not satisfy what he calls the "tragic spirit." He says that, in principle, we could see any of the following:

1. A bad man goes from bad fortune to good. This does not work for tragedy, however, because somehow our sense of justice is violated, and we feel no sympathy for him. We don't want to see the villain rewarded.

2. A bad man goes from good fortune to bad. This does not work either, because we feel that this is proper; the bad man *should* fall, and thus we don't feel the sadness that we should.

3. A virtuous man goes from good fortune to bad. This also does not work because, while we might feel sorry for this man, somehow we wouldn't stand in awe of what happened to him. We don't want to see random accidents happen to people we like.

This leaves the man in the fourth category. The true tragic spirit, Aristotle says, is present when *a reasonably good man suffers because of something wrong he has done.* "It remains," he writes, "to see the fall of a man who is not wholly good or bad, but suffers through an act of his own." He uses the Greek term *hamartia*—which is best translated as "error." It's this term and its definition that provide the key element.

Aristotle's statement is often misinterpreted to mean that the tragic hero must have some defect in his personality. Critics and teachers often call this defect a "tragic flaw" and say that the character has some sort of emotional or psychological weakness that makes him mess up. Oedipus is said to have this flaw because he is arrogant and proud, considering himself above the law. In fact, nearly all tragic heroes seem to possess this last defect, setting themselves above the moral code; the term *hubris* is used to describe this kind of pride. In some studies, you will find *hubris* used to mean the tragic flaw in general.

But this misses the mark. When Aristotle uses the term *hamartia* (error), he means that the character makes a mistake. The tragic hero misjudges a situation and chooses the wrong option. It's a matter of logic, not emotion; of intelligence, not passion; of mind, not of heart. It's what he *does*, not what he *is*, that forms the core of the issue. Thus, when Oedipus decides to defy the gods, it's a deliberate action—in short, what we've already called an act of shame.

Ah, but, you may say, what is it that has caused the character to make this bad decision? Surely, if Oedipus hadn't been so cocky, he wouldn't have tried to escape the prophecy. If Hamlet hadn't been so wishy-washy, he'd have finished his uncle right off. If Romeo were in control of his hormones, he'd have waited a couple of days more. And you would be right: Bad decisions are often caused by imperfect personalities.

But they are also often caused by smart people well in control of their emotions who make them for good and sound reasons. They think they are doing the right thing, but somehow they go wrong because they don't have all the facts, or they misread the facts. When Romeo marries too quickly and in secret, he thinks he's doing the right thing because he knows Juliet's parents would have stopped their romance if they had waited. When Oedipus decides to leave Corinth, it's because he thinks he's protecting the king and queen who, you must remember, he believes are his true parents.

Then why should he suffer? If the mistake is unconscious, how is it really an act of shame? Well, perhaps ignorance is, in a way, a kind of "tragic flaw" in itself. Or perhaps tragedy as a genre has to insist on absolutes and makes no allowances for good excuses (just as your parents might make no allowances for your getting poor grades). Or perhaps tragedy likes to function in this somewhat ambiguous, gray world, leaving the ultimate decisions up to you.

Nemesis

The term *nemesis* comes from the name of the Greek goddess of vengeance in classical mythology. Nemesis was one of the minor deities, whose job it was to seek vengeance on wrongdoers. The word itself, therefore, refers to any person or force that seeks to right a wrong and that wants to make a guilty person pay. The nemesis provides the punishment.

Notice the terms *person* and *force*. In some plays, the nemesis appears as another character who is part of the literal world of the play. Thus, when Troy Maxson fathers a child out of wedlock (an act of shame in his world), it's his wife who punishes him. She promises to take care of the baby but will no longer be a wife to him.

In other plays, the nemesis may be part of the tragic hero's own personality; her guilty conscience preys on her until she makes herself pay, often by committing suicide, going mad, or some other way. In O'Neill's *Mourning Becomes Electra*, Lavinia has convinced her brother to murder their mother; her final act in the play is to lock herself away in her cold, empty house until she dies.

The nemesis may also appear as some symbolic force. In *Fences*, we see Troy often speaking aloud to "Mr. Death," challenging him to a showdown. In the end, death wins. Keep in mind, however, that even when the nemesis appears as a *literal* character, she still has a *symbolic* component. Thus, Troy's wife Rose appears as a literal character/nemesis, but her role also has symbolic connotations in the play: She represents woman, wife, mother, stability, Christian values, and perhaps a number of other ideas. There's a reason for her name.

Identifying the source of the nemesis is an important clue to the meaning of the play. Consider the nemesis to be, in a way, the *antagonist* of the play, and ask yourself the kinds of questions you would ask of a character fulfilling that function. If it's an external character, where does it come from? What does it represent? In Shakespeare's *Macbeth*, if the nemesis is the three witches, where do they come from? Are they like gods? Or abstractions of Macbeth's own mental state? Are they hallucinations or projections? Are they forces of nature or just evil old women? Are they foils in some way to the tragic hero?

Innocent Victim

We've noted that the act of shame that initiates the tragedy has to be significant enough to bring about suffering and insight. Clearly, stepping on a bug or shoplifting a pack of cigarettes is wrong, but are they big enough crimes to qualify as tragedy? Sometimes even committing murder isn't enough; as we asked before, suppose the killing were an act of self-defense?

To provide the necessary scope to turn a nasty deed into an act of shame, therefore, there must be somewhere in the play a person who gets hurt without cause; somebody who happens to be in harm's way and gets caught up in the fateful sequence of events. This character is an *innocent victim* and may appear, as the nemesis does, in any number of forms.

The victim might be an individual. In *Fences*, Troy harms several people: He cheats on his wife, steals money that rightfully belongs to his brother, and abuses his children so badly they leave him. The victim might also be a whole community—this is one reason we earlier noted that a tragic hero is typically somebody of responsibility, like a king. Oedipus brings great harm to his city, causing the innocent populace unwarranted suffering.

Classical tragedy is a style of drama that is typically serious, but not necessarily sad. It shows us noble characters, above us in some way, who suffer some terrible fate because they have made at least one crucial error. However, the play often ends on a note of calm or hope; there is some sense of value the experience provides, both to the tragic hero and to the audience. Something has been affirmed or redeemed, and there has been a validation of a universal moral code. In this sense, a tragedy is often a good thing, and even though it ends in exclusion and death, it has a sort of upbeat ending after all: If we're not entirely happy, the people in the play are at least somewhat better off.

What Kinds of Tragedy Are There?

Over the years, tragedy has developed many variations. While the plot pattern remains relatively constant, changes have usually involved matters of social class. In its early manifestations, tragedy appeared most often in societies that were clearly divided into class structures: notably Athenian Greece, Elizabethan England, and seventeenth-century France. Thus, a tragic hero who was "above us" was usually a king, a prince, or an aristocrat. During the eighteenth century and afterward, many of these class distinctions dissolved; emerging middle and merchant classes became more visible, and dramatists began to write serious plays about characters at lower social levels, creating tragic heroes from these emergent classes. Thus, George Lillo tried to draw in *The London Merchant* a tragic hero who was nothing higher than an apprentice to a businessman. Later, John Millington Synge took as his central figure in *Riders to the Sea* a poor fisherman's wife on an island in the Irish sea. And August Wilson, as we've seen, wrote about an average neighborhood guy in *Fences*.

To accommodate these shifts, several categories have been named: *domestic tragedy*, *bourgeois tragedy*, *folk tragedy*, and others. The differences between them and classic tragedy are essentially minimal, and it serves little purpose to spend time isolating each one. What's important to remember is that these subgenres do give a tragic dignity to plays about common people.

Tragedy shows us a world that is, at bottom, good. While men may misbehave, they are eventually punished. Thus, the writer of tragedy sees the world as ultimately hopeful.

Questioning the Play

1. After your first reading of the play, what mood are you left with: somber or uplifting? What sort of ending does the play suggest: happy and hopeful, or sad and depressing?

2. What clues does the play give you that help you define the universal moral code of the play's world? Does this code have any relation to the world in which you live? Or is there something in the play's efficient cause that you might want to investigate?

3. What constitutes the play's act of shame? Does it seem to be a universal idea, or does it seem relative to the specific world of this play? In what ways does this act have larger resonances: Who else is affected by what the tragic hero has done?

4. What is the nature of the tragic hero's suffering? Is there something either unique or universal about it?

5. What important insights does the tragic hero achieve? Is he at any moment in the play functioning partly as a *raisonneur* character?

6. Does the play seem to end with some sort of redemption? If so, how is the new world better than the old?

7. Who functions as the play's tragic hero? In what ways is she elevated above the rest of us, either in character, in position, or in areas of responsibility?

8. Can you determine what her *hamartia* might be? How is this idea thematically linked with the rest of the play?

9. Who or what constitutes the play's nemesis? Where does it come from? What does this tell you about the play's symbolic action?

10. Who or what constitutes the play's innocent victim? Is it a person or a collective group? Does this victim have any symbolic connotations?

7

Classic Comedy

Comedy is sometimes called the "evil twin sister" of tragedy. At first glance, it seems relatively easy to define: It's a kind of play that's funny and makes us laugh. But this encompasses an extremely broad range, from outrageous knockdown farces where people chase each other and slam doors in a desperate attempt to get out of a ticklish jam, to comedies of manners, wherein people sit in chairs, drink tea, and exchange witty remarks. Furthermore, there are great works of literature that are called comedies that aren't funny at all. Dante called his masterpiece *The Divine Comedy*; it's about a journey through hell and doesn't have a chuckle anywhere. Therefore, we sometimes even have to take "laughter" out of the picture.

We call a play a comedy because, like tragedy, it presents us with a playwright's attitude toward the world. Also like tragedy, the genre of comedy has taken on different shapes and forms over the centuries. We'll first examine those elements that are usually attributed to what we'll call *classic comedy* and then examine some variations. Following that, we'll look at laughter: When a comedy is actually funny, what are some of the devices that make us laugh? Finally, we'll examine the different kinds of comedies that exist and see how a *comedy of intrigue* differs from, say, a *comedy of manners*.

What Is the Mood of a Classic Comedy?

While classic comedy isn't necessarily funny, its mood is generally one of delight and joy. Sometimes people say that "tragedy ends in a funeral, while comedy ends in a wedding," and in many ways (both literally and symbolically), this is true. We leave a classic comedy feeling hopeful, optimistic, and usually satisfied: There's been a happy ending, the guy has got the girl or vice versa, and all the fools have been vanquished—a cause for celebrating.

But there's also something a little condescending and perhaps even cruel about classic comedy. Aristotle spoke very little about it, except to say that, while tragedy shows us people "above us," comedy shows us people who are "below us." Although he used those terms in their social context (*above us* meaning kings, and *below us* meaning slaves and women), we can use them in their larger context. Thus, as tragedy deals with characters who are noble, wise, and superior in quality, comedy contains characters who are foolish, ludicrous, and inferior in quality. We admire tragic characters; we mock comedic ones. Consider: Why is it that we laugh at a man slipping on a banana peel rather than rush to his rescue? Why don't we instead feel some pity for this poor misguided wretch and call an ambulance?

Some critics have tried to solve this conundrum by saying that "tragedy is what happens to me; comedy is what happens to you." Or "comedy is tragedy two weeks later." This suggests a matter of involvement. When we watch a tragedy, we somehow empathize with the tragic hero; on the other hand, comedy often requires us to stand apart from and outside the events. We must be uninvolved spectators.

However, sometimes it's a very fine line that separates the two. Imagine yourself watching a performance of Shakespeare's *King Lear*. Toward the end of the play, Lear, an old man, enters carrying the dead body of his daughter. When we see him with her, we are sad too, because we empathize with such suffering. But then suddenly, Lear stubs his toe and utters a loud "Ouch!" This odd sound suddenly takes us out of the illusion. It isn't Lear grunting; it's the actor playing Lear who is. We see him for what he is: a thin, middle-aged man wearing makeup and a costume and carrying an actress who is probably ten or twelve pounds heavier than the actor can bear and who's trying not to breathe too deeply so we'll think she's "dead." We have now become detached, objective spectators. The spectacle of this poor old man trying not to drop this overweight ingenue strikes us as ridiculous, and we chuckle.

But then the actor stumbles because his robe gets caught beneath his foot. He drops the actress; she lands with a loud, hollow thud (maybe she bounces a bit). Now we are more than disconnected: We are superior. We in the audience feel that the struggling actor is an incompetent fool, unlike us. We don't do such stupid things. Our condescension makes us laugh louder.

But wait: Now the actor is suddenly completely still. We see that he's dropped her not because she was too heavy but because he's just suffered a massive heart attack. Now we are not superior but engaged. Are we back in tragedy country again?

We need somehow to reconcile these two opposing attitudes and understand that comedy is at the same time both joyous and mocking. It celebrates happiness, but it also makes fun of pain. It engages us, but we're also a little detached. And at the end, it's a little cruel.

What Sort of World or Society Forms the Setting?

Unlike classic tragedy, which takes for its playing field the universe, classic comedy is typically set in a specific society. This society may be a particular country, a particular kingdom, a particular social class, or even an extended family. It's any specific and more or less unique group of people who have organized themselves into a culture and created a set of rules that govern how they should live.

We can describe this unique world by the rules it has laid down. Sometimes these rules are fair and just, and sometimes they're unfair and artificial. For example, we live in a society (contemporary America at the start of the twenty-first century) that is governed by written rules set down in the Constitution, the Bill of Rights, and many laws. We all consider these rules fair and just (at least in theory). But we are also governed by a set of unwritten rules that are sometimes just as binding; however, these unwritten rules are not at all fair or just. For example, until fairly recently the unwritten rules were that men wore pants, and women wore dresses; women stayed at home and tended the house, while men went forth to earn the bread; husbands controlled the household finances, while wives ruled the kitchen.

Although none of these rules were written down, our culture still subscribed to them because tradition supposedly indicated how sensible they were. But, of course, they were not at all sensible: Why should only women wear dresses? What if, on a very hot day, Steven decided he'd be cooler wearing a skirt? Some people would look at him and not think twice. Some would mock him and make jokes. Some people might feel so threatened they'd want to take him out to a country road and beat him to death.

Clearly, in this case, there is something seriously wrong here. The problem isn't Steven; he's thinking quite clearly. It certainly is a hot day. Common sense says he has a point. The problem is clearly with the unwritten rule about proper clothing; it has imposed an artificial restriction on Steven's freedom. No, the problem is with society, which because of this artificial rule has blocked Steven from following his heart. This society is flawed. This is the world of a classic comedy: a blocked society that has some set of unwritten codes that are unfair and restrictive.

For example, in Oscar Wilde's comedy *The Importance of Being Earnest*, the society is upper-class Victorian England, and the rules that govern lives are an elaborate set of customs about how people should behave with each other. Even worse, it has a set of unwritten codes that dictate who can marry whom. Jack Worthing wants to marry Gwendolyn, but he is blocked because her aunt, Lady Bracknell, doesn't think he's marriage material. Yes, he lives on the right street in London (although on the wrong side, but that, she says, can be changed), and yes, he has a fashionably rich income; but he has no idea who his parents were. He was found in a handbag left by mistake in the cloakroom of a train station. Well! This won't do. As she says to him:

> To be born, or at any rate, bred in a handbag, whether it had handles or not, seems to me to display a contempt for the ordinary decencies of family life that remind one of the worst excesses of the French Revolution. And I presume you know what the unfortunate movement led to! (act 1)

Jack is prevented from achieving his heart's dream because he is blocked by society's unwritten rule about proper parents.

Many classic comedies are like this: Two young lovers are kept from each other by some unfair impediment. In Shakespeare's *Midsummer Night's Dream*, the blocking element is the law of Athens, which says that if daughters don't marry the men their fathers want them to, they can be killed. Sometimes the blocking element is the girl's father or other relative who controls the money and the permission and who wants the girl to marry somebody else who is richer or more socially advantageous than her beloved. In Molière's *The Miser*, the father insists that his daughter marry a rich man instead of the seemingly poor man who is courting her.

In more profound classic comedies, the blocking element is, as shown by Lady Bracknell's remarks, some attitude or idea that characters hold. In many comedies by George Bernard Shaw, people in power hold onto romantic ideals or conventions that are outdated or inappropriate. In *Major Barbara*, Barbara has joined the Salvation Army, rejecting her wealthy father's money and position. His name is Undershaft, and he's earned his millions by manufacturing munitions. Barbara is convinced that helping the poor learn to live with their suffering will get them into heaven. Undershaft believes, on the other hand, that being poor is a terrible crime, and the only way to redeem people's souls is to amass enough wealth and power to force governments to change. He says his evil money will do more good than her pious prayers. The action of the play, which for the most part consists of lengthy discussions about this issue, results in Barbara's coming to accept her father's point of view and rejecting her own. In this case, the blocking element has been a set of false ideals that prevent people from living real and authentic lives.

To repeat: The world of a classic comedy is a society that is blocked by false, inappropriate, or unjust rules or attitudes; a society dominated by authority figures, minions of the law, or fools. These blocks keep the agent of action from her goal. Because of this, we can safely generalize that the basic conflict in a classic comedy is between *man and society*.

What Typical Plots Does a Classic Comedy Have?

Although comedies may be of very different types, the one thing they all share is a plot that has a happy ending. The smart people triumph over the stupid, and the guy gets the girl. The blocked society is freed; the flawed society is made better, and dreams are fulfilled. All this is usually symbolized by a celebration: There's usually a dinner or a wedding in the offing, and all are invited.

Thus, while classic tragedy often demands that somebody be excluded, classic comedy insists on everybody being included. It's in this sense—the happy ending—that Dante's *Divine Comedy* is a comedy.

To get to that happy ending, most classic comedies use the traditional well-made play structure, moving from the state of equilibrium to the climax, resolution, and new state of equilibrium that brings us to a better world in which the blocks have been removed. What sets one comedy apart from another is the rising action; that is, the sorts of strategies the agent of action generates in order to win. Four distinct kinds of strategies typically appear:

- A romance is pursued.
- A trick is played.
- A lesson is taught.
- A "green world" is visited.

After we examine each, we'll turn our attention to one moment that all of them have in common, something we'll call a *cognitio*.

Pursuing a Romance

As we mentioned, most classic comedies are about love. A young man loves a young woman but is blocked by a law, a parent or other authority figure, or some blind spot in one of the lovers themselves. When the block comes from the authority figure, the plot become a series of attempts by the young lover to get around the old folks. The pattern is as old as fairy tales: Rapunzel is locked in a tower by an old witch, and the only way the Prince can get to her is to climb up her long braids.

In Oscar Wilde's *The Importance of Being Earnest*, Jack Worthing has to somehow overcome Lady Bracknell's objections to his being an orphan by convincing her that he is worthy (of course, you noticed the pun in his name); he can do so only when it's discovered that his true lineage shows him to be a member of a high enough social class. (However, he meets an additional blocking element in Gwendolyn herself, the girl he's courting. She is convinced that she can only love and be happily married to a man whose real name is Earnest; in order to win her, therefore, Jack determines to get himself christened Earnest—even though he's slightly over twenty years old!)

This tradition of "getting the girl" over the objections of the old folks goes all the way back to the earliest roots of classic comedy. The great Roman comedies of Plautus and Terence, all of Shakespeare's comedies, the masterpieces of Molière, every Restoration comedy, nineteenth-century farce, and major musical or opera of the past two hundred years, not to mention all those romantic comedies that fill the movie screens every summer—are all about clearing the way to the wedding.

Playing a Trick

Sometimes the agent of action has to resort to setting up an elaborate scheme of deception; the plot revolves around a large and extended trick he plays on his antagonist.

When a young lad wants the young lass, he has to get around the old codger (*The Importance of Being Earnest*). If a poor young man wants to get the treasure, he has to get around the wicked dragon (*Major Barbara*). If a young lass wants to keep her parents from finding out that she's dating a man who's not of their faith, she has to get the young lad to pretend to be what he's not in order to fool them (James Sherman's *Beau Jest*). Think of your favorite TV sitcom: There's no doubt at least one episode in which somebody pretends something in order to impress a previous lover.

Sometimes we in the audience are in on the secret, and sometimes we're just as surprised as the antagonist. It's up to you to decide which is funnier or more satisfying.

Teaching a Lesson

In some classic comedies, the blocking element is ignorance. Somebody doesn't understand something or know how to do something. In order for the agent of action to achieve her goals, some form of teaching has to take place. Of course, the teacher winds up learning almost as much as the pupil, and the play ends with both characters somehow being changed. George Bernard Shaw uses this pattern; he was an active political reformist and used his plays to propagandize many of his own ideas, so the "teacher" in his plays

is often a *raisonneur* for Shaw himself, and the lessons that character teaches are what Shaw wants his audiences to believe. In *Major
Barbara*, we've noted how Undershaft teaches his daughter many
of his own political views; but while he teaches her about politics,
she also teaches him something about her spiritual values.

Sometimes teaching and trickery work together: The teaching
goes along with maintaining the secret. Much of the fun of James
Sherman's *Beau Jest* comes from the Jewish girl trying to teach her
Gentile boyfriend some of her culture; all he knows about Jews is
what he learned from appearing in an amateur production of *Fiddler on the Roof*.

Interfacing with the "Green World"

Classic tragedies take place in an absolute universe; it exists, and
we either have to accept its universal moral values or suffer the
consequences. Classic comedies, however, exist in a particular society that, as we've seen, is flawed. But there might be other societies out there that are better than the one you're in. You live in
the city, but there are also small towns, villages, countrysides, forests, and so on—any number of places where you could live. Some
classic comedies, therefore, contrast one society with another, allowing the "better" society to somehow influence the "worse." This
works in several ways.

Some plays begin in the flawed society, which we can call the
real world; the action involves some characters running away from
this place and going to the other place. While in that second place,
they are somehow transformed, educated, or changed in any number of ways. After a period of time, they return to the original world
and, because of their experiences, are able to make that first world
better. Many of Shakespeare's great comedies are of this sort, and
because the place into which the characters retreat is often a forest, an important twentieth-century critic, Northrop Frye, in his
book *Anatomy of Criticism*, has named this place the *green world*.

Consider *A Midsummer Night's Dream*. The play begins in Athens, where the cruel duke is going to impose upon the young lovers
the law that says they must marry whomever their fathers choose

or they must die. Worse yet, one of the women loves a man who loves another woman. This world is blocked on many levels.

In order to escape both the cruel law and their unbending parents, the two sets of lovers decide to escape into the nearby forest. In this magical place, they meet fairies, become the victim of Puck's silly mistakes, and come to their senses about whom they really love. At the same time, the king and queen of the fairies are quarreling; they take their quarrel into the green world and somehow manage to reconcile. And also at the same time, the duke and his queen (who were also doing a bit of quarreling) also enter the forest, and a series of events changes the duke's mind about the law. When morning comes, they all return to the city magically changed, and the play ends with not one, but four, weddings.

We can consider the *green world* to mean any place away from "here," where interesting and sometimes wonderful things happen that change people. The first act of *The Importance of Being Earnest* takes place in town, while the second and third acts take place in the country, and it's in the country that Algernon meets and falls in love with Cecily, Jack discovers the truth of his heritage, and Lady Bracknell is forced to give in. At the end of the play, they all trundle back to London, wiser and happier.

Hollywood writers often call this kind of story "the fish out of water" scenario. Many contemporary plays and films create several variations on it, such as these:

Sometimes we leave the real world and stay in the green world. Folks from one place (the city?) move to the other (the country?) and have a slew of adventures that ultimately change them and then decide to stay. Nearly all the great plays of Aristophanes are of this type: In *The Birds*, two disgruntled Athenians, fed up with the corruption of the city, build a kingdom in the sky and, through a series of comic events, manage to change the world.

Sometimes we stay in the real world, but somebody from the green world comes to visit us and somehow makes us a little better. Shaw's *Pygmalion* (and its musical permutation, *My Fair Lady*) are of this type: Liza comes from the "streets of London," a world in which people are authentic; she spends time with Professor Higgins in his world, where people are vain, pompous, and blocked. Ultimately, she wreaks some small changes in him.

Sometimes it works in a negative way: The green world visitor is not so nice after all, and we come to realize how good we have it as is. Molière's *Tartuffe* is like this. Orgon is obsessed with religion and, convinced that Tartuffe is a holy man, gives all his time, attention, and fortune to him. Tartuffe upsets Orgon's household and threatens to ruin him. But he proves to be a fraud and is arrested, and Orgon ultimately sees the error of his ways.

Sometimes we begin in the green world and are forced to leave it because it is a place of magic and illusion and not a place of reality after all. We've already met two such examples. In *A Doll's House*, Nora has to leave this place of false values and lies. In *The Glass Menagerie*, Tom has to leave this house of illusions and dreams. (Are these last two plays comedies? Perhaps they are.)

These four major strategies—pursuing a romance, playing a trick, teaching a lesson, or interfacing with a green world—appear in one form or another in most classic comedies. Sometimes a comedy will mix and match several of them. All classic comedies show how a wrong society contrasts with a right one, usually changing the former into the latter. And all of them lead us to a happy ending.

The Importance of the *Cognitio*

Classic comedies share with all other types of plays the need for a central climactic moment. If the play is at all well-made, in the Aristotelian sense, it will build to a moment of recognition and reversal. In classic tragedies, this moment is often a moment of insight, in which the tragic hero comes to some enlightenment. In classic comedies, this moment is called a *cognitio*. The term comes from Latin and means "knowledge." Other words with the same root include *recognize*, *cognition*, and *cogitate*.

Often the society of a classic comedy is blocked by some mystery or secret. This secret gets in the way of the pursuit of love and, once it's cleared up, we can once again get on with the wedding. Or this secret prevents a young hero from achieving some other goal: obtaining his family fortune, becoming employed, understanding who he really is after all. Or the young hero's got himself into a terrible predicament; his fate is about to be crushed, and all will be lost—and then somebody or something comes along and reveals the truth. In Plautus's play *Mostellaria* (*The Haunted House*), the young man is forbidden to marry a slave girl whom he loves, until somebody notices that the necklace she always wears was given to her by her father just before a storm wrecked the boat they were traveling in and separated his twin children. The girl, it turns out, isn't a slave at all, but a freeborn citizen, whom the young lad can now marry.

This device pops up in many guises: The truth is revealed by a bracelet, a birthmark, a long-lost set of papers, or a deathbed confession. In *The Importance of Being Earnest*, you'll recall that Jack Worthing doesn't know who his true parents were; however, in the nick of time, this mystery is solved. It turns out that he's really a distant cousin of Gwendolyn's. Even better, it turns out that his real name isn't Jack after all; it's really—well, I won't reveal the ending, but perhaps you can guess.

Sometimes the moment of *cognitio* comes when a villain is unmasked. This is clearly the moment in a murder mystery when the detective identifies the killer; it's also the moment in *Tartuffe* when the emissary from the king comes in at the last minute to identify Tartuffe as the hypocrite he is and to save Orgon from losing his entire fortune.

The secret is not always one of identity. In those comedies that involve playing a trick on somebody, the *cognitio* appears when the trick is exposed. When the parents in *Beau Jest* learn they've been tricked, they generously forgive their daughter, and all is mended.

In those comedies that involve teaching a lesson, the *cognitio* appears when the teacher suddenly realizes what his student has actually become, how she's surpassed him, or how she's taught him more than he's taught her. In *Pygmalion*, the moment occurs when Higgins and Liza are fighting, and she shows him her true inner strength; he cries out in delight, "I said I would make a woman of you and I have. I like you like this!" (act 4).

In green-world comedies, the *cognitio* often appears when characters realize what lesson they've learned and understand that it's now time to go home.

What Characters Appear in a Classic Comedy?

Once again, Aristotle was the first to identify and categorize the elements of play structure in comedy that still hold true. While he says very little in his *Poetics* about comedy, his *Ethics* lists three types of comic characters. These were later elaborated on by Northrop Frye in *Anatomy of Criticism* and provide an extremely useful analytical tool for us. This section borrows from these two sources.

The three kinds of characters are:

- *alazon* (also called the "blocker")
- *eiron* (also called the "teacher")
- buffoon

The Alazon

The Greek word *alazon* originally meant an "impostor," in the sense of somebody being in disguise or not revealing his true nature. Over time, it has come to mean any person who is not "real" or "authentic." We have seen how this trait appears in those characters who serve as blocking forces in a blocked society; to that end, it might be useful to rename this character the *blocker*. Thus, the blocker is the person who stands in the way of a free, healthy life.

In order to get to the happy ending, the block has to be eliminated; thus, this person has to be changed. The father who won't let the boy marry his dream girl has to change his mind; the ignorant person has to be educated; the self-deluded woman has to come to her senses; the pompous and opinionated parents have to be put in their place.

Typically, one character is the primary blocker, but very often this role can be assumed by any number of characters in the play. In *Major Barbara*, clearly Barbara is a major blocker to herself, because her ideas about religion and politics need to be changed—she needs to be educated. However, at the same time, her father also has some frozen ideas of his own that need to be thawed out; so Undershaft can also be thought of as a blocker.

The blocker is perhaps the most important character in classic comedy for you to identify because the ideas this character holds and the behaviors she engages in are the ones that the playwright is mocking. In a sense, she is like a negative *raisonneur*. Examining the statements this character makes, the positions she holds, and the particular kinds of objections and attitudes she has provides clues to the play's meaning.

(Note that you can also find blockers in serious plays as well. Which of Tennessee Williams's characters in *The Glass Menagerie* holds onto the past so long that she becomes almost foolish and dangerous? Which central character in *A Doll's House* takes the whole play to finally come to her senses about how wrong society has been to her?)

The Eiron

The original meaning of the Greek word *eiron* was "self-deprecator," that is, somebody who mocked, ridiculed, and poked fun at himself and others. If you think of a blocker as a bowling pin (something that's set up for the sole purpose of being knocked down), the *eiron* is the character who does the knocking down; it is any character who deflates, defeats, educates, tricks, or in any way works on a character to eliminate the major block of the play. We can also give this character a clearer name; let's call it the *teacher*.

This teacher may be a fool, an actual professor, a young lover, a schemer, or—in many ancient plays—a cunning and wily slave. The emperor walking naked in the street is a blocker; the young boy who's not afraid to call out that the emperor has no clothes is the teacher. Lady Bracknell is a blocker; Jack is her teacher.

Also note that just as more than one character in a play can be a blocker, more than one character can also assume the role of teacher. In fact, the same character can be both at different times. A wonderful example of this appears in act 2 of *Major Barbara*. The setting is the Salvation Army where Barbara, believing that religion is what people need, has gone to work. Early in the act, she confronts a man who has beaten his wife; the passion of her beliefs causes him to see the error of his ways: He's the blocker to her teacher. However, later in the act, Barbara is shocked when her father offers to give the charity several million pounds of his ill-earned fortune; her boss accepts the offer—destroying Barbara's whole belief system. In that instance, she is the blocker (needing to be educated), and her father is the teacher. And still later—in the third act—Undershaft himself is changed by Barbara, as their blocker and teacher roles are reversed.

Also, you'll find it useful to realize that, just as there are variations on the blocker figures in noncomedies, so there are variations on teachers. If Nora in *A Doll's House* is a sort of blocker, needing to be educated, who does the teaching? And what about Amanda in *The Glass Menagerie*: If she's living in this illusory dream world, who brings her out of it? (That is, if you believe she ever *does* come out of it.)

The Buffoon

The main action of a classic comedy stems from the conflict between the blocker and its corresponding teacher; therefore, to put the matter most simply, a *buffoon* is any other character in the play. This character might be a sarcastic bystander, a surly waiter, a smart-mouthed confidant, somebody from the community who happens by, or any number of variations. There are several typical functions served by a buffoon.

Serving as a foil to one of the main characters. Western heroes have their silly sidekicks, romantic heroes have their buddies, Don Quixote has Sancho Panza. In *Major Barbara*, her younger brother Stephen serves this function—he's rather stupid and silly and gets in the way a lot.

Providing for a moment of comic relief that has little to do with the action but is entertaining in its own way. Good examples of this are Bottom and his thespian cronies in *A Midsummer Night's Dream*.

Serving as a raisonneur. In *Tartuffe*, Molière puts into the mouth of one of Orgon's servants some of his most pointed attacks on the kind of foolish obsession that has made a blocker out of Orgon.

Serving as a utilitarian character. This is someone who brings about important plot moments, as does Miss Prism in Oscar Wilde's *The Importance of Being Earnest* when she reveals the secret of that play's *cognitio*.

What Is "Funny"? Sources of Laughter

When we began this chapter, we took special care to define *classic comedy* by its plot structure and typical characters. We deliberately removed *funny* from our definition, going only so far as to say that a comedy should end happily. However, most comedies are meant to be funny and to make us laugh. Therefore, to truly understand what a classic comedy means, it's important to examine how the playwright provokes laughter in us.

Many theories have been offered to explain why humans laugh. Nearly all of them assume what we've already seen: Comedy requires the viewer to be at some remove from the event, so that laughter comes from our feeling superior and safe. Within these broad parameters, there are several special devices that appear in plays:

- incongruity
- rigidity
    bodily
    mental: *idée fixe*
    emotional: the "humours"
- Freudian psychology
    hostility
    sex jokes
- topsy-turvy

Incongruity

This device calls for juxtaposing things that we don't normally think belong together; the laughter stems from recognizing the contrast between what we expect and what we actually get. A tall woman dancing with a short man seems *incongruous*; we usually think of their sizes being the other way around. An old *New Yorker* magazine cartoon shows an image out of a Frankenstein movie: Igor is running into the laboratory; in the distance, we can see villagers coming over the hill in troops, brandishing torches, pitchforks, and other weapons. The caption reads: "It's the condo board!" The incongruity comes from a condo board being associated with a Frankenstein movie; these things just don't belong together.

An incongruous moment occurs in act 2 of *The Importance of Being Earnest*: Gwendolyn and Cecily have just met. They've decided to become instant friends, until their conversation leads them to believe they are both in love with the same man. Just then, tea is served.

Their conversation now turns into an exchange of insults over tea, butter, muffins, and cake. Finally, Gwendolyn has had enough:

> You have filled my tea with lumps of sugar, and though I asked most distinctly for bread and butter, you have given me cake. I am known for the gentleness of my disposition, and the extraordinary sweetness of my nature, but I warn you, Miss Cardew; you may go too far!

To which Cecily replies:

> To save my poor innocent trusting boy from the machinations of any other girl, there are no lengths to which I would not go!

The incongruity stems from the use of lumps of sugar as weapons in a quarrel, as well as from the fact that the two women are talking about a most uncivil rivalry while engaged in a most civil activity.

Verbal humor in the form of puns is another type of incongruity: Using a word in a context where it doesn't belong calls our attention to the contrast between what is expected and what actually happens. Shakespeare loves such wordplay. If you read the opening lines of *Julius Caesar*, you will find a whole conversation built around puns on various words associated with making shoes: *cobbler*, *soles*, *awls*, *recover*, and so forth.

Rigidity

As human beings, we like to think that we are intelligent creatures, aware of the world around us and able to adapt to situations as they occur. We are creatures of the mind, soul, and spirit. Our bodies are flexible organisms, temples of our being, houses in which our intellect lives. We are in control. If there's a banana peel in the middle of the road, we notice it and either pick it up or step around it. However, every so often, something happens that calls this noble assumption into question. We don't see the banana peel—for the moment, our awareness has slipped; we aren't observant creatures after all but have tunnel vision instead. Even worse, we step on the banana peel and fall flat on our backs. For the moment, our glorious "temple" becomes nothing more than a collection of bones and muscles, subject to the same laws of gravity as a stone.

A renowned critic named Henri Bergson first described this phenomenon in an essay titled "Laughter" and called it an occasion in which "the mechanical is encrusted on the living." He pointed out, "The attitudes, gestures and movements of the human body are laughable in exact proportion as the body reminds us of a mere machine." Machines don't think; machines don't adapt; machines don't grow; machines fall and break. In human beings, this rigidity takes several forms: bodily, mental, and emotional.

Bodily Rigidity

We've already hinted at this comic device in our example with the banana peel. Our bodies, in a sense, betray us; for a moment, we are not human at all, just an inert piece of clay, subject to abuse. Every time somebody takes a pratfall, gets gouged in the eye, has his nose poked, gets his finger stuck in a child's toy, or in any other way reminds you of a *Three Stooges* movie, this person has become momentarily less human and more machinelike. However, remember that in comedy the abuse must be painless: Larry, Curly, and Moe are never *really* injured.

Another way in which our bodies betray us is to require of us certain attentions. As humans, we may dream and plan, but as animals, we have to eat, sleep, and eliminate our bodily waste. Sometimes these things have to be done immediately, and when they do, we are once again reminded of our "mechanical" nature: We're embarrassed in a classroom when our stomach starts to rumble while the professor is lecturing, or—worse—we have to leave a movie in order to go to the restroom . . . very quickly.

At the end of act 2 of *The Importance of Being Earnest*, Jack and Algernon are in a bitter quarrel, blaming each other for the apparent failure of their love quests. In the middle of all this, Algernon is stuffing his mouth with muffins. Jack calls his attention to this ludicrous moment:

How can you sit there, calmly eating muffins, when we are in this horrible trouble, I can't make out. You seem to me to be perfectly heartless.

And Algernon replies:

Well, I can't eat muffins in an agitated manner. The butter would probably get on my cuffs.

Mental Rigidity

This comic device appears whenever a person becomes fixated or obsessed by any one central idea, and this fixation causes her to be excessively unreasonable. It is often given the name *idée fixe*, which is a French term meaning, as you'd suppose, a "fixed idea," or sometimes called a *comic obsession*. The person *must* have things this certain way because no other way is at all possible. A cartoon illustrating the use of this device shows a skeleton sitting by a telephone; the skeleton is covered with spider webs and has clearly been sitting there a very long time. A detective is there, holding the telephone to his ear. The caption is a voice on the other end of the phone that says, "Your call is important to us!" Clearly, the person had been on hold for years, fixated on the idea that if he waited long enough, he would get through.

The Importance of Being Earnest has several characters with fixed ideas: Lady Bracknell, obsessed by the idea that only a person of a specific social class can marry her niece; and Gwendolyn and Cecily, who are both insistent on only marrying men whose names happen to be Earnest.

It often helps to understand this device if you think of its parallel in classic tragedy: The tragic *hamartia* is often caused by this same sort of blindness, but in a more serious way. Think of Oedipus, fully determined at no matter what cost, to discover the truth about Thebes's plague. If it weren't for the other devices that make these plays tragedies, they might easily become comedies.

Emotional Rigidity

Sometimes a character will let her emotions take over; her mind shuts down, and she goes out of control. People who get angry at the drop of a hat; people who are always jealous, no matter what happens; people whose libidos are so strong that sex is on their minds constantly—these characters have become emotionally rigid.

There is a historical basis for this theory of emotional rigidity dating back to the early Renaissance. At the time, it was thought that the body contained four basic fluids that run through our systems and control our behaviors. These fluids were called *humours* and included choler, blood, yellow bile (or phlegm), and black bile (or melancholy). When these were properly balanced, all was well, but when one fluid became too predominant, the poor creature was afflicted; he became "ill-humoured," and depending on which fluid was the culprit, might be phlegmatic (ornery), choleric (hot-tempered), bloody (passionate), or melancholic (moody).

How many sitcoms can you think of in which one character is obsessed by sex or drink, and the jokes are always about lust or alcohol? A typical device in a farce is a man who is cheating on his wife being chased around by his mistress's husband, who is quick-tempered, murderously jealous, and dangerous. Indeed, the farce is often kicked off by the excessive sex drive of the wayward husband.

In a *comedy of manners*, you will often find that the buffoon characters are the ones who are out of emotional control. They are made to look ridiculous because they are in contrast with others who *are* in control, and the plays become divided between the "in-group" and the outside "wanna-bes." Thus, you meet an old woman like Lady Wishfort (in William Congreve's *The Way of the World*) who longs to be seduced, or Sir Fopling Flutter (in William Wycherley's *The Man of Mode*), and other fops who are obsessed with fancy clothes and extravagant posing.

Again, there is a tragic counterpart to this excess of emotion: When we talked about *hubris*, the overwhelming and arrogant pride that such a character as Oedipus had, we were in similar territory. Consider Romeo's hot temper and rash judgment, and Juliet's silly obsession with tragic love—in another story, these emotional excesses would be funny.

Freudian Psychology

Sigmund Freud is known as the father of psychoanalysis, being one of the first to recognize the importance our unconscious plays in our daily lives and how much of what we do is controlled by impulses that lie below the surface of our conscious minds. He noted that all humans are driven by certain basic needs like shelter, food, safety, and sex. In primitive societies, people went around satisfying these needs at will: When a caveman was hungry, he would eat whatever was available; when made angry, he might kill whatever made him angry; when sexually aroused, he might rape. However, we don't live in a primitive society; we have set up laws and codes of conduct that prohibit such spontaneous and aggressive behaviors. For the most part, we control ourselves; we've learned the art of repression. But repression isn't always easy: We are aroused by many things but can't always gain instant satisfaction. Still, our demanding unconscious won't be ignored, and since it can't express itself in action, it has to find another outlet. Jokes are one way of releasing this tension.

Freud claims that jokes are a safe way for us to deal with dangerous impulses. He noted two key areas in which this happens:

Hostility

Jokes often come from that center of our unconscious that controls fear. We may have leaders whom we don't like but can't confront. Our boss might be a jerk, but he is our boss. Our teacher might be inept, but she still controls the grades. We can't always confront these power figures, but we can deal with the hostility we feel by making fun of them. We can draw political cartoons of them, laugh at one-liners about them on late-night television, imitate them in comedic sketches, or wear silly masks of them at Halloween.

One way we express this hostility is by taking some feature or event and exaggerating it: If the leader has an unusual nose, we'll draw her with a very large one. If the leader has trouble understanding a foreign culture, we'll put him in a sketch in which he totally embarrasses himself in front of a foreign visitor. This results in caricature, parody, or satire. Today you most often see this sort of laughter generated by sketch-comedy shows such as *Saturday Night Live* or *Mad TV*.

Sex Jokes

In our discussion of emotional rigidity, we pointed out that the contrast between our "human" nature and our "animal" needs is often a source of laughter. Freud went a little further down this same road. He argued that, while we publicly suppress our sexual nature, we are still creatures of urges. Moreover, we often consider these urges slightly sinful, dangerous, or wicked. Often there's a tension here: Our desire to control ourselves fights against our desire to explore that "dark" side. One way, therefore, to relieve this tension is to poke fun at it; and this fun results in the "dirty joke."

Many comedies have either their entire story line based on a dirty joke or at least one or two scenes in which sex becomes the subtext. Aristophanes' *Lysistrata* is the classic example of the former. Here, a group of Athenian and Spartan women vow together to withhold sex from their husbands until they stop their long war. Gradually, the men grow more and more aroused. As this torture goes on, we see them appearing with larger and larger phalluses and hear them groaning with pain and desire. Ultimately, of course, the women win: The dirty joke is that sex is more important than politics.

Topsy-Turvy

This device refers to any situation in the play in which your normal expectations are turned upside down. Things are backward, and our expectations of what is "normal" are suddenly called into question. What is normally bad becomes good, and so the gangster becomes the guy we root for. What is normally "powerful" becomes "subordinate," and so the servant or butler turns out to be smarter and more competent than the master. What is normally the province of the man becomes the activity of the woman, and so the girl gets out and fixes the flat tire.

Topsy-turvy appears in several ways:

When things are not as they should normally be. Consider again *Major Barbara:* In a usual comedy, the young lad conspires with the maiden to outwit the nasty father. In Shaw's play, however, it's the father and the young lad who conspire to outwit the maiden.

When characters behave against their type. We don't expect anybody to be so stupid as to mistake a baby in a carriage for a manuscript in a handbag, but that's exactly what Miss Prism does in *The Importance of Being Earnest.* We normally expect women to wear women's clothes, and men to behave like men, but consider Brandon Thomas's play *Charley's Aunt* or the movies *Tootsie* and *Some*

Like It Hot; in all three examples, men dress up and disguise themselves as women—and get away with it for the longest time.

When the long arm of coincidence saves the day. We don't expect the ex-nursemaid (now tutor) to have the key to anybody's true existence, nor to show up at just the exact moment when she's needed, nor to provide the solution to the mystery—but Miss Prism does all these things. Earlier, we noticed that many plays depend for their *cognitio* on the last-minute recognition of something as silly as a birthmark or a bracelet.

When the ending is not what we expect. This particular device will be more prominent in chapter 10, when we discuss tragicomedies and talk about the plays of Chekov. Normally, we expect comedies to have a happy ending. In the best of all worlds, the *Cherry Orchard* would end with Ranevskaya saving the orchard and attending a couple of weddings. Chekov turns this convention topsy-turvy: She loses the orchard, nobody gets married after all, and worst of all, somebody dies at the end! And yet Chekov still insisted on calling the play a comedy.

What Kinds of Comedy Are There?

Classic comedy comes in a wide variety of subcategories. We'll describe only a few of the most common. Please note that in all of these forms, you will find blockers, teachers, and buffoons, but they might take on different surface characteristics. Also be warned: These various categories are defined by the leading characteristics of these plays, and you should not consider them to be totally distinct from each other. One play might have several of these characteristics mixed together in various ways as one category blends into another.

Comedy of Manners

Comedies of manners are usually set in wealthy, sophisticated, leisured worlds and deal with the antics of smart, socially insulated people; almost nobody ever has a job or works for a living in such a play. The world in which they live is usually quite narrow and controlled by very specific codes of conduct; often the smart and witty people form a sort of in-group and poke fun at the wanna-bes who can't quite match their wit, elegance, and culture. The plot is typically a love chase, in which a seduction—as opposed to a wedding—becomes the ultimate goal. Language is important, because much of the humor comes from clever wordplay. To that end, the plot is often very slight, and most of the scenes involve conversation. Typical characters who appear might be:

- reluctant lovers: The man pursues a woman who pretends she doesn't want him but who actually does.
- elderly men and/or women: These are often people who are too old for the love chase but who want to be in the game anyhow.
- silly pretenders: These consist of fops, country bumpkins, or others who try to fit in but only manage to look ridiculous.

Examples include:

- Shakespeare's *Love Labor's Lost, Much Ado about Nothing*
- Wilde's *The Importance of Being Earnest* and *Lady Windemere's Fan*
- Philip Barry's *The Philadelphia Story* and *Holiday*

Commedia dell'arte

Historically, *commedia dell'arte* flourished in sixteenth-century Italy, and it traveled to France, England, and Germany, where it took on slightly different aspects. The plays were improvised: The company would have an outline of the plot and the basic matter of the scenes, but the dialogue, stage business, and pantomime would be made up on the spot. Over the years, many stock bits of business, some of the dialogue, and most of the characters would become formalized through repetition. The action, very much like the Roman comedies of Plautus and Terence, were often about how young lovers deceived their elders. Later writers would adopt many of the characters and plots of these improvised pieces: Most of Molière's plays are commedia dell'arte in spirit and form, as are many Restoration and nineteenth-century comedies. To some extent, even *The Importance of Being Earnest* has many roots in commedia dell'arte.

Many of the characters who first emerged in these sketches became classic stereotypes and still exist in various forms today. These include:

- the young lovers, called *inamorata*
- a doddering, foolish old man, often the father, called *il pantalone*; when this old fool isn't trying to stop the young lad, he himself is often chasing after a young girl and making a spectacle of himself in the process
- a cowardly, braggart, pompous soldier, whose boasting exceeds his deeds, called *il capitano*
- a supposedly learned pedant—often a doctor or a lawyer—who pretends to know much but actually knows very little, called *il dottore*; his dialogue is often filled with academic-sounding nonsense
- a clever, scheming, witty servant, whose schemes and wiles often move the plot along, called by many names, such as *pedrolino*, *scaramouche*, *arlecchino*, *harlequin*, and so on

If you take a look at Burt Shevelove and Stephen Sondheim's *A Funny Thing Happened on the Way to the Forum*, you'll see how commedia dell'arte itself borrowed much from Roman comedy, because these characters all appear in one form or another. In *Uncle Vanya*, you'll see how Chekov uses these old stereotypes and plays topsy-turvy with them: There's the foolish old man who is also a useless scholar married to a young girl; there's the doctor who's reduced to a feeble failure; there's the young girl longing for him but losing out; there's the servant (Vanya himself) who is neither clever, scheming, nor witty and whose end is very sad.

Comedy of Intrigue

While a comedy of manners relies more on language, the *comedy of intrigue* relies more on plot. It, too, is a love chase, but its emphasis is on the many complicated schemes the young lad goes through. Although many of the same kinds of characters appear as in Roman comedy and commedia dell'arte, it is more concerned with disguises, tricks, sudden coincidences, and revelations. Famous examples include Ben Jonson's *Volpone* and Shakespeare's *Twelfth Night*, *Measure for Measure*, and *All's Well That Ends Well*.

Comedy of Humours

We discussed *humours* as a device for causing laughter that is built on the theory of emotional excesses. *Comedies of humours*, therefore, are plays in which many of the characters are drawn as emotionally obsessive or in which the plot stems from the ridiculous behavior of a central character who is similarly out of control. Molière made a career with comedies built around such obsessions: Orgon's religious zeal in *Tartuffe*; Argan's hypochondria in *The Imaginary Invalid*; Alceste's hatred of humanity in *The Misanthrope*; and Harpagon's miserliness in, of course, *The Miser*. In Neil Simon's *The Odd Couple*, Felix's obsessive neatness conflicts with Oscar's generic sloppiness.

Classic comedy shows us how a blocked society is turned into an open, healthy society. The action comes about when a teacher character somehow defeats or transforms a blocker character, freeing her way to a happy ending. Everybody is included in the real or symbolic celebration or wedding at the end. We enjoy laughing at the follies and calamities of these characters as they overcome their obstacles, but at the same time, we feel a little safe, secure, and superior. The writer of comedy has an attitude of joy mixed with cruelty, and for that reason, there's always something a little sad about a comedy.

Questioning the Play

1. Comedy typically requires the audience to be somewhat removed and "superior" to the action, and the mood of a comedy can range from being gently humorous to savagely mocking. What is the overriding mood of this play?

2. When the play begins, how is the world "blocked"? What characters are in charge, what false ideals or unrealistic beliefs permeate the world, what self-deceptions are at work, or what unjust laws are in effect?

3. Of the four types of plot strategies, which is operative in this play? Is there more than one? Why do you think the playwright has chosen these and not others?

4. If the play is primarily about pursuing a romance, what is there about the lovers that makes them so attractive to each other? What particular virtues does the playwright elect to be important? What does that say about the kind of world the play is set in?

5. If the play is primarily about playing a trick, what is the nature of that trick? Is it harmless or deliberately cruel? If someone gets into disguise, why are they choosing that specific one? Is the playwright making any sort of comment about the institution that disguise might represent? (For instance, many Restoration heroes disguise themselves or their friends as fake clergymen in order to bring about pretended marriages: Does this imply any particular attitude toward the Church?)

6. If the play is about teaching a lesson, what is the lesson to be learned? Is it of value only to the world of the play, or does it have any larger repercussions? Does it have any applicability toward your own life?

7. If the play is about interfacing with a "green world," in what ways is the green world better, worse, or just different from the "real world"? Which world changes which at the end? For better or for worse? In what ways? Which world do you think the playwright prefers or wants us to prefer?

8. What *cognitio* appears in the climax? What is the nature of the disclosure? Does it have resonance only in the play, or does the playwright intend for it to have relevance to the audience's world as well?

9. Which characters fill the role of blockers? How are they flawed or mistaken? In what ways are these qualities symptomatic of the blocked world that opens the play?

10. Which characters fill the role of teachers? How are they contrasted with the blockers? Which attitude or ideal does the playwright seem to favor?

11. Who are the buffoons? What functions do they fulfill in the play? Are they similar in ways to either the blockers or the teachers?

12. What are the sources of laughter that seem to be most prominent in the play? Why do you think the playwright has made use of the ones she did?

13. What *idées fixes* do any of the characters hold? How do these reinforce any of the blocking elements that began the play? How are they contrasted?

14. What elements of topsy-turvy, if any, are used? Precisely what is switched with what? Why has the playwright made these choices? How does it contribute to the overall meaning of the play?

15. If the play fits into the categories of any comedic subgenre, which would it be? What specific element (plot, humor, verbal wit, and so on) seems to be more prominent than any other? How does this relate to the blocker-teacher relationship?

8

Melodrama

At first glance, *melodrama* ought to be simple to define. You imagine something exciting: An evil villain pursues a fair-haired hero, or a winsome heroine, or both; there's a chase involving many hair-raising adventures of danger and near destruction; and—oh, delicious terror!—there might even be a ghost about the place, coming back to haunt the old house, or the cloud of some deep mystery that must be solved before ultimate disaster occurs. You might remember some R-rated flick you saw, perhaps from the Indiana Jones or Dracula school. Furthermore, you would probably claim this kind of play was fun to watch: You get hooked in early, have a few good scares, a moment of near disaster, but a sure and certain happy ending.

To some extent, all of these apply to melodrama; it *is* fun to watch and *does* provide us with a few good scares. Because of this, it's easy to define a melodrama as "a tragedy that never quite grew up." In a way, both types of play are serious; both are about important, sometimes life-and-death issues. But consider these differences: Tragedy raises complicated questions of morality, what's right and what's wrong, and very often fails to come up with an answer. Thus, one could argue that Oedipus does right just as easily as one could argue that he does wrong. Melodrama, on the other hand, reduces these sometimes complex questions to a much simpler state. In a melodrama, the division between right and wrong is clear: The good guys are right, and the bad guys are wrong.

Another difference lies in their use of characters. Tragedy shows us people who are complex; remember that a tragic hero is neither all good nor all bad, but somewhere in between. The characters in melodrama, on the other hand, are more likely to be one-dimensional: They're typically all good or all bad. And finally, as we watch a tragedy, we are made aware that there is an issue here: The play is trying to illustrate a point; somehow we become intellectually involved: Are the gods all powerful or not? As we watch a melodrama, however, we are concerned primarily with the outcome of the story: Will the good guy escape in time? Thus, tragedy is a serious play that typically deals with serious *issues* in a somewhat subtle and complex manner. Melodrama is a serious play that typically deals with serious *dangers* in a more obvious fashion.

All this makes it sound as though there were something juvenile or simplistic about these plays, and that we don't have to take them seriously. But this is wrong: There are many classic melodramas that are, in fact, quite profound. Plays such as Euripides' *Medea*, Lillian Hellman's *The Little Foxes*, or David Mamet's *Speed-the-Plow* are, by definition, melodramas, but they still manage to deal with mature, complex, and thought-provoking matters. So, our definition is not so simple after all.

It will help to take a look at the history of this genre. Originally, during the Renaissance, melodrama was a form of musical theater. It was partly sung and partly spoken and thus appealed more to the emotions (as music typically does) than to the intellect. During the nineteenth century, melodramas gradually evolved into completely spoken plays, but they were greatly influenced by the Romantic movement prevalent in Europe. Romanticism was a cultural attitude and a philosophical outlook on life that stressed individual achievement over both society and the universe: A typical Romantic hero was strong-willed, passionate, and self-determined. He might be a renegade or outlaw, like William Tell, Faust, or Victor Hugo's Hernani.

In addition, stages during the nineteenth century began to evolve from simple platforms separated from the audience into quite complex machines of magic. It became possible to use lighting, scenery, and costumes to create elaborate effects: thunderstorms, horse races, narrow escapes from railroad trains—all onstage before your very eyes. Soon enough, playwrights began to write into their scripts exciting scenes that would take advantage of these effects. And finally, changes in styles of acting appeared. Players strove to play as large as their characters were: They used bold gestures, adopted body positions indicating strong emotions, and spoke in rich voices strong enough to project into auditoriums that now seated thousands of spectators.

Moving into the twentieth century, plays that could accommodate this passionate outlook on life, this dramatic use of the stage, this bold extravagance, and this fascination with strong effects continued to be quite popular, and the genre exerted a strong influence on many writers. Some of these writers, however, became interested in trying to use this form to express some theme or idea rather than simply to give the balcony a good show. Today, therefore, writers employing the genre tend to encompass both attitudes: the desire to put on a good show, and the need to express an idea.

What Is the Mood of a Melodrama?

While it is indeed an oversimplification to call melodrama "a tragedy that never quite grew up," it's still a good place to start, because melodrama and tragedy do share some of the same features. As we said, both are serious. While we don't look at melodramatic characters with the same sense of awe and amazement that we do characters in classic tragedy, we don't look down on them and mock them either. Rather, we are more likely to empathize with them and see their struggles as similar to ours. Furthermore, while the stakes in a melodrama may indeed be high—in Ibsen's *An Enemy of the People*, it's the safety of an entire town—they are not so profound as the foundations of our moral existence.

Therefore, the predominant mood of a melodrama is one of suspense. We want the agent of action to win, but the antagonist proves harder to defeat than we at first thought. The dangers are more severe, the risk of failure more intimidating. The "escapes" become narrower and narrower. And victory, when it appears, is all the more sweet. (Keep in mind, however that suspense can come in very small doses as well as large: Whether or not Nora in *A Doll's House* sees the fatal envelope before Torvald does is just as vital a question as whether or not the screaming heroine will escape the clutches of the murderer before the cops arrive).

What Is the World of a Melodrama?

At first glance, the world of a melodrama might seem to be the most ordered and stable of all the genres. In classic tragedy, we see a moral code that has been violated and needs to be restored. In classic comedy, we see a flawed society being transformed into a healthy one. In melodrama, we enter into a place that seems split down the middle. We are in some world or society that is torn between two opposing forces: good and evil. The playing field may be as vast as outer space or as small as a living room, and the struggle may be public or private, but these two forces are always there: Somebody who represents good opposes somebody who represents evil.

In *Medea*, the playing field is a kingdom; in *Speed-the-Plow*, it's the offices of a film studio; and in *The Little Foxes*, it's a family business. But in each case, you can clearly identify this polar opposition. However—and this is what makes the world of melodrama such a nice place to live in—good almost always triumphs. We might add, therefore, to the description of the mood of a melodrama that it is upbeat; it makes us happy when right defeats wrong.

Or does it?

Because what's "right" and what's "wrong" may be quite relative things and depend to a great extent on the culture in which the writer and audience live. For instance, most action-adventure movies you see involve some killing, and your reaction to the killing probably varies. Usually, when the good guy kills a bad guy, that's a good thing, and "right" has prevailed. However, if the bad guy kills the hero, that's a bad thing, and "evil" has won. But isn't it still killing? Doesn't it still involve the deliberate taking of a human life? When is murder applauded, and when is it condemned?

Serious writers of melodrama use this ambiguity to their advantage. They present a world that is divided into what appears to be right and wrong but yet still leaves us in doubt as to which side wins. Medea certainly seems right to despise Jason for his treachery and to seek revenge—but is it right for her to murder their two small children?

On the surface, therefore, it appears that the central conflict in melodrama is *man against man*.

What Typical Plot Patterns Does a Melodrama Use?

A major difference between classic tragedy and its offspring, melodrama, is that the latter is typically more concerned with plot, while the former is more concerned with character. In melodrama, we are more interested in what happens and whether it will end properly or not; we are less interested in how these events transform the personalities of the people involved. That is, melodrama makes us wonder, Will Medea get away with her crime? rather than, How has this crime affected her? What kind of woman will she be afterward?

With these differences in mind, here are some characteristics of melodramatic plotting that are typical:

Somebody Is in Danger

This danger may be personal harm, illness, or great loss of either life or property. Sometimes the agent of action is holding onto a deep personal secret, which somebody else is desperately trying to discover (think of Nora's "crime" in *A Doll's House*). Often the agent of action wants to get away from a bad place (a prison? a totalitarian society?) while the villain wants to keep him there. Occasionally, the danger is nature run amok: There's a terrible storm coming, or mutated atomic ants are on the rampage devouring the world.

The Stakes Are Very High

Death, of course, ranks at the top of the list, but other things the agent of action might also be close to losing could include freedom, reputation, fortune, property, or a loved one. Therefore, there is often a great sense of urgency in a melodrama.

There Is an Object over Which the Two Opponents Struggle

Since this object is often a person, we'll discuss that possibility a little later on, in our section on characters in melodrama. However, this object might be a valuable treasure of other sorts: a stash of gold, a secret formula, the Maltese Falcon, or control of the kingdom. Some *center of attention* is created that becomes the most important thing in the world of the play. The object that the playwright chooses provides a clue to the meaning of the play. Sometimes this object is vast: Luke Skywalker and Darth Vader are struggling over the existence of the entire civilized universe—the destinies of billions of people are at stake. The object might be a tad smaller, perhaps control of a large corporation, and the playwright is saying something about greed. Perhaps it's the throne of a kingdom, and the play is about ambition. Or perhaps it's the right of minorities to vote, and the play is about justice. Or perhaps it's something ironic; the brothers in Sam Shepard's *True West* fight to the death over a screenplay credit!

Time Is Often a Major Obstacle

The clock is running out, and we have only weeks, days, hours, or seconds in which to save ourselves. Medea has one day to set her plans in motion; in *Speed-the-Plow*, Charlie Fox has until 10:30— minutes away!—to get Bobby Gould to change his mind. Think of the countless action-adventure shows you've seen in which a countdown starts around the middle of the second act. James Bond has seven seconds to defuse the bomb; Captain Kirk has minutes left before the dilithium crystals dissolve.

The Agent of Action's Fortune Vacillates Frequently

Classic tragedy tends to send its hero down a relatively smooth and clean descent: Once Oedipus sets out to discover the truth, he gets one bit of bad news after another until all the fatal pieces fit. Melodrama, by contrast, likes to play cat-and-mouse with its hero. He starts out in a good place, when a small trouble occurs. He gets out of this small trouble and catches his breath, only to encounter a bigger one; he gets out of that jam, but before he has time to enjoy his new life, along comes an even bigger one. Every time Regina, in *The Little Foxes*, thinks she's gotten power over her brothers, something happens to take it away—a new discovery, a new plot twist, or an unexpected event. We're living in a seesaw world.

Theatrical Effects Are Important, and the Plot Includes Some Variety of the "Big Scene"

Remembering that melodrama sprang in part from romanticism— a literary movement that stressed feeling over intellect—it shouldn't surprise you that melodrama loves to play upon an audience's emotions, giving them the biggest scare, the most important shock, the greatest tearjerker, or the most surprising discovery. In melodramas of the nineteenth and early twentieth centuries, these scenes are almost comic in their clumsiness. You find writers hooking audiences in with dark and ominous foreshadowings ("Something terrible is going to happen, I know it!"), inspiring them with heroes who make bold decisions to take strong action ("As God is my witness, I'll never go hungry again!"), shocking them with surprising coincidences or unexpected revelations ("It is true; it is I, your long-lost mother!"). Today, melodramas still use the *big scene* as a sort of cliff-hanger, a moment that can be milked for all the sensationalism it contains.

Medea has a terrible moment onstage in which she struggles with herself over whether or not to kill her children in order to make her cheating husband suffer, and then goes offstage to do it. The chorus, and we, wait in terrible anticipation as the deed happens. Even so "intellectual" a melodrama as Arthur Miller's *The Crucible* has a big scene: John Proctor's wife is trying to save her husband from hanging and so tells a lie to the court. In order to test her, they bring Proctor in and ask him some questions that will either support or deny that lie. The tension in the room as Proctor tries to guess which answer he must give is nearly as "hair-raising" as Indiana Jones's struggle with the runaway airplane.

The favorite spot for such a big scene is often the end of an act because it provides terrific curtain lines. The first act of *A Doll's House* ends with Nora alone on the stage, trembling in fear after Krogstad has threatened blackmail, muttering to herself, "Corrupt my little children! Poison my home! It isn't true. It *couldn't* be true!"

The "Big Scene" Shows the Ultimate Reversal

Because a melodrama plays roller coaster with the fortunes of the agent of action, writers of melodrama will squeeze that character as hard as they can before they save her. Our hero faces utter ruin, tension is at its highest peak, when something miraculously happens to reverse the situation. Or she seems perched on the brink of success, when she's zapped without mercy and plunges to her doom. What causes this incredible reversal varies from play to play. If you recall our discussion of crisis in chapter 3, we noted that any of the things that come along to make things worse can also operate to make things better. Thus, this last major reversal might come from inside the character, from another character, or from some external force, even an act of nature. The source helps reveal the play's meaning.

Very often, this sudden upswing in fortune is accompanied by the "biggest" scene of all and contains a line or two of surprising intensity and power. In a moment of extreme pressure, a character is likely to be letting his guard down, operating on instinct rather than conscious design, and is most vulnerable. In this moment, he often cries out a phrase or a line that he would normally have kept hidden. This line is so strong that it gives us an instant insight into the personality of the character, while at the same time shifting gears for him irrevocably.

I like to define this moment as a "Torvald moment," because one of the most famous ones appears in *A Doll's House*. Torvald, you'll recall, is reading the letter from Krogstad, who has decided not to pursue his blackmail of Nora. Torvald is so relieved he calls out spontaneously, "Nora, I am saved!" Nora quietly then asks, "And what about me?" And Torvald catches himself with, "Of course, you too. We are saved." But it's too late. He has shown his true colors by what he's said when the chips were down.

In *The Little Foxes*, two such powerful moments occur. In the first, Regina has lost all hope of getting the upper hand on her brothers because her husband—an invalid bound to a wheelchair—will not release to her the bonds that she needs. They've had a quarrel; she's just said to him, "I'm waiting for you to die; I'm wanting you to die" (act 2), and he is about to leave the room when he suddenly suffers a heart attack. As he desperately tries to climb the stairs for his medicine, she stands there absolutely quiet and still, watching him struggle and die. Her Torvald line is her *in*-activity.

The second big moment plunges Regina back down permanently. During the investigation of the death, it is discovered that the husband was on the stairs when he died. Just before it looks as though she's won forever, one of her brothers, who's been struggling with her for control of the family business, says to her, very calmly, "I say to myself, things may change. I agree with Alexandra. What is a man in a wheelchair doing on a staircase?" (act 3). And it is clear that she's trapped once again, this time for good.

What Sort of Characters Are Typical?

Recall that classic tragedy deals with characters who are, by some definition or other, "above us," while classic comedy shows us people who are "below us," in the sense that we feel somehow superior to their foolishness. The people who typically inhabit melodramas are "more like us," in both their sociopolitical status and their personalities. But, more important, they tend to be less extreme than characters in the other two genres. That is to say, they are neither as guilty as those in classic tragedy nor as ludicrous as those in classic comedy. They don't suffer from *hubris*, nor are they turned into machines by extreme passions and humors.

Nor are the characters in melodrama typically as complex as those in the other two genres we've discussed. Keep in mind that melodrama is more interested in plot than in character. Generally speaking, therefore, characters are typically drawn in broad strokes, with little texture or subtlety. Indeed, the characters in popular nineteenth-century melodramas were extreme stereotypes; in the most famous one of all, Harriet Beecher Stowe's novel *Uncle Tom's Cabin*, we have Simon Legree—wickedness incarnate; Eliza—suffering victim; Topsy—funny little comic relief; Eva—the pure innocent child who dies; St. Clare—the good master; and so on.

While modern melodrama characters have grown beyond such clichés, they are still relatively one-dimensional. Often they are almost comedic in the sense that they are dominated by one of the four humours or an *idée fixe*, and we come to understand them completely early in the play. As the action unfolds, they don't change—or if they do, they change very little, rarely experiencing the same sort of maturation or achieving the same depth of insight as do Oedipus, Tom in *The Glass Menagerie*, or Nora in *A Doll's House*. According to this description, you might argue that Willy Loman in *Death of a Salesman* is a melodramatic character: He has the same position at the end as he had in the beginning. He never understands what he's done to his family, and he never stops dreaming his foolish dream; he even commits suicide because of it.

It follows, therefore, that the dialogue of melodramatic characters is often not what we'd call complex; it rather consists of a continuing series of position statements, epigrams, or repeated phrases that give us the essence of their personalities in quick, broad strokes. Instead of getting character development, we often get character illustration. The salesmen in David Mamet's *Glengarry Glen Ross*, for instance, are easily identified by their attitudes toward their jobs, which never change. Levene sees it as a sport: "A man's his job." Roma always refers to it in Darwinian terms: "I say this is how we must act. I do these things which seem correct to me *today*." And Aaronow is confused—he's always a bit behind, is made the butt of jokes, and says as his last line, "I hate this job" (act 2).

With these generalizations in mind, let's look at typical characters who appear in melodramas:

- the good guy
- the bad guy
- the character in distress
- the outsider
- other characters for comic relief and in subplots

The Good Guy

Since melodramas show us a world divided into good and evil, it's obvious that there'll be characters who personify these forces. Typically, the agent of action is the *good guy*: a character who is on the side of "right," or at least what supposedly stands for "right," since, as we've noted, this position is always relative. However, you can usually see the good guy as a *raisonneur* character and study his actions, decisions, and speeches as representing the author's point of view. Detectives in mystery stories are on the side of justice; revolutionaries such as Dr. Stockman in Ibsen's *An Enemy of the People* are on the side of honesty and truth; even Nora could be considered a good guy because she believes in self-realization.

However, the good guy is not always the agent of action. Some of the more interesting melodramas are driven by people who are not so good: Regina in *The Little Foxes* is manipulative, Medea is vengeful, and Roma in *Glengarry Glen Ross* is corrupt. These characters are closer to the next type.

The Bad Guy

The *bad guy* is the character who obviously stands for the values that the playwright feels are wrong: lying, killing, manipulating, betraying, and so on. To this end, you might consider this character a sort of topsy-turvy *raisonneur;* that is, a negative role model.

Given the *raisonneur* attributes of both the good guy and the bad guy, it follows that a major clue to the meaning of a melodrama lies in their interaction. Analyze them on the symbolic level, and you should be able to determine what idea or value is in conflict with its opposite. Which wins? Which loses? In *The Little Foxes*, it's clear that Regina is a bad guy: She engages in all sorts of double-dealing, and her brothers are very much like her. The good guy role is filled both by her husband, whom she disposes of in the third act, and by her daughter Alexandra. Alexandra has watched all these goings-on with continuing alarm and with growing insight. In her last confrontation with her mother, she delivers what's clearly a *raisonneur* speech:

> Adie said there were people who ate the earth and other people who stood around and watched them do it. . . . Well, I'm not going to stand around and watch you do it. (act 3)

This hints that Alexandra is at least equal to her mother. But then the following exchange takes place:

> REGINA: Well, you have spirit, after all. I used to think you were all sugar water. We don't have to be bad friends. . . . Would you like to come and talk to me, Alexandra? Would you—would you like to sleep in my room tonight?
> ALEXANDRA: Are you afraid, Mama?

At this, Regina exits, alone. We are left with the image of Alexandra onstage, now dominant after all. So, has innocence beat corruption? Youth defeated age? Honesty triumphed over—what? You decide.

Are there melodramas in which the bad guy wins? Of course. However, try to examine whether or not there's irony involved here: That is, is the playwright making some judgment about this victory? Is it a true victory? A permanent victory? Or a false one? In other words, the fact that the bad guy wins doesn't necessarily mean the writer is a pessimist; she may have irony up her sleeve.

The Character in Distress

We touched upon this above briefly as a plot device: For the good guy and the bad guy to have a proper struggle, the playwright needs to provide something for them to struggle over. In some of the best melodramas, the object of the struggle is a person: somebody who is wanted by both sides for reasons of their own. This character serves to personify whatever idea the writer is trying to convey and to give dramatic life and power to an abstract concept. Thus, if the struggle is over control of a large corporation, the playwright might invent somebody who is currently the CEO, and who will either stay or go, depending on who wins. The fight for control of the family fortune in *The Little Foxes* centers in part on those bonds that Regina needs in order to buy a larger share of the company than her brothers can, but it also centers in part on Alexandra. She's Regina's daughter, and like a princess in a medieval kingdom, is eligible for marriage. But to whom? If Regina's brother has *his* way, she'll marry his son (a dull lout) in order to keep the fortune in the family. If Regina's husband has *his* way, Alexandra will get away from this household and marry a man she loves. If Regina, on the other hand, has *her* way, she'll keep Alexandra unmarried as long as she can in order to use her as a bargaining chip. Thus, Alexandra becomes the center of a great deal of plotting and quarreling.

The Outsider

The struggle between good and evil over control of the object often gets heated and intense. Because part of the job of a melodrama is to keep the audience wondering how the plot will turn out, audiences can lose sight of the real issue in the play. Therefore, to present a cooler, perhaps more objective, point of view, the writer often inserts a character who stands a bit outside the struggle and is not contaminated by it. Perhaps this character has come into this bizarre green world from someplace else and represents a standard against which to measure the struggle of the good guy and the bad guy. While they battle over power and control, this outsider puts their struggle into a broader perspective; she lets us know that somewhere else this power struggle means perhaps something different, or perhaps even nothing at all. In this respect, the *outsider* is partly a foil and partly a *raisonneur*.

Medea, for instance, is consumed with anger and jealousy, while her unfaithful husband, Jason, is concerned with protecting his children, his new wife, and his newly found power. Neither is objective. Into this mix, Euripides inserts a scene between Medea and a man named Aegeus. He's the king of a nearby country who is passing through. He encounters Medea, who helps him solve a riddle that puzzles him. In return, she enlists his help, telling him her story. He then offers to provide her sanctuary in his own country, providing she can get there on her own. His point—which might be the point of the play—is that he cannot get involved in this emotional struggle. It's better to remain levelheaded and impartial. In this respect, he represents a kind of moral code: In a world of bickering and animosity, he stands for sanity, fairness, and objectivity, qualities that both Medea and Jason certainly lack.

Other Characters for Comic Relief and in Subplots

Some melodramas are richer in texture than others, with a broader story to tell and a wider collection of characters. We will look at two types of additional characters.

Comic relief. Many early melodramas included characters who provided comic relief, and they often played upon bald stereotypes. These characters included neighbors, servants, weird relatives, and bizarre local yokels who would pop in and out of the play seemingly at whim. They range from the cartoonlike Topsy in *Uncle Tom's Cabin*, through a gaggle of Irish, German, or Yankee bystanders in the plays of Dion Boucicault and others, down to, to some extent, the confused and bewildered Aaronow in *Glengarry Glen Ross*.

Characters in subplots. Sometimes a writer tries to juggle two stories at the same time, one of which somehow echoes the other. While the upper-class people are having their struggles, their servants or neighbors or relatives might also be having struggles of their own. Or while the main plot involves bad deeds, the subplot might deal with good ones. *The Little Foxes* is a modern example of this. While Regina is struggling with her brothers and busy with her schemes, Alexandra welcomes home her ailing father, spends time consoling Birdie, and puts off the unwelcome advances of her cousin. She exerts a healthy influence on folks, while her mother and uncles are exerting an unhealthy one.

A melodrama is a serious play that puts more emphasis on plot than on character and typically shows a struggle between personifications of good and evil, a struggle in which good most often wins. It typically deals with high stakes and personal danger to an agent of action. Its plot is complicated, with a series of reversals that tend to drive the agent of action to near defeat or near victory and then is topped off with a climax that provides a sudden and final reversal. Some writers, however, switch around some of these characteristics in a topsy-turvy manner, depending on their vision.

Questioning the Play

1. How do the elements in your play compare or contrast with those found in a classic tragedy? (Does your play have, for instance, a tragic hero without *hamartia*?) What meaning do you think lies in that difference?

2. How do the principles of right and wrong emerge in your play? Has the playwright laid down and clarified two opposing forces? Which side, if any, does the playwright seem to be on?

3. What degree of importance does the playwright place on plot versus character?

4. How has the playwright structured the plot to include a series of reversals? Do these reversals seem organic to the story, or do they seem contrived for the purpose of suspense?

5. Where does a big scene occur? How has the playwright built the play toward that moment? What is the cause and the nature of this major reversal?

6. Is there a "Torvald moment" in the play? How does it come about? What does it say about the true identity of a character and/ or the overall meaning of the play?

7. Which characters represent the good and which the evil? What do these terms mean in the context of the play?

8. What is the object over which the two opponents struggle? Who functions as the character in distress? How does this center of opposition operate to keep the plot moving? What symbolic associations do you think it has?

9. Is there an outsider in the play? How does this person function as a *raisonneur*?

10. Does the play have any subplot? If so, how does this subplot relate to the main plot: Does it echo, contrast with, or somehow reinforce the theme?

Farce

If we call melodrama a "tragedy that never quite grew up," we can say *farce* is "comedy at maximum overdrive." It's typically a very funny play that deals with extremely dangerous situations. People are pushed to the extreme edge, either physically or emotionally; they are often one narrow step away from total disaster; their bodies take complete possession of their minds—and yet we laugh. It's a genre that goes all the way back to the beginning of drama.

Farce first appeared in Greece during its classical period in the fifth century BCE, primarily in the plays of Aristophanes. These boisterous works were part political satire, part outrageous burlesque, part musical comedy, and part *Mary Poppins*–like fantasy. A typical plot is the one in *The Birds*: A pair of Athenian citizens are fed up with the corruption and poverty in Athens and decide to find a better place to live. They ascend to the clouds and enter the realm where the birds live. After some effort, they convince the birds to organize and build their own city, halfway between earth and heaven. Ultimately, this happens, and the play ends with the two Athenians now quite literally "on top of the roost." Along the way, several characters show up to profit from the scheme and engage the Athenian heroes in a series of comic bits that almost seem to come directly from scenes in *The Three Stooges*. Plot is not as important as individual bits of nonsense: The work is more a revue than a play. People get kicked and beaten, duped, deceived, and tricked; jokes are made about sex, eating, and eliminating; and the whole thing descends more and more into the ridiculous and the ribald.

This sort of comedy faded away after Aristophanes and was replaced by the classic well-made comedy we discussed in chapter 7, in which plot became more organic and characters became a little more human. The two forms are very different from each other, so that the earlier, Aristophanic comedy is called "Old Comedy," while the more familiar, plot-driven form is called "New Comedy." However, while New Comedy gained popularity and became entrenched in the centuries to follow, traces of the outrageous shtick of the other form continued to appear in various guises. Throughout the middle and later years of the Roman Empire, popular writers created a variety of outrageous plays collectively labeled "Atellanian Farce." At the same time, there developed a whole history and tradition of popular entertainments at such events as fairs, festivals, and church holidays involving strolling players, clowns, jugglers, mimes, storytellers, Punch-and-Judy puppet shows, and other kinds of theatrics that used many of the same burlesque bits as Aristophanes: bawdy jokes, broad plotlines, and physical comedy. (Judy was always beating Punch because he was doing something stupid in the household—a sort of medieval version of *The Honeymooners*).

Around the seventeenth century, the commedia dell'arte troupes used many of the plotlines from earlier farces and many of the outrageous bits from popular entertainment. These players in turn influenced the formal theater and the work of Molière, William Congreve, William Wycherley, and other writers of the seventeenth and eighteenth centuries. Today, you might be most familiar with this sort of material in sketch-comedy on *Saturday Night Live* or in the films of such clowns as Buster Keaton, Charlie Chaplin, Adam Sandler, Jim Carrey, and others. Out of all these various influences emerged the genre we're looking at now.

What Is the Mood of a Farce?

Like classic comedy, farce allows us to feel superior to other human beings and to laugh at their misfortune—except that "life-threatening danger" is a more accurate description. Typically, a character in farce is doing something he's not supposed to be doing (cheating on his wife, leaving work or school when he's not supposed to, or pretending to be somebody else) and runs the risk of losing everything he holds precious and going down in ignominious defeat. He has to do something—anything—to avoid the disaster that will occur if he's found out. And, of course, events conspire to bring him to the brink of ruin: The wife shows up just when she's not supposed to; the incriminating letter falls into the wrong hands; or the person who can penetrate the disguise walks into the room. (Note that use of the masculine pronoun is deliberate here; most farces are about cheating husbands and rarely about cheating wives.)

Because of its fondness for near disaster, farce has a sense of urgency. Often time is quickly running out, and impending doom is just around the corner. The hero has only days or minutes to get out of his predicament; the husband cheating on his wife suddenly hears his wife's voice coming down the hall and has seconds in which to hide his mistress. Farce is always out of breath as people hurry, scurry, dash in or behind or under hiding places, or slam their way in and out of doors.

In addition to this mood of breakneck speed and impending disaster, farce often has a sense of crudeness about it: It's typically concerned more with the physical side of life than the intellectual. Jokes are made about bodily functions: The old man, barely able to walk, still gets aroused by a well-endowed maiden; somebody passes gas in the middle of a love scene; Charlie Chaplin tries to eat a steamed boot as though it were Fettuccini Alfredo. Think of all the jokes you know that make fun of people who are hearing-impaired or have other disabilities, people who lisp, or people who just don't speak English as we do. These stereotypes may all be politically incorrect, and they are certainly offensive, but farce, as we'll see, includes them all.

Another typical mood in farce is a sense of violence. Servants are beaten by their angry masters; clumsy oafs fall into holes, slam into doors, have windows fall on their fingers, get trapped inside rotating clothes driers, and even get their genitals stuck in the zippers of their pants. But face the truth: Watching somebody else squirm in agony makes us howl with laughter.

What Is the World of a Farce?

The world of farce is filled with danger, urgency, violence, and pain—not a friendly place. Whatever can go wrong, will. It seems as though there were a dark and malevolent force at work; some evil that makes objects turn against you, messes up your world deliberately, sets traps and deceits for you at every turn. In other genres, the world seems to at least have some absolute rationality: Classic tragedy, for example, is set against a universal moral code that is ultimately proven sound; comedy shows us a false or blocked world moving toward some ideal true or open world; melodrama provides us with personifications of right and wrong. All of these genres imply that beyond and behind us exists some ideal place where order prevails. None of these assumptions, however, can be considered true in farce. What we have is *man against chaos*.

In Thornton Wilder's play *The Matchmaker* (the basis for the musical *Hello, Dolly!*), young Barnaby Tucker expresses this idea in a famous line. When things are looking very bad for him, he delivers a speech that distills the essence of farce perfectly: "It began getting desperate about half-past four and it's been getting worse ever since. Now I have to take a bath and get slapped all over!" (act 4).

Later, when we discuss at length various styles of drama, we'll examine what is meant by *theater of the absurd*. We'll define it as a play that deals with a world that has no order or meaning, and we'll make the point that absurdist plays such as Samuel Beckett's *Waiting for Godot* are often very funny. That's because, in their hearts, they all want to be farces.

What Typical Plots Appear in a Farce?

Farce takes place in a world devoid of reason. Our agent of action is probably the only "sane" person around. Granted, he may not be the nicest person (after all, he could be a philandering husband!), but he still serves as our focal point. When plunged into this world of lunacy, the agent of action has essentially three choices that, alone or in combination, form the basis for most farce plots.

The Agent of Action Has to Hold the Chaos at Bay with All His Might

He struggles to keep his mind focused on the rational, to pursue whatever his goal might be with clear purpose, and to avoid being turned mad himself. Think of Alice, dropped into Wonderland or stepping through the looking-glass. She's suddenly surrounded by a mad hatter, one insanely murderous queen and another who turns into a sheep, a knight who can't stay on his horse, and a croquet match played with flamingos for mallets—it's enough to drive anybody over the edge. You also see this pattern appearing in prime-time television sitcoms. A typical plot has a happily married guy living near his relatives, all of whom, in their loony ways, provoke him into one bizarre crisis after another.

Let's look at a famous American farce that displays this pattern. In Joseph Kesselring's *Arsenic and Old Lace*, Teddy Brewster comes to visit his aunts; he learns that they have been quietly poisoning lonely old men (in order to put them out of their misery), that his uncle thinks he's Teddy Roosevelt charging up San Juan Hill every time he goes upstairs, and that his own brother is often mistaken for Boris Karloff (a role, by the way, originally played by Boris Karloff— how farcical is that!). Poor Teddy has to keep the cops from finding out about his senile old aunts and hauling them off to jail.

In *The Matchmaker*, Thornton Wilder again puts the essence of farce into the mouth of a character. Horace Vandergelder, dressing to go off courting a young widow, says to the audience, "Ninety percent of the people in the world are fools and the rest of us are in great danger of contagion" (act 1).

The Agent of Action Has to Descend and Become
Part of This Mad World in Order to Survive

Often the agent of action is thrust into this bizarre world by accident. If he's cheating on his wife, he has to set up a series of lies and thereby create a mad world of his own, which he now has to live in and make real; if he has lied, saying that this woman is a foreign diplomat, he now has to go to any length necessary to make that lie real. One of the greatest examples comes from Billy Wilder's film *Some Like It Hot*. Two musicians have witnessed the St. Valentine's Day massacre in Chicago; to avoid being caught by the criminals, they must join an all-girl band. They have to pretend to be girls—and you can probably guess what insanity follows.

In *The Matchmaker*, Vandergelder himself becomes an example. Further along in the speech quoted above, he lets us know that he has decided to take a bold step:

Since you see I'm a man of sense, I guess you were surprised to hear that I'm planning to get married again....After many years' caution and hard work, I have a right to a little risk and adventure, and I'm thinking of getting married. Yes, like all you other fools, I'm willing to risk a little security for a certain amount of adventure. Think it over. (act 1)

The Agent of Action Decides to Attack the Madness of the World

Sometimes the agent of action becomes a sort of super-teacher figure, charging Don Quixote–like against impossible odds, trying either to make the lunatics of the world see the idiocy of their ways or to bring about some change in them. In Mary Chase's *Harvey*, Veta Louise Simmons tries to cure her brother, Elwood P. Dowd, of his belief that his best friend is an invisible giant rabbit named Harvey. She goes so far as to try to have him committed. Of course, she finds in the psychiatric hospital a world that's even more bizarre than her home life and ultimately decides that maybe Dowd is the sane one after all! She then has to find a way to get Dowd safely out of this "madhouse."

Often the role of teacher is taken by the playwright herself, and she uses the play to attack what she sees as the idiocy of the real world she lives in. When this happens, farce moves into *satire*. Sometimes the writing pokes gentle fun at our bizarre practices, as in the musicals *Of Thee I Sing* (George S. Kaufman, Morrie Ryskind, George and Ira Gershwin's spoof of presidential politics) or *How to Succeed in Business Without Really Trying* (Abe Burrows and Frank Loesser's attack on corporate hypocrisy). In the 1960s, a vicious attack was made on the Johnson administration in a play by Barbara Garson called *Macbird*, which drew farcical parallels with Shakespeare's *Macbeth*. Again, you find many examples in electronic media: Sketch-comedy shows such as *Saturday Night Live* or *Mad TV* are weekly attacks on the lunacy of our times.

Within these three broadly generic story patterns, several plot devices appear.

Deceit

Farce begins when somebody sets up a lie, and then it involves the weaving of a complex web of strategies, obstacles, reversals, and near misses before the ultimate success.

The Matchmaker starts this way. Horace Vandergelder is the employer of Barnaby and Cornelius. In his absence (he's off to New York to find a bride), the two men decide to fake an explosion in the store and go off for an adventure. They must then take care not to be seen by their boss. And, of course, in many farces, from Georges Feydeau's *A Flea in Her Ear* to Michael Frayn's *Noises Off*, somebody has to lie incessantly to hide the fact that he or she is cheating on a spouse.

Love Chases

Somebody is lustfully pursuing somebody else, either for marriage or for fun. Like most good comedies, farce involves romance and can be about a boy getting a girl. However, love isn't always pure: Farce reveals two very different kinds of romance. We'll label them *true-love chases* and *false-love chases*.

The first type is an authentic courtship: In *The Matchmaker*, Cornelius really wants to woo Irene Molloy, and we in the audience want them to get together because they're nice people who deserve happiness.

But in false-love chases, this pattern is subverted in several ways:

It's turned topsy-turvy because the woman is chasing the man. Nowadays, in the twenty-first century, this might not seem as bold and outrageous an idea as it was in the past, but many farces get their fun by seeing women behave contrary to type. Thus, Wilder has Dolly Levi pursuing Horace Vandergelder and, once she's seen him, Minnie Faye setting her eyes on Barnaby Tucker.

It's inappropriate because the man is all wrong for the woman. Usually it's because the man is an old fool who thinks he's young enough to handle a youthful bride; this story line goes all the way back to Plautus and Terence and, of course, is echoed in Burt Shevelove and Stephen Sondheim's *A Funny Thing Happened on the Way to the Forum*, wherein the lusty young lad's old and decrepit father is chasing after the maiden. In *The Matchmaker*, clearly Vandergelder also falls into this category.

The chase is not about love but about lust. Marriage isn't the objective; seduction is. *A* doesn't want to marry *B* so much as to bed her—or to continue to do so. A whole library of such chases were written in France during the last part of the nineteenth century by such writers as Georges Feydeau, Augustin Eugène Scribe, and Eugène Labiche, who were almost as prolific as today's sitcom writers. Their formulas proved to be so popular and so enduring that the name of a distinct subgenre has emerged to describe these lustful romps: Today, we call them *bedroom farces*.

Getting the Treasure

Somebody has to seize an important object before it's too late, or at least prevent somebody else from getting it first. This object might be a letter that incriminates the erring husband or a document that proves his innocence. One of the earliest English comedies is a precursor of this: In the anonymously authored *Gammer Gurton's Needle*, the whole town is turned upside down in a frantic search for a missing needle—that turns up in the pants of one of the characters.

The Long Arm of Coincidence Plays a Disastrous Role

Remember the operative rule in farce is that what can go wrong, will. In *The Importance of Being Earnest*, you may recall that Jack's "dead brother" shows up five minutes after Jack has "buried" him. In *The Matchmaker*, it just so happens that Barnaby and Cornelius walk into Irene Molloy's hat shop ten minutes before Vandergelder shows up; later, it just so happens that the table in the restaurant at which they are seated is *precisely* next to the table occupied by Vandergelder; and then it just so happens that they all wind up in the same living room in the third act. (However, sometimes the long arm is benevolent: When Cornelius is presented with the restaurant bill and realizes that he has no money, it just so happens that he is given a wallet by a man who found it on the floor because it was lost by Vandergelder himself—how coincidental can you get?)

Misunderstandings Get People into Trouble

People get directions wrong all the time in farce. If I say eleven o'clock, I may very well mean 11 PM, but you are, of course, going to hear 11 AM. If I send a message with my servant for you to meet me at Twelfth Street and Third Avenue, he's obviously going to tell you Twelfth Avenue and Third Street. And what about confusion of people? When I'm expecting my cousin (whom I've never met) to show up at the train wearing a red hat, and another woman gets off the train also wearing a red hat, you can be sure I'll confuse her for my cousin. So, when I offer to take her home, to buy her dinner, to put her up in style, this stranger will bless her good luck, while my real cousin stands waiting for five hours at the train station. Shakespeare's earliest comedy builds scene after scene on this device, as one long-lost twin is mistaken for his brother; there's a good reason it's called *A Comedy of Errors*.

Sometimes this misunderstanding is based on a device known as *quid pro quo*. The term comes from the Latin, which means "this for that." It's often used in a legal context when discussing contracts. In farce, this device occurs when two people are talking about something, and each assumes—erroneously—that the other has the same meaning in mind. A classic example appears in the musical *Fiddler on the Roof*. Tevye is invited by Lazar Wolfe, the butcher, to discuss an important matter. Tevye thinks he wants to talk about buying a cow. Lazar wants to discuss marrying Tevye's daughter. The audience, of course, is in on the joke and gets to laugh at how confused it gets when Tevye can't understand why Lazar sees this purchase as a cure for his loneliness!

Disguises: Somebody Needs to Pretend to Be Somebody Else

The disguise is usually either to get somebody out of trouble or to help somebody achieve some goal. A young man will pretend to be rich to fool his girlfriend's father, or a single girl will pretend to be married to get a job or to adopt a baby or for some other reason. We mentioned this device (playing a trick) in chapter 7 as one of the four main story lines of classic comedy. In farce, this disguise is carried to ridiculous extremes and often involves a man pretending to be a woman. There seems to be something intrinsically funny about a man dressed as a woman: Guys in drag have been a staple of burlesque for centuries. In Brandon Thomas's play *Charley's Aunt*, the young hero dresses up as his rich aunt from Brazil ("where the nuts come from!") in order to safely court his proper girlfriend. Of course, a man falls in love with him/her. *The Matchmaker's* Barnaby, in order to escape detection, winds up putting on a lady's hat and coat. And on and on.

An interesting and somewhat inexplicable extension of this device worth noting is that, while men dressing as women seems funny, the reverse is not necessarily true. In those comedies in which women dress as men—as in Shakespeare's *As You Like It* and *Twelfth Night*, or in Caryl Churchill's *Cloud Nine*—the playwright isn't using this disguise to get laughs but to achieve some other purpose. While Shakespeare's women wear trousers to protect themselves in hostile or uncertain environments, Churchill has her women cross-dress because she's making a political point about gender expectations. Many contemporary artists follow her lead and use gender disguise for satirical purposes.

Closely Related to Disguises: Hiding

People in farces are always getting themselves into the wrong place at the wrong time, and the only recourse is to find a place to hide; almost anything will do in an emergency. Such scenes are very common in world drama. For instance, people hide:

- in Richard Brinsley Sheridan's *School for Scandal* behind a folding screen
- in Ben Jonson's *Volpone* in the next room
- in Thornton Wilder's *The Matchmaker* under a table
- in Pierre Augustin Beaumarchais's *The Marriage of Figaro* under a rug on the seat of a chair
- in Neil Simon's *California Suite* outside on the window ledge

and so on, *ad infinitum.*

Objects Wreak Havoc with People's Lives

Things seem to have a malevolent life of their own, determined to do evil. If there's a letter, it will fall into the wrong hands. If there's a machine, it will break down. If there's a door, it'll get stuck. If there's a zipper, someone will get some body part caught in it. If there's a handkerchief, it will get lost and then found by the wrong person . . . But wait: Isn't that what happens in *Othello*? There's just a chuckle and a death separating farce from classic tragedy!

A Whole Series of Complex and Convoluted Events Transpires

Just a cursory glance at the lines of action in *The Matchmaker* is almost enough to confuse you. Dolly Levi is after Vandergelder; he's after Irene; she's after Cornelius; Barnaby and Cornelius are hiding from Vandergelder while at the same time trying to get a kiss from the ladies; Dolly is trying to help them because if she can get Irene attached to Cornelius, she'll be free to go after Vandergelder; Vandergelder has a niece who is running away with her boyfriend and has to avoid being caught. Have you got all that?

In a farce by Tom Stoppard, *On the Razzle*, a character muses to himself. You don't need to know the details of what went before in order to understand the disasters that lie ahead:

> Why do I have a sense of impending disaster? Sonders is after my niece and has discovered the secret address where I am sending her to the safe keeping of my sister-in-law . . . who has never laid eyes on him, or, for that matter, on Marie either since she was a baby—while I have to leave my business in the charge of my assistant and apprentice, and follow my new servant, whom I haven't had time to introduce to anyone, to town so that I can join the parade in a uniform I can't sit down in and take my fiancée to dinner in a fashionable restaurant. One false move and we could have a farce on our hands. (act 1)

All these complexities and pitfalls, of course, lead to the play's convoluted and intense climax.

Events Become More and More Convoluted, Building Toward a Scene of Chaos

Madness descends. The universe is out of control. Attempts to find any degree of rationality are next to useless. Plot twists have led us down an ever-narrowing path, until there's nothing left to do but explode. Chaos. Nearly mindless physical activity. Beatings. Narrow escapes. Ridiculous sword fights. Chases. Noise. Confusion. Vandergelder bumps into Cornelius at the restaurant (remember how they just happened to be at the same place at the same time) and goes after him. Cornelius, Barnaby, Irene, and Minnie Faye run out, just as Vandergelder discovers his wallet is missing and starts to look for it, just as his own niece and her fiancé enter; Vandergelder goes after them, but they run off, and at the same time, the band strikes up a polka, and Mrs. Levi goes after Horace—there's no way out of this maelstrom—except to ring down the curtain at the end of the act.

This chaos is often heightened by doors: things for people to go in and out of and—best of all—to slam and make noise with. Doors are so common in great farces that they've almost become a hallmark: As soon as the curtain goes up on Frayn's *Noises Off*, you'll see nine different ways to come in and out of the room; you don't need the program to tell you you're in farce country.

Eventually, It All Gets Cleared Up with a *Cognitio*

You will recall that a *cognitio* is a moment in which the mystery is cleared up, the answer is discovered, and the mistaken identities are all unveiled. And it's always a good discovery: The slave girl turns out to be freeborn after all and in fact not the sister of her boyfriend; the girl pretending to be a guy is really a girl, and the guy pretending to be the girl is really her long-lost twin brother, who has the same tattoo on his cheek that she does. The culprit confesses his misdeeds and gets the heroine off the hook; and, of course, he's forgiven. Farce, like comedy, *includes*.

This *cognitio* often provides an extremely important clue to the play's meaning. The playwright often creates the secret that is revealed to make some comment about life as she sees it. Thus, if the secret is about somebody's real gender (a man pretending to be a woman all along), the play may well be commenting on society's gender expectations. If the secret is about a long-lost relationship, the playwright might be commenting on the dangerous line that lies between truth and illusion—how, after all, can we ever be really sure who anybody truly is? If the secret is about a treasure long hidden or a family scandal long buried, the playwright might be commenting in some way on the relations between past and present.

What Sort of Characters Appear in Farce?

Generally speaking, we've noted that, in tragedy, a tragic hero is "above us"; in comedy, characters are "below us"; and in melodrama, "a lot like us." How, then, do characters in a farce relate to us? Since they behave so foolishly and get into so much silly trouble, we might say they are "very far below us." But the issue goes deeper than that.

Consider: A typical plot shows a relatively "sane" person trying to cope with an insane world. How often have you looked around and thought the people in your world were extremely stupid: your folks, with their outmoded attitudes; your boss, with his inflexible rules; your teacher, with her useless assignments? Or how often have you fantasized about running away from the mundane, leading a secret life filled with adventure, danger, and lust? Or how often have you watched older people, or people with disabilities, and secretly feared growing old or becoming handicapped?

All of these characters are typical farce creations. To some extent, therefore, we might say that these plays are extended Freudian psychological jokes. What we see enacted before us is an exaggerated extension of our secret ideas, longings, and terrors. Thus, we can generalize and say that the characters in farce are personifications of our secret selves.

Within these parameters, the following are some specific types.

The Sane Person

This is often the agent of action (or teacher), who is trying to make her way through a mad world inhabited by a variety of fools (or blockers) with or without the help of third parties (or buffoons).

The Fool

Fools fall into three recognizable categories.

The Blockhead: The Fool Who Is Defeated by Nature

This fool represents what Henri Bergson was talking about when he described laughter as a response to "the mechanical encrusted on the living." There is something basically robotlike about blockheads: They are as stupid and dull as machines, or they have been cruelly cheated by nature in some other way. Many contemporary sitcoms have in their cast at least one person who is a little slow. In *A Funny Thing Happened on the Way to the Forum*, the young girl whom Hero wants is a typical "dumb blond" caricature, who is so dense she can't even remember Hero's name: All she can be is—as her song suggests—"lovely."

Blockheads often have some outrageous defect or other. In Feydeau's famous play *A Flea in Her Ear*, a pivotal character has a cleft palate: Too much fun is generated by the inarticulate sounds he makes when he doesn't use his prosthesis, and entirely too much fun is made when he *loses* it! People who limp, very fat women, foreigners who butcher our language, men who are impotent—farce ridicules them all, "political correctness" notwithstanding. You'll note that there's something distinctly Freudian about this, since we are laughing at things that otherwise might frighten or embarrass us.

The Inflexible: The Fool Who Is Defeated by Himself

This category contains all those characters who are in the grip of an *idée fixe*, or a passionate humour—the person unable to wrap his mind around any concept or belief other than the one he's been living with forever. We described these characters in chapter 7 and pointed out that one subgenre, comedy of humours, is entirely built upon characters who are out of balance. The difference is that in farce these characters are more exaggerated, more obtuse, and rarely, if ever, come to their senses. Hysterium, in *A Funny Thing Happened on the Way to the Forum*, is always terrified of the future: so terrified in fact that he's named after his quirk. The bragging soldier also appears, as Miles Gloriosus—the man so in love with himself that he is his own ideal. Other farces contain a whole catalog of over-sexed vixens, horny young men, drunken loafers, slightly insane relatives, jealous husbands, and pompous old ladies.

The Dotard: The Fool Who Is Defeated by Time

Farce is exceptionally cruel to the elderly. Into this category fall all the old men who go chasing young vixens, and all the old women who go chasing young studs. In *A Funny Thing,* we see both examples: Hero's dad is after his girl, and Hero's mom is after the hunky soldier. In *The Matchmaker,* Vandergelder, another old fool, is after Irene, a maiden half his age.

The Lover

In addition to three categories of fools, we find two types of lovers. This makes sense because, as we've seen, there are two kinds of love-centered plots. *True lovers* are those we could call "normal" types: the young lad pursuing the virtuous and desirable young lass. *False lovers* are any of those varieties we've suggested above: old men chasing young girls, old women chasing young men, any woman chasing a man, and—of course—any spouse cheating on his/her mate in an illicit affair.

The Knave

Knaves are a form of buffoon, ancillary characters who add to the fun. However, in farce, they often actively create mischief. They are not just foils to others but very important utilitarian characters. Sometimes they cause trouble because they mess up the message: Thus, we find any number of silly servants or slow-witted messengers. At other times, they cause trouble out of a sense of deviltry: because they love to see people suffer farcically; in this sense, they often are a form of *trickster,* a character in many myths who goes around stirring up the universe. Any number of Shakespeare's clowns are like this: Puck in *A Midsummer Night's Dream,* or Touchstone in *As You Like It.*

The long tradition of the clever, scheming servant who sets up complicated plans in order to procure his master's fortune or his own freedom runs from Rome to Broadway and includes Plautus's wily servants, Beaumarchais's Figaro, and Pseudolus in *A Funny Thing Happened on the Way to the Forum.* Thornton Wilder does a topsy-turvy spin on this when he created Malachi Stack in *The Matchmaker,* rather than cause a disturbance, Stack is the one who is able to help, when he hands over Vandergelder's lost wallet to Cornelius and thereby saves his skin.

Generically, farce is a comic look at the cruelty of the universe. It loves to squeeze its agent of action into the worst possible situations, delights in making things hard for him, and is fraught with confusion and chaos. The playwright who deals in farce treats the world as a mad place, and yet, because she gives the play a happy ending, still sees hope for us.

Questioning the Play

1. How close in mood is your play to the description of farce's mood described at the beginning of this chapter? Does it seem to have the speed, urgency, and cruelty of the genre?

2. What is there in the basic situation that is causing this world to go mad? If the play qualifies as farce, why do you suppose the playwright has chosen this genre to tell her story?

3. Which of the three general plotlines does the play use? How does the agent of action interface with the insanity of the world around her?

4. What might the playwright be suggesting by the kind of insanity he creates? Is the world gone "mad" in any particularly unique way? Are all the "fools," for instance, foolish in the same way or in some related way? In other words, consider the characters in their symbolic mode, and make whatever discoveries you can.

5. Which of the farce plot devices appear in your play? As in the question above, examine them to see what, if anything, they have in common, or how they might contrast with each other.

6. Are there, for instance, related love chases—a true one versus a false one?

7. What is the nature of the treasure that's the object of a search? Is it real, illusory, emotional, or nonsensical? As small as a needle, or as large as a fortune? What might it signify?

8. What sorts of misunderstandings occur: Confusions in language? Directions? Identities?

9. What sort of disguises are used? Do people play with gender roles? Is there some political or social comment on gender that this makes?

10. What is the nature of the *cognitio*? What has been hidden, and what might revealing that truth signify?

11. Examine the characters on their symbolic level: What might their relationships suggest?

12. What sort of fools does the playwright draw? What defeating force is most prevalent in the play?

Alternate Genres

Over theater's history, a wide variety of genres beyond the four we've examined has developed. Authors have adapted these conventional forms in order to find new ways to express their ideas. Essentially, however, these alternate genres all contain some elements of the basic four; we might even be right to call them *subgenres*. In this chapter, we'll examine two of the most important of these and then suggest a method for understanding any others you may encounter.

Drama

Drama is a relatively late development in the history of playwriting. Early plays dealt with either fully tragic or completely comic materials, a distinction that dates all the way back to Aristotle. You'll recall he observed that tragedy dealt with people "above us," while comedy looked at people "below us." It wasn't until the middle of the eighteenth century that writers began to look at the gray area in between and ask, What about people like us, of the same social status and with the same kinds of needs, problems, and personalities that we more or less average folks have? Thus, in 1731, George Lillo wrote a play called *The London Merchant* that took for its hero a young lad who works for a successful London merchant, but who hooks up with a bad woman, steals and kills for her, and is hanged. In 1722, Sir Richard Steele wrote *The Conscious Lovers*, about a pair of young lovers who want to get married against the wishes of their fathers but *seek to get their permission first*—no trickery or teachers defeating blockers, but serious people going about serious business in a serious way.

From these departures emerged a genre that was somewhere in between the poles of tragedy and comedy; late in the eighteenth century, it became known as *drame*, although today we call such a play about "average folks" simply a *drama*. We can define this, now, as a serious play in which the universe is reduced in size. While a classic tragedy pits man against a universal moral code, exploring how his actions affect a large population, a drama is often about a private struggle, a family situation, or a character grappling with some form of social injustice or another. Thus, the playing field, while important, is somehow smaller. We've studied two such plays already: *A Glass Menagerie* and *A Doll's House*. Nearly all contemporary American plays, such as Suzan-Lori Parks's *Topdog/Underdog* and Nilo Cruz's *Anna of the Tropics*, are of this genre.

Characters in drama don't fall into easy categories; nor are there recurring plot patterns that we can identify. The ending may be happy or sad, depending on the author's particular vision. The plays are always hybrids; therefore, the best way to approach them is to apply the criteria of the other four genres and see what conclusions we can draw. Thus, we might ask whether or not Nora might have any of the characteristics of a tragic hero: She's not the head of the household, but she's important. She has made a bad judgment call—a sort of *hamartia*—when she forged her husband's name. She does achieve a major insight about her life when she comes to understand how she's been wronged. She does make an ultimate sacrifice in that, while she doesn't lose her life, she does leave her family. But has a universal moral code been broken?

At the same time, we can ask whether Nora has any of the characteristics of a comedic character: Is she a blocker or a teacher? Is she defeated and transformed, or does she defeat and transform her husband? Have we moved from a false society to a true one? Is there a *cognitio*?

What about some of the elements of melodrama or farce: How much of the play is about character, and how much is about plot? Can we divide the characters into good guys and bad guys? We may think Torvald is nasty and self-important, until we take into account the times he lives in and the conventions that order his life and determine whether or not he can keep his job. However, is he a kind of farcical false lover in that he doesn't really love Nora but rather the conventional life that Nora helps him live? And don't forget: Nora is saved by the sudden appearance of a letter and the marriage of Krogstad with Mrs. Linde—certainly, these are the long arms of coincidence at work.

Again, there are no right or wrong answers here. Examine the efficient, formal, and final causes and determine for yourself what Ibsen is trying to accomplish.

Tragicomedy: The Work of Chekov

Tragicomedy seems easier to define, and it began somewhat earlier in history, first emerging in the work of Euripides and coming into full fruition around the time of Shakespeare. Perhaps writers began to feel somewhat restricted by the dictum that a tragedy had to end unhappily. Why couldn't the tragic hero somehow be rescued or redeemed without having to die? Thus, Medea murders her children but gets her revenge, in a sort of "happy ending." And in Shakespeare's *A Winter's Tale*, we have a bad-tempered and jealous husband who orders his wife imprisoned and her suspected lover poisoned. But at the end, he sees the error of his ways, and his wife is restored to him. In a similar fashion, why couldn't a play that would otherwise be a comedy have an ending that was dark? Thus, Ben Jonson's *Volpone* is about a lying, deceitful nobleman who seduces wives, cons his friends out of their fortunes, and misbehaves in almost a farcical way. But at the end, he's caught and severely punished for his tricks.

Playwrights and critics gave a great deal of thought to these questions, and the term *tragicomedy* first appeared to mean "tragedies with happy endings." Some critics put the work of Euripides in this category, and during the eighteenth and nineteenth centuries, as more and more plays fell into this neutral territory, tragicomedy became almost synonymous with drama; that is, *any* play that didn't fit into a neat pigeonhole. In the twentieth century, the term lost some of its original connotation; today, works that don't fit neatly into classical patterns are often labeled *modern* or *postmodern*, and the term *tragicomedy* somehow seems outdated. Therefore, it's all the more important to look at each individual play on its own merits. Again, your chore is to examine the four causes and ask yourself, How is this play like and/or different from traditional plays? And why?

A good way to demonstrate this process is to examine the work of one writer who, more than any other, most fully explored this hybrid genre. Anton Chekov was a nineteenth-century Russian playwright who insisted that his plays were essentially comedies, but their effect on audiences is always one of sadness. They are about societies that are blocked by illusions, but they never show these societies getting better. The plays use typical comedic characters and almost farcical situations and yet somehow turn them into the material of tragedy; and the endings are certainly far from happy.

Chekov's most celebrated play is *The Cherry Orchard*. We'll describe what's in it and ask ourselves, How are these elements comic and yet sad? How are they tragic and yet funny?

The play's setting is a country estate several miles outside Moscow, toward the end of the nineteenth century. The owner of the estate, Madame Ranevskaya, lives in Moscow and travels a great deal, so neither she nor her brother lives on the estate. Holding down the fort is her ward named Varya and an old servant named Firs. Also in residence is a man named Lopakhin: He used to be a servant on the estate but has gradually worked himself up to be a wealthy landowner. He and Varya have a sort of on-again, off-again courtship, and everybody expects them to get married eventually.

Other characters include Madame Ranevskaya's daughter (Anya), a young man she's in love with (Petya), a neighbor who is always coming to borrow money (Pishchik), Ranevskaya's brother (Gayev), and a governess (Charlotta) who is still, for some inexplicable reason, part of the family.

The play begins when Ranevskaya and her retinue arrive for the summer. It quickly emerges that the family is facing a crisis: They are running out of money. Lopakhin has a plan: sell off bits of the old estate for homes and use the income to save themselves. The problem with this plan is that in order to do that, the family will have to cut down the cherry orchard that has grown there for generations. Time and again, Lopakhin urges Ranevskaya to make that decision. She hesitates, unable to face her responsibility. Ultimately, the estate has to go up for auction in order to pay off its debts. It turns out that Lopakhin himself buys it—and the former servant is now the owner.

Two other plotlines also involve romances: We see the Anya/ Petya and the Lopakhin/Varya relationships progress, but they do not in fact get married. At the end of the play, everybody goes back to the city; the only major change we can see is the loss of the farm. In the very last scene, the old servant (Firs) has been left alone in the shut-up house. He wanders onstage, lies down on a couch, and quietly dies.

Even with this short and somewhat superficial plot summary, we can see some familiar comedic elements. Let's look at them one at a time and see what odd topsy-turvy kinds of things Chekov does with them:

1. If it's a comedy, we would expect a "false, blocked world" to be replaced by an "authentic, open world"; that is, a world domi-nated by illusions and unrealistic ideals should give way to one that is more sensible and rational. Madame Ranevskaya would hopefully wake up to the realities around her and go through some change. But she doesn't. At the end of the play, once the orchard has been lost, she leaves for the city, without gaining any insight at all.

2. The play looks like a "green world" comedy: People come out to the country and are supposed to be transformed. But they're not. They leave in pretty much the same condition they were in when they arrived. Furthermore, a green world is supposed to be a place of richness and life. Yet here is the stage direction Chekov provides for the setting of an outdoor scene:

A field. Off to one side is an old abandoned shrine. Nearby are several fallen rocks that once were tombstones. Off in the dis-tance, we can see bits of the cherry orchard. Beyond them, there is a telegraph wire and, far in the distance, a small town. It is near dusk and quiet. (act 2)

An old abandoned cemetery far out in the country. The end of the day. Quiet. Near desolation. Life is only glimpsed far off in the distance. It's no luscious, magical *A Midsummer Night's Dream*–like place; what sort of topsy-turvy trick is Chekov playing here?

3. A classic comedy ends on a positive, happy note; there's sup-posed to be a celebration, a sense of a wonderful future ahead. The end of *The Cherry Orchard*, on the other hand, is all about loss. The

old ways, symbolized by the destruction of the orchard and the death of Firs, are lost. No good times ahead here.

4. Classic comedies are supposed to end in weddings, unions, and celebrations: The young guy wins the gorgeous girl over the objections of the old folks; they get married, and the world is renewed. In *The Cherry Orchard*, in addition to the Anya/Petya and Varya/Lopakhin romances, there are four other love stories (involving minor characters) running through the play. Not a single one of them ends happily; nobody gets married.

5. Many classic comedies feature clever servants who set up schemes to help their masters get away with lustful alliances. Usually these schemes work, and the servants, although rewarded, go back to being servants. In Chekov's play, however, the "clever servant" is Lopakhin. And like every good servant (or in his case, ex-servant) should do, he tries to set up a scheme: He keeps telling the old lady how to save herself. She doesn't listen, and he winds up buying the estate. The servant has become the master; and once again, we're in comedic topsy-turvy.

6. Notice how Chekov uses many devices to arouse laughter. Nearly all the characters are either obsessed by an *idée fixe* or in the grip of some overpowering attitude: Ranevskaya's brother (Gayev) is always going off on some bizarre conversational sidetrack and playing imaginary games of pool with himself. The neighbor is always borrowing money. Varya is always cleaning and spying on Anya. Ranevskaya herself is guilty of being as inflexible as a machine, unable to make a decision.

Chekov juxtaposes many moments that don't belong together, so there is an overwhelming presence of the incongruous. One small example will stand for many: At the start of act 3, the governess is sitting with some others and complaining that she doesn't know who she is, who her parents were, where she comes from, what her purpose in life is—and all the time she's munching on a cucumber. Thus, Chekov juxtaposes the serious and the philosophical with the ludicrous and the mundane.

The incongruous appears throughout the play in other forms as well, most notably in how people react to each other: Time and again, one character will express his or her deepest longings about love or life; while you would normally expect another character to respond to that, just the opposite happens. The other character all but ignores the first and goes on about his or her own preoccupations. People don't listen to each other. People don't connect to each other. Or in the middle of an intense moment, some bizarre and unrelated thing occurs that doesn't seem to fit: At one point, Varya and her sister are talking about how serious the financial crisis is, and Lopakhin sticks his head into the room, moos like a cow, and then disappears. There seems to be no logic at work. (Of course, all of these incongruities are deliberate on Chekov's part. There are reasons people don't listen to each other: because their own private issues are strongly preoccupying them. There's a reason Lopakhin sticks his head in just when they're talking about selling the estate. You figure it out.)

There's a great deal of physical shtick in the play: For instance, one character is always stumbling over himself, a chair, a step—indeed, he's nicknamed "Two and Twenty-Troubles." At one point, this character has just had his world shattered by something his girlfriend has said, and as he makes his exit, he falls down the stairs.

In comedies, a clue to the meaning of the play lies in the relationship between the blocker and the teacher; in tragedies, it often lies in the interaction of the tragic hero and her nemesis. In *The Cherry Orchard*, there is certainly a very strong dynamic between Ranevskaya and Lopakhin. But is she a blocker or a tragic hero? Is he a teacher or a nemesis?

A careful reading of the play reveals how Chekov carefully uses very traditional devices of comedy, turns them topsy-turvy, and expresses a serious and sympathetic attitude toward the world. Thus, to say that *The Cherry Orchard* is a comedy that ends sadly or a tragedy that ends happily is to greatly oversimplify the very subtle and important ways in which the author blends the funny with the sad to create a hybrid form all its own.

Classifying Subgenres

Drama and tragicomedy are perhaps the two most important variants of the major genres, but they aren't the only ones. Over time, a wide range of what we might call *subgenres* has appeared, with many different labels. Indeed, there are almost as many subgenres as there are writers creating them. But they are all variants of the four major ones we've described.

It's almost useless, therefore, to try to list or define them all. An easier and perhaps more accurate way to talk about subgenres is to ask two specific questions of any play: First, is it *plot-driven* or *character-driven*? That is, are we more interested in what happens (the twists and turns of the plot's complications) or in the people to whom it happens (their insights, revelations, changes)? Second, is the play *serious* or *funny*? That is, is the author interested in making us laugh all the time, part of the time, or not at all?

With these two questions in mind, we can create a chart with four windows:

	CHARACTER	PLOT
SERIOUS		
FUNNY		

Asking these two questions of any given play, we can decide roughly where to put it on the chart. Thus, a classic tragedy is typically very short on plot and very long on character; that is, we are less interested in how and why the tragic hero falls than we are in what insight he achieves, what sort of redemption he has, and what it all means. We also know that a farce is almost all plot, with very little interest in character development. Therefore, we might place those genres on the chart thus:

	CHARACTER	PLOT
SERIOUS	Classic Tragedy	
FUNNY		Classic Farce

And we might fill in the rest of the chart with other genres that come to mind:

	CHARACTER	PLOT

	CHARACTER	PLOT
SERIOUS	Classic Tragedy Domestic Tragedy Drama of Ideas Tragicomedy	Melodrama Drama Sentimental Comedy
FUNNY	Comedy of Humours Satire	Romantic Comedy Comedy of Manners Comedy of Intrigue Classic Farce

There is a risk of oversimplifying all this and becoming more concerned with where to put the play on the chart than with trying to understand why the playwright has written what he has. If he's turned the conventions of comedy into something serious, as Chekov has done, it's important to analyze his possible reasons. When you examine a play like *Major Barbara* by Shaw and discover that he's taken many elements of comedy of manners and used them to tell a serious story, or when you see that a writer like Samuel Beckett has used many of the devices of farce in such a bleak play as *Waiting for Godot*, ask yourself, Why? What unusual insight do we gain by such borrowings?

Remember, there are no right or wrong answers in play analysis; there are only well thought out ideas. The various genres are only tools to help you hone your own opinions.

Questioning the Play

1. Which of the four basic genres does your play seem closest to?

2. What characteristics of those genres does it have?

3. How do the characters compare with those associated with the basic four genres?

4. What plot devices from these genres does the playwright borrow? How does she use or alter them?

5. What clue does the ending of the play give you?

6. Does the playwright seem to be using topsy-turvy ideas in order to stress her attitude toward life? If so, what elements is she turning upside down: Plot? Characters? The functional aspects of character?

7. In what ways is your agent of action like a tragic hero and/or like a blocker?

8. In what ways does your play contain a nemesis and/or teacher figure?

9. What clues do you get in researching the author's life and times? How does the material cause help you understand this play?

10. Where would you place the play on the chart? Why?

Part Three: **Styles**

In addition to having various attitudes about the world they live in, playwrights often have differing interpretations of how the world itself is actually constituted. The question essentially is not, What do I think of reality? but rather, What is reality? Is it something that exists independently of us, or is it something that we shape and control by our perceptions of it? Take the question of a red rose, for example. Does "red" have any meaning on its own? Does the color exist by itself in nature, or is it only a particular set of light waves that our brains perceive, translate, and interpret?

To take this a step further: What about this flower-thing itself? Does it exist? Is it real, in and of itself? Or does it only stand for or reflect some other existence that lies beneath or behind it? Is the true reality what we see on the surface, or does this true reality lie someplace below, behind, or above, in some other time/space dimension that we cannot penetrate, that's invisible to us, wherein such things as "beauty" or "justice" or even the true rose actually exist? (Notice that we haven't raised the question whether we like the rose or not; that's the province of *genres*.)

This kind of questioning can become very complex, and any good course in philosophy will go into much greater detail than we do here. Suffice it to say that over the course of history, various playwrights have defined reality in different ways. This definition is reflected in a play's *style*.

How do these different "definitions of reality"—these styles—come about? What forces work on a writer to shape his or her beliefs about reality? We have to look to the efficient cause for answers. Often the definition writers adopt is a product of the culture in which they live; they more or less accept the predominant worldview of their times. Or this definition may have been strongly influenced by scientific discoveries or social upheavals that changed the world drastically. To some extent, therefore, these differing views are best understood in light of the specific history that is associated with them. Thus, *realism* refers to a worldview—and a style of theater—that became prominent late in the nineteenth century, partly as a result of a rapidly increasing number of scientific and sociological discoveries. *Expressionism* was a direct response to the chaos and horrors of postwar life in Europe (especially Germany) around the 1920s and 1930s. *Theater of the absurd* came into vogue during a period of intellectual despair and nihilism that became prevalent around the world in the 1950s.

As we describe these various "isms," we'll base our definition on nine different components. We'll describe these components here and then apply them to the different styles that have developed. Keep in mind, however, that not every play you read will fall completely and neatly into any one category.

1. The Concerns of the Author

By *concerns of the author* we mean the particular subject or idea the author seems most interested in. Some writers take society as their subject and are interested in exploring how social forces affect our lives: Is the world all about money, or machines, or politics? Other writers take the individual mind as their subject and are interested in human psychology: Is the world all about people, or relationships, or families? Others take the human soul as their subject and are interested in how people find spiritual comfort and inner peace: Is the world all about religion?

2. The Point of View of the Author

The *point of view of the author* does not mean the attitude the author has about her subject; that, again, is the province of genres. In the context of styles, *point of view* refers to where the author is placing the audience; that is, in either an *objective* or a *subjective* position. Let's explain.

When we speak of having an *objective* position, we mean that we who are watching an event are standing outside, looking from a distance as disinterested spectators. Every set of eyes that looks on will see the same thing. Conversely, when we speak of having a *subjective* position, we mean that we are in the middle of the experience, seeing it through only one set of eyes and thus getting only a limited idea of what's happening.

Think of a football game: If you're up in the stands, you're watching from an outside, objective position, seeing the whole picture. You know where the ball is, what the fullback is doing, and even how the coach is responding to the play. If you're the center in the middle of the line, surrounded by players, you can't see the whole picture at all, but only a very limited part of it. You have only a vague idea where the fullback is at this moment and hardly a clue what expression might be on the face of the coach. You are, therefore, in a subjective position.

There's a vast difference in how we interpret the events, depending on which point of view we are taking. If we are outside the event, we're in a better position to grasp and understand what's happening. If we are inside the event, we are apt to be confused, disoriented, or even frightened. This should be fairly obvious in the football analogy; here's how it works in the theater. Imagine the set shows us two rooms, joined by a door. A man sits in one room and hears a knock. Sitting in the audience, we can see the other room and so we know who is knocking. But the man in the room can't see and doesn't know. For us, it's only the maid bringing in tea. For him, it might be his sister, his girlfriend, or the serial killer who's been on the rampage. We're comfortable; he's momentarily surprised or even terrified. We understand; he's confused. The author has taken care to give us an objective point of view.

If, however, the set only showed us the one room (in which the man is sitting), and the knock comes, we are in the same position as the man because we don't know who it is either. We are now, therefore, in a subjective position: We see the events as he sees them, or—as the more common phrase has it—through his eyes. We're as frightened, confused, or disoriented as he himself is.

3. The Comprehensibility of the World

Therefore, the point of view from which we see the world has a great influence on how we understand it. But that assumes that the world can be understood—that it is *comprehensible*. It assumes that scientists from Sir Francis Bacon and Galileo to Albert Einstein, Werner Heisenberg, and the proponents of the new physics can uncover the truth about the way the world works; that at bottom, once we have the information, we'll understand it all. If someone dies in a car accident, it's logical and human to search for a reason for that accident: Some would say it's the will of the Lord; others would blame the rain and the third martini; others might look to corruption in the Department of Transportation that led to bad road construction.

But perhaps, once we get to the bottom of it, we discover that there are no rules or principles. There is no order or sense to what happens; everything is random chance. Perhaps there is no explanation for that traffic accident other than that sometimes things just happen that you can't explain but you have to accept all the same.

Writers can fit anywhere in this continuum.

4. The Construction of the Plot

When we discussed plot as one of the elements of play structure, we described what we called the well-made play pattern. This pattern described a time line on which certain events happened in a certain order so that one event flowed logically from another: When *A* happened, *B* was the result, and then *C* was the result of *B*, and so forth.

But remember, there are plays in which events do not happen in this logical, "normal" fashion: Just because *B follows A* does *not* mean that *B is the result of A*. We mentioned plays that work backward—in which *A* follows *B*; there are also plays that skip around in time—*A, D, C, L, F, B*, and so on—arranged in some sequence that either has meaning only to the author or—more significantly—perhaps has no meaning at all, which itself is its meaning.

Ask yourself, then: Are the events therefore causal and linear, random and illogical, or somewhere in between?

5. The Substance/Texture of the Characters

In some plays, the characters are meant to be fully textured human beings, with ideas, feelings, personalities, passions, and foibles that are very similar to ours, and we say they are "three-dimensional" and "lifelike."

In other plays, the characters are meant only to represent or suggest types of people and are not ever supposed to be taken for real. In the medieval morality play *Everyman*, for instance, we meet such folks as Riches, Good Deeds, Confession, and Knowledge and have entered the world of analogies, where the characters are personifications of abstract ideas.

In satires or farces, the characters might have only one or two personality traits; the author has exaggerated those traits in order to make fun of them. We saw this in our discussion of laughter, as we met characters affected by their "humours" or folks dominated by an *idée fixe*. They might, as in melodrama, be somewhat more complex but still only represent some moral position, as we saw in the way in which the good guy differs from the bad guy.

6. The Setting

While the actual scene design of any particular production of a play is often a creative interpretation by the designer, some plays call for very specific scenic elements. For one reason or another, the author wants a particular environment to be shown, providing a particular mood or feeling. Remember how, in *A Doll's House*, the two doors in the room had symbolic reverberations. Remember also how Chekov described the second act of *The Cherry Orchard*, with its bleak cemetery suggesting an ironic, topsy-turvy green world.

Whatever symbolic associations the playwright had in mind when he suggested these specific elements, he still meant for them to look like real places. No matter what the door stood for, it was still, objectively speaking, a lifelike door. It had a normal door size and structure, and people could go in and out of it by twisting a normal-looking knob and opening it on its normal-looking hinges. The setting, in other words, imitated real life.

In some "isms," however, the setting is deliberately distorted. For a character trapped in a cell, who longs for freedom, the door might take on a whole different meaning. It might become the main focus of the character's every waking thought and loom large in his mind. Thus, the writer may demand that the physical door used in the set be, say, fifteen feet high, six feet wide, with a handle perched ten feet above the floor—as gigantic in shape as it is in symbol. In a famous play of the 1930s, Elmer Rice's *The Adding Machine*, this office machine is not just a computing tool, but a gigantic and distorted landscape: One scene in the play calls for the central character (a man called, by the way, "Mr. Zero"; see our discussion above about abstracted characters) literally to be trapped on the surface of the machine, wandering through the keys like a rat in a maze. Objects, furniture, even the walls themselves may be distorted, fragmented, or exaggerated in any number of ways, visually suggesting what the world looks like from someone's subjective point of view.

7. Language

In the same way that character and setting can be judged on a continuum from very lifelike to very abstract or distorted, so can the language that is used. At one extreme is language that is supposed to suggest real people talking the kind of colloquial, casual prose that sounds familiar to our ears. At the other extreme is language composed of words selected for their sounds alone: words devoid of rational meaning as such. An example of this last case appears in Samuel Beckett's *Waiting for Godot*, when the character Lucky begins a long monologue that is largely nonsense syllables composed of a variety of guttural and plosive sounds. When Lucky speaks, he sounds like a machine sputtering as it fails ... which, in a sense, is what Lucky is.

In some plays, writers use language to achieve certain psychological effects. In Arthur Miller's *Death of a Salesman*, for instance, Willy imagines speaking to his brother, Ben. Ben responds to many of Willy's questions or statements with a recurring phrase: "When I walked into the jungle I was seventeen. When I walked out I was twenty-one. And by God I was rich." After the third or fourth time Ben says this, it ceases to have meaning in itself but simply becomes a sad litany. In Sophie Treadwell's *Machinal*, the main character finds her life dull and mechanical: She hates her tedious job. We get a sense of how tedious it is when she walks into the office:

STENOGRAPHER: You're late.
FILING CLERK: You're late.
ADDING CLERK: You're late.
STENOGRAPHER: And yesterday.
FILING CLERK: The day before.
ADDING CLERK: And the day before. (act 1)

The effect is that none of these speakers are human (note their "names") but machines in human form. The heroine lives in a world of robot-people.

8. Form: Presentational/Representational

Form (which is either *presentational* or *representational*) refers to the relationship between the people on the stage (actors/characters) and the people watching (audience).

Traditional theater practice has developed the convention of separating the playing area (i.e., stage) from the viewing area. Most often, there's a physical and psychological barrier set up between the two that typically is not crossed. This barrier is often called *the fourth wall*; the term comes from the idea that most interior sets show us three walls, and we in the audience are expected to imagine there's a fourth—one that would close that world off from our view.

Some plays make use of this fourth wall; we in the audience are ignored as the actors go about their business. *A Doll's House* is such a play, as are August Wilson's *Fences*, Suzan-Lori Parks's *In the Blood*, Donald Margulies's *Dinner with Friends*, David Auburn's *Proof*, and almost every play written in the early to mid-twentieth century. These plays are known as *representational*; the playwright represents the artificial world as a real one.

Other plays break this fourth wall; the characters in the play are fully aware that we are sitting out there and actively interact with us. They talk to us, show us things, explain things to us, take us into their confidence, and generally invite us to share with them their experiences. These plays are known as *presentational* because, as the term implies, they present the play to us. Thornton Wilder's *The Matchmaker* is such a play: Mrs. Levi, Horace, Malachi Stack, and others all find moments to come down to the front of the stage and chat with us. So are Wilder's *Our Town*, Richard Greenburg's *Take Me Out*, and David Henry Hwang's *M Butterfly*.

It's important to note that presentational elements have to be deliberate. Many plays, such as those of Shakespeare, Restoration and eighteenth-century tragedies, and some corny nineteenth-century melodramas have characters speaking soliloquies to themselves. Hamlet's "To be or not to be" speech is probably the most famous example. These are *not* presentational because the character is not speaking to *us*; he is simply speaking aloud, and we, invisible and unseen, are simply overhearing him.

Finally, many plays mix these two forms, as in *The Glass Menagerie*. Between each of the scenes, Tom speaks to us and give us some background material, shares some of his philosophical musings, and at the end, confesses his secret remorse. However, once the scenes themselves actually begin, they are completely representational, as we once again find the fourth wall set up.

9. The Playwright's Definition of the World

The *playwright's definition of the world* is essentially a summarizing statement of the rest: as simple a description as possible of how the writer defines reality.

These nine components form the building blocks of the various styles. As we further explore each "ism," we'll notice how each is typically used. Again, keep in mind that few plays are "pure" styles; most have some qualities of one and some of another. These definitions are only tools for you to use in order to make your own judgment about the individual play you're analyzing.

11

Realism

Background

The simplest way to define *realism* would be to call it a style that attempts to depict life on stage as it is actually lived by the members of the audience. It shows us so-called everyday events happening to people like us who live in a world like ours and tells its story in a way that makes it appear logical and believable.

However, two factors complicate this definition. The first is the reference to the *audience*, because realism is actually a relative concept. As cultures change and modes of behavior mutate, the way in which people live their "everyday" lives also changes. To members of a Restoration audience, the fact that the characters in a play wore extravagant clothing, moved in a rather stiff and formal gait, spoke in well-modulated and articulate sentences, and behaved with control and decorum did not seem unusual at all. Thus, to them, a play like William Congreve's *The Way of the World* would easily qualify as realism.

So, this easy definition doesn't really do the job. We'll need to define this style by taking the audience out of the picture and look at what is in the text itself.

The second factor to consider is that the term *realism* itself is fairly *modern*. Up until the middle of the nineteenth century, few audiences or critics much concerned themselves with wondering whether plays should reflect the world as it was seen: Everybody assumed that they knew what the world was like and that plays reflected it more or less accurately. When controversy did arise, it came not from the "what" but from the "how": What did people mean by *accurately*? The answer seemed obvious: *accurately* meant "believable." We had to be able to lose ourselves in the illusion and accept that what we were seeing could actually be happening as we watched.

To that end, whole catalogues of rules were invented that were designed to make sure that plays were "believable" to the audience. Among these rules emerged three that often pop up in play analysis. These are known as the *three unities*: *time*, *place*, and *action*.

Unity of time. This rule held that the action of a play should take place in the time it took for the performance. If a play lasted two hours, the events in the play should only take place over two hours, since for the audience only two hours had passed. This notion was gradually expanded, until it was agreed that a "day" was a proper length of time for a play, but then controversy arose over what constituted a "day": Was it twelve hours or twenty-four?

Unity of place. This rule dictated that the action should take place in one location. After all, if the audience doesn't move, why should they believe the actors have? If we're in a room in France now, how can we possibly be in the countryside later? Again, this rule was often bent: Eventually, the "one place" could be different locales in, say, the same castle or the same general vicinity. But even that caused problems: If the play was supposedly set in a throne room, why should the audience believe that servants or common people were present, since such people weren't allowed in a throne room! To solve that problem, plays came to be set in "neutral" space, a place that looked something like a room, but wasn't intended to actually be a room. It was just "a place where the action occurred."

Unity of action. By this rule, the play could only tell one story; there was no allowance made for subplots—thus effectively knocking Shakespeare out of the picture. After all, realistically speaking, people could only concentrate on one story at a time. Kings couldn't inhabit the same story as commoners, and so forth.

These rules were clearly arbitrary, but they gave order and boundaries to the theatrical universe and thus satisfied a seventeenth- and eighteenth-century culture that was itself ordered and confined. They continued to dominate playwriting up through the middle of the nineteenth century, when such Romantic critics and writers as Johann Wolfgang von Goethe, Johann Friedrich von Schiller, and Victor Hugo aggressively broke them. Such writers stressed that the world was not a controlled and confining space but a wild and extravagant one. Plays, to them, were depictions of bold and heroic outlaw characters who roamed through forests and cities alike, came from a range of social classes, and had passionate and hair-raising adventures that carried through time and space. Feeling was everything, and Romantic posing took the place of intellectual debate. It didn't matter that the characters weren't like the people in the audience. They weren't supposed to be; rather, they were supposed to be idealizations of what people *should* be like. Furthermore, logic didn't matter; what did matter was a rousing good story well told.

It was as a reaction to this sort of Romanticism that the idea of *realism* as we use it today came into prominence. New writers protested that these stories were false exaggerations of life; the characters were cardboard clichés; the situations were contrived in order to provide dramatic effects and startling curtains; and the whole theatrical experience was phony. These criticisms reflected other ideas that were gaining currency at the time: The ideas of Charles Darwin, Sigmund Freud, Karl Marx, and others had begun to show that life was a phenomenon to be studied and understood scientifically, not one to be exaggerated and distorted.

In this cultural setting, it began to be important to some dramatists that the theater reflect this new view of life. The characters should be motivated not by an artificial passion but rather by the same complex web of desires, ambitions, hopes, and fears that we all share. Events should not be "startling," but a tightly connected string of causes and effects. This concern was expressed in an essay by Émile Zola entitled "Naturalism on the Stage," written in 1880. Here is a key passage from the essay:

> I am waiting for [writers] . . . to put a man of flesh and bones on the stage, taken from reality, scientifically analyzed, without one lie. I am waiting for them to rid us of fictional characters, of conventional symbols of virtue and vice, which possess no value as human data. I am waiting for the surroundings to determine the characters, and for characters to act according to the logic of facts, combined with the logic of their own temperament. I am waiting until there is no more jugglery of any kind, no more strokes of a magical wand, changing in one minute persons and things. . . . I am waiting, finally . . . until

[dramatists] return to the source of science and modern arts, to the study of nature, to the anatomy of man, to the painting of life, in an exact reproduction.

There are several key ideas to note here:

1. Adopting a scientific framework, Zola refers to characters in plays as "human data," implying that we should be studying the behavior of people in the same way we study the behavior of bees or beans.

2. He makes reference to characters being motivated by their surroundings, the first inklings we get that environmental determinism belongs on the stage.

3. He clearly dislikes contrived plots, filled with false reversals and climaxes.

In a way, Zola brings us back to the point made at the beginning of this chapter, that realism is supposed to depict the real world *as it is*. However, he has clearly also defined what that *is* refers to: a phenomenon that obeys laws of nature and logic.

Before we begin to apply the various components of style to realism, we need to address an important issue. You'll notice Zola used the term *naturalism*; many students mistakenly think it is another word for realism, when it's really quite different. Consider that Zola and his colleagues were part of not only a literary movement but a political and social movement as well. Beginning in the mid-nineteenth century, what's now known as the Industrial Revolution had begun to peak. Machines and factories replaced cottage industries. Cities grew larger and larger, and this growth brought with it all the evils of urban blight: slums, pollution, poverty, and an ever-increasing split between the haves and the have-nots. Throughout Europe and America, organizations were established to combat the evils of unrestrained capitalism and exploitation. Part of this reform, naturally enough, involved calling attention to the problem. Thus, writers chose for their subjects such previously unmentionable topics as prostitution, unemployment, cruel working conditions in factories, and drunkenness and put the evils of their times onto the stage in order to shock their audiences into awareness.

Simply put, therefore, naturalism is a style like realism that focuses on the gritty details of social problems. Naturalism is more about content, and realism is more about form. With this in mind, let's apply the various components and see how they are used in realism.

What Are the Concerns of the Author?

Remember that *realism* is a relative term. Certainly for writers of naturalistic plays, the author is concerned about the impact the evils of society often have upon the human spirit: whether the dangers of capitalism or the inhumanity of slum landlords. However, there are two ways to approach such a subject. The writer might be very anxious to expose the issue and concentrate her play on the facts; to that end, the dialogue will be filled with speeches denouncing this or that evil, characters will give us facts about how many people die every year from this disease or that, and the plot will be clearly contrived to bring about the worst-case scenario. Plays that take this approach are considered to be *issue-driven*.

On the other hand, the writer may be less concerned about the specific issue and more concerned with the people who are affected by it. The playwright wants to show us how these characters are changed; so these plays are *character-driven*. To that end, the writer will write a more traditional well-made play, with the kind of plot and characters we examined in part 1.

The former is illustrated by the kinds of plays we've described above as *naturalistic*. We learn a great deal about the institutions of the day and the traps that ensnare the characters. But as society moves on, these plays quickly become dated.

Plays that take the latter approach tend to be the better plays because, while the issue may be dead, the characters still interest us. Examples of this are seen in many of Ibsen's plays. Something bad is going on outside, but we never get a clear picture of what it is. In *An Enemy of the People*, for instance, we learn that the town's famous waters (which people travel many miles to bathe in) are polluted, but we don't know exactly how it happened. What we do see is how the townsfolk all turn against the one man who wants to speak the truth and so ultimately destroy everything about him but his fighting spirit.

What Is the Point of View of the Author?

If the playwright takes the position that he is offering up scientific data for us to peruse, clearly then he is taking an objective position. He wants us to stand outside the events and to watch them almost as though we were medical students sitting in an operating theater.

Of course, there never really is such a thing as total objectivity in any play. Part of the playwright's job is to pick and choose what to show us; out of the infinite number of possible characters he can create, he has decided to show us these particular ones. He makes these choices, obviously, because they illustrate a point he is trying to make: There's a good, sound reason why Ibsen sends Nora out of the house.

And certainly, as we watch the play, our sympathies are gradually drawn to one character over another. One person becomes the agent of action and another the antagonist. We like some folks, and we dislike some others. True objectivity is impossible, as it goes against the very impulse that draws us to drama in the first place: our empathic response to another person, and our tendency to take sides in a struggle.

Nevertheless, within these limitations, the realistic play becomes objective when it tries to let the audience see all sides of the story. We may dislike Torvald, but Ibsen allows him to present his point of view about his position in the bank, why he distrusts Krogstad, and how important it is for him to uphold his reputation.

It's this sort of objectivity that applies to a realistic play: The audience may be drawn to one side or another, but it sits outside the play and watches from the stands.

How Comprehensible Is the World?

Writers of realistic plays convey the idea that the world, at its core, is a completely comprehensible phenomenon. As Zola has indicated, if we put people in certain situations and apply certain stimuli, we should, in principle, get predictable responses. If we dig deeply into whatever mystery confronts us, and if we work hard and smart, we can always find an answer. Characters and events in realistic plays may strike us as strange and unworldly, but they always behave in ways that we can ultimately understand. This is especially true in fantasies, such as *The Wizard of Oz* or the Harry Potter movies, where characters follow their own logic and obey their own rules. Scarecrows don't really sing and dance, lions never talk, and men made out of tin don't come to life. But if such humanlike creatures really existed, they would surely feel pain, have fear, and possibly die, for the world of Oz still obeys the laws of mortality.

It's this distinction between what can really happen and what could possibly happen that Aristotle meant in the *Poetics* when he talked about the laws of probability and necessity, and how a good drama has to obey them. The *probable*, he says, is what might logically happen in a set of given circumstances. He contrasts that with what he calls the *possible*, that which is actually true no matter what the circumstances. The two don't necessary have to meet: What's possible doesn't always have to be what's probable. In other words, it's quite impossible for me to fly; the true facts of life as we know it forbid this. But if I could fly, it is probable that I would have to learn how to do it, that I would make some mistakes, and that I could ultimately succeed. So, you can see how *probability obeys the laws of logic*, while *possibility obeys the laws of reality*.

It's in this sense that a fantasy is, at its core, a highly realistic play. The world may be unfamiliar, but we can understand it. It is as comprehensible as Ibsen.

How Is the Plot Constructed?

When we say that nature follows the laws of cause and effect, we imply that it follows a direct and linear path from event to event. I step on the banana peel, and then I slip. The slip comes after, and is caused by, the step.

The plots of realistic plays also follow these laws. These plots typically move forward in a direct chronology from one event to the next, and each event always somehow causes the next to happen. We can describe the plot of such a play through a series of "therefore" connections—with a few "howevers" tossed in to provide us with some plot twists.

Thus, in *The Glass Menagerie*:

Amanda finds out that Laura hasn't gone to typing school;

THEREFORE, she must find another way to provide for her;

THEREFORE, she begins to work on Tom to help her find a husband;

THEREFORE, Tom gets a friend to come over for dinner;

THEREFORE, Amanda fixes up the place and prepares a special dinner;

THEREFORE, the Gentleman Caller shows up;

HOWEVER, Tom has forgotten to pay the light bill;

THEREFORE, the lights go out;

THEREFORE, Laura and the Gentleman Caller can have a serious conversation;

THEREFORE, Laura begins to bond with the man;

HOWEVER, the man reveals he is engaged;

THEREFORE, Amanda's plans are thwarted;

THEREFORE, she turns on Tom;

THEREFORE, Tom leaves for the last time;

THEREFORE, Tom feels guilty; and

THEREFORE, he tells us his story as a sort of confession.

Nearly all realistic plays are essentially of this type: chronological, causal, and linear.

With, of course, some interesting exceptions. Some plays, as we noted earlier, seem to string events together logically, even though the events are shown to us out of sequence; they are *nonlinear*. Here, for example, are the scene indicators for Donald Margulies's *Sight Unseen*:

Scene 1: the present
Scene 2: four days later
Scene 3: an hour before scene 1
Scene 4: fifteen years earlier
Scene 5: a few hours after scene 1
Scene 6: continued from the end of scene 2
Scene 7: a few hours after scene 5
Scene 8: seventeen years earlier

What is one to make of this? In every other respect, this is a completely realistic play: It follows all the guidelines we're looking at. But what's the point in switching around times like this? Is Margulies showing us some other relationship between the various events than time? Are there emotional connections? Are there bits of exposition that are saved for the end in order to surprise us?

What Is the Substance/Texture of the Characters?

Characters who appear in realistic plays are meant to be three-dimensional and lifelike. We are to assume they operate from psychological motives and instincts that are like ours, whether they speak in prose or blank verse. If you take a look back at chapter 4, which examined characters as one of the key Aristotelian elements, we always assumed the characters were realistic. The three key elements we discussed apply to all realistic characters:

- goal: What specific thing does the character want to achieve?
- at stake: How is the character vulnerable; what does he most dread losing?
- strategies: What sort of approach does the character embark upon in order to accomplish that goal?

Many textbooks on playwriting or on acting suggest other questions: What is the character's background? What is the character's environment like? What sort of animal image does the character conjure? What is the character's rhythm of speech or movement? You can apply as many or as few of these as you like. The point to remember is that, if you come up with an answer that makes sense according to the world as you see and live it, that character is probably in a realistic play.

What Is the Setting?

We have examined at various places in this book how the play's setting is an important clue to the play's meaning. We noted, for instance, that the "world" of a classic tragedy is typically large, involving as it does a universal moral code. A classic comedy, we observed, uses a particular society as its playing field, and a drama might be located in an even more limited space: the family's living room, for instance.

In a realistic play, the setting plays a different sort of role. Because the intent of realism is to examine the world as a scientific phenomenon, it is often concerned with the effect a person's environment has upon her character development. If we're looking at a world governed by the laws of cause and effect, clearly important causes are *place* and *time*. A woman born in a London slum in the nineteenth century will turn out very different than a woman born in a mansion in New York City in the twentieth; and a realistic play will be likely to make full use of these differences. Therefore, the specific environment needs to be examined very carefully. Consider the following elements:

The Immediate Surroundings: Where the Onstage Action Is Placed

Is it a well-furnished room, containing expensive furniture and accessories? Is it a crowded slum kitchen? Is it a lushly planted, well-maintained city park, or—as we saw in *The Cherry Orchard*—an abandoned, weed-ridden cemetery? Consider the psychological effect this place has on the characters. We referred to the setting of *A Doll's House* earlier and noted how it looks like a well-furnished upper-middle-class room in a nineteenth-century house. We also noted that Ibsen calls for only two doors: one leading outside, and one leading to Torvald's room, providing Nora with only two possible options—leave the house entirely or succumb to Torvald's influence. Clearly, as the action of the play demonstrates, this is a very important psychological determinant.

The Larger Society Outside This Particular Location

This element is a combination of both space and time that raises broad questions about several factors.

The Economic Picture

Are we upper, lower, or middle class? Are the characters concerned about their survival, or is it not at issue? Is the outside world secure or in crisis? Recall that *The Glass Menagerie* takes place during the Great Depression of the 1930s, and notice how the fear of poverty drives Amanda to desperately seek a husband for Laura. However, people in a Noel Coward comedy almost never worry about money; their world is secure enough to allow them to think more about love, courtship, and sex.

The Cultural Picture

What are the ideals and mores that the world considers valuable? Is it a conservative time, in which people are expected to behave according to very rigid social rules? Or is it a time of change, revolution, and transition in which people can exercise freedom? Jean Baptiste Racine's seventeenth-century French tragedy *Phèdre* is about a woman who happens to desire her stepson; in her time, admitting out loud such a heinous thought would have been a crime worth committing suicide over. Were she to be a character in a romping 1970s farce set in America, such a thought would hardly be a bother, and she would probably act on her desires and feel no pangs at all. How is Nora a prisoner of her times?

The Political/Historical Picture

Are there current or recent world events that have influence on the characters? *Mother Courage and Her Children*, by Bertolt Brecht, takes place during the long Thirty Years War in Europe, a world in which everybody is scrambling for a way to earn a buck; a world in which Mother Courage, in order to keep herself alive, must ultimately sacrifice all of her children to the war machine. Arthur Miller's *All My Sons* is set a few years after the end of World War II; during the play, we learn that the father of the family had sold shoddy airplane parts to the government, causing the deaths of many pilots. When this secret comes out, he kills himself.

In sum, the setting of a realistic play is typically very carefully laid out for us because it exerts an important influence on the lives and fortunes of the play's characters.

How Is Language Used?

The language spoken in a realistic play is also supposed to reflect the lives of the audience. Thus, in a contemporary play, we would expect the language to be colloquial, informal, filled with slang where appropriate, and to generally display the rhythms of average speech. Certainly, within these broad parameters, there is room for variations. Ethnic, class, geographic, and economic differences color the way in which we speak. Furthermore, what we are trying to accomplish in a situation is also a factor. Thus, well-educated and intelligent people seducing or impressing each other in a drawing room would use language differently than street punks scoring a drug deal with a gang leader in a dark alley. The same well-educated, intelligent people might speak differently to a police officer who's stopped them for speeding, while one of those street punks might modify his speech if he were applying for an important job.

What Is the Form?

Nearly all realistic plays are representational. We in the audience are distant, unattached observers of a scientific demonstration in progress. The events on the stage are happening in another world that we are not a part of and that takes no notice of us. The famous "fourth wall" is up.

Please note, however, that some plays use a combination of both representational and presentational elements. We noted how, in *The Glass Menagerie*, Tom sometimes addresses the audience directly and at other times steps into a representational scene as a character. What about Shakespeare and other Elizabethan writers who often write long soliloquies for their characters? Or Restoration writers who provide their characters with what's called *asides*? Where do these fit?

It depends on each situation. Remember that when Hamlet is alone on the stage and speaking "To be or not to be," he is not addressing the audience but rather speaking his inner thoughts aloud to himself. Similarly, when Romeo appears in the fourth act and describes the dream he's had, he is not telling *us*; he's merely fixing it in his memory. These characters are in representational plays.

On the other hand, when the character speaks an aside, he is taking the audience into his confidence; he is telling us what his fears are, what his plan is, how he immediately reacts to something that's just happened. Thus, the first thing the Duke of Gloucester (in Shakespeare's *Richard III*) does is tell the audience that he is a villain and plans to take over the throne. He knows we are powerless to stop him and delights in making us squirm a bit. These moments are essentially presentational moments in an otherwise representational play.

And there are plays that are what might be called "totally presentational," in which the audience actually plays a role. One example would be *Waiting for Lefty* by Clifford Odets. The audience for the play is supposedly an audience at a union rally: At the end of the play, the union organizers urge the audience to strike. The audience members at its premiere actually did stand up and begin shouting. During the 1960s and 1970s, many plays sent the actors into the audience, to actually confront and speak to individuals and sometimes to invite them onto the stage to join in.

How Does Realism Define the World?

For writers who chose realism as their style, the world is a place that obeys natural laws of cause and effect. It is comprehensible and therefore able to be studied and eventually controlled. It is a place of order, logic, and rationality, where what you see is what you get. It is as objective and scientifically valid as a laboratory experiment.

Questioning the Play

1. When was the play written, and how do the life and times of the author influence her choice of this style? Is she writing during a time of political and social change? What, in other words, is the efficient cause?

2. Apply the three unities to the play: Does it adhere to them or violate them? How does this affect the action? What influence might it have on the meaning?

3. Would you describe your play as issue-driven or character-driven?

4. Apply the concepts of probability and possibility to the play. Do the events seem to lean more toward one or the other? Why?

5. To what extent is the plot typical of the well-made play pattern? Are the events in the play related causally, even though they may not be linear? If they are not linear, how and why has the playwright made the play nonlinear? What purpose might be served by either approach?

6. How would you describe the characters? In a realistic play, their literal aspect is usually more important than their functional or connotative aspects, but how would you apply all three of those aspects, and what conclusions can you draw?

7. How does the setting affect the characters, the action, and ultimately the meaning of the play?

12

Symbolism

Background

Actually, all plays are *symbolist* in one way or another. Out of all the possible events that could happen to a character, the dramatist selects only those that somehow dramatize the theme. Out of all the possible characters who could inhabit the world that's created, she chooses some and ignores others. And to those that are chosen, she takes special care to give personalities, actions, and lines of dialogue that also dramatize her theme. It's always important, therefore, to ask, Do these events and characters mean more than their literal sense? For instance, there is some significance, in *A Doll's House*, to the fact that the men in Nora's life come from different backgrounds: Her husband, a banker, represents financial security. Krogstad wants to find some dignity and suggests social stability. And Dr. Rank comes from the world of medicine. In short, every time you analyze a character according to his or her *connotative aspect*, you're entering symbolist territory.

That being understood, therefore, please note that when we talk of *symbolism* as a style, we are referring to a specific kind of play that was popular during a particular time period and that uses symbols of a special kind and in a unique way. As in the case of realism, this style has specific historical roots. Almost as soon as realism came into vogue, reactions to it arose. Some critics, painters, theorists, and eventually playwrights began to chafe under its apparent restrictions, taking issue with the idea that life was only what we saw or only how we reacted to environmental stimuli. The true reality, they claimed, does not lie on the surface at all, but rather somewhere below or behind, in a realm of the spirit, in some vague and mysterious time and space that is normally hidden from our sense. What we see, hear, taste, touch, or smell are only symbols of other things.

Actually, this was not a new idea. Philosophers and clergymen had been saying something similar since the time of Plato. He divided our existence into that which existed in our temporal world and that which existed in a pure form in what he called an *ideal* world. The tree that we look at is only a kind of representation of the ideal of "treeness," which we can never directly experience. We observers have to remember this when we look at things and be careful not to mistake the surface illusion for the hidden reality.

This view of reality permeated art prominently in the Middle Ages because of the symbolism developed by the Catholic Church. For instance, in a famous medieval drama, *The Second Shepherd's Play*, the shepherds bring three gifts to the infant Jesus: a bird, some cherries, and a tennis ball. This moment is heavy with hidden significance: There are three shepherds bringing three gifts—God is three-in-one: Father, Son, Holy Spirit. The bird is a symbol of Heavenly Grace. The cherries are a fruit—the blossoming of new life and richness. They are red—the color of Christ's blood, which was shed to redeem humanity. The tennis ball is round and limitless—like the earth itself, the mortal realm in which we live, which is unending, and over which Jesus is said to reign.

Late in the nineteenth century, as a reaction to the scientific claims of realism, poets and dramatists deliberately returned to this mode of thinking and set out to write about this strange hidden world that lay behind the mask of surfaces. The movement was also known by such terms as *neoromanticism*, *impressionism*, or *idealism*. This hidden world was almost indescribable; the goal was less to understand and define this world rationally than it was to experience it emotionally. The idea was that we can't ever really "see" what is hidden; we can only "feel" it as something inexplicable but powerful.

This movement began to surface first in France among a group of poets such as Stéphane Mallarmé, who wrote lyrical, dreamlike poems, and dramatists such as Maurice Maeterlinck, who wrote plays that sought to evoke a mood rather than tell a story. In Germany, Richard Wagner adapted many symbolist features in his grand operas, seeking a fusion of music, spectacle, and drama to hint at a world that lay beyond words.

At about the same time, Irish writers such as William Butler Yeats wrote short plays about Ireland's mystical past that were designed to stir the heart with their beauty and to pique the imagination by tales of mystery and supernatural events. In Sweden, many of August Strindberg's plays, and in Russia, even Chekov's major works used some of the techniques we'll describe below.

As a historical movement, however, symbolism had a relatively short life. Few writers working in this mode wrote really masterful works, and audiences soon wearied of these lyrical and moody pieces. More important, the ever-encroaching Industrial Revolution and the rise of Socialism and Marxism, the shattering effects of the Russian Revolution and World War I—these stated loud and clear that there really wasn't a beautiful world underneath after all. Nevertheless, as we said earlier, many of the features of symbolism are still found in contemporary works.

What Are the Concerns of the Author?

Writers of symbolist plays are not interested in the scientific nature of reality. They are more interested in a world "behind" the one we see. External actions and dialogue are useful only insofar as they help us enter some spiritual, emotional state in which we experience the mystery of the world. The essence of this experience is to be emotional rather than intellectual.

One of the most important symbolist writers, Maurice Maeterlinck, wrote an essay on the subject, "The Tragical in Daily Life," in which he argues that there is more truth and reality to be found in the sight of an old man sitting quietly in a candlelit room, listening to the darkening silence around him and patiently waiting, than there is in all the dramas about "lovers who strangle their mistresses or captains who conquer in battle." He goes on to state:

> One may even affirm that a poem draws the nearer to beauty and loftier truth in the measure that it eliminates words that merely explain the action, and substitutes for them others that reveal ... I know not what intangible and unceasing striving of the soul for its own beauty and truth. And so much the nearer, also, does it draw to the true life.

Maeterlinck follows his own advice in a famous short play, *The Intruder*. The setting is a rather dark room in an old castle. A blind old man, referred to only as "Grandfather," sits with his children and grandchildren. Offstage, his daughter-in-law is failing after a very difficult birth. Grandfather is uneasy, sensing that something is wrong. Outside, the wind blows strangely; there are odd whisperings and murmurs in the dark, and the old man begins to fear that somebody is approaching. The rest of the family are upset by his unease and try to reassure him. The evening grows more tense; suddenly, the baby offstage cries out with fear. The others all rush to see what's happened, and the old man is left onstage—blind, alone, anxiously groping his way to the door, and crying, "They've left me all alone!" (act 1).

While nothing much actually happens onstage, a mood of suspense and melancholy is created, and a great deal happens behind the scenes. For one thing, the woman offstage dies. We only learn about it indirectly: We hear a "frightened cry" from offstage, the family is frozen with terror, a nun appears and makes the sign of the cross, and the family walk slowly into the next room. In other words, nobody actually *says* that the mother has died, but we understand it through symbols. But we also understand it emotionally: We have been caught up in the mood of dread and sadness that Maeterlinck has created onstage.

Another thing has "happened" in the play—but again, not on the surface. A spiritual event has occurred: death has come visiting. Now, you might argue that saying "the mother dies" and "death has come visiting" is saying the same thing; but if you give the concepts a little more thought—and a little more "feeling"—you will see that the first is a physical act, more in the nature of a reaction to other forces. The mother is a passive figure, responding to nature's inevitability. She essentially does nothing; something is done to her.

The second, however, is a symbolic personification of an abstract concept, a force with a will of its own. It generates activity. It creates a situation that forms the basis for what happens in the play, in the same sense that Nora in *A Doll's House* does. In a dramaturgical sense, death is really the agent of action of this play. In other words, Maeterlinck is not interested in telling us a story of a woman who dies, but rather he wants us to experience the emotions that come to us when we realize that "death comes calling."

We have to learn, in reading Maeterlinck and writers like him (including Chekov) to look for that other level of reality that the surface can only suggest to us.

What Is the Point of View of the Author?

We may not clearly understand what this hidden world is all about, but nevertheless the author wants us to experience it as she does. Like the author, we are all trapped in the surface world, trying to catch a fleeting glimpse of what lies behind or below. To that extent, we can identify the point of view of a symbolist play as objective.

How Comprehensible Is the World?

Comprehensibility, of course, is absolutely the wrong word to use in describing the symbolist vision. After all, I've just spent the whole first part of this section explaining that these writers look for a truth that *cannot be explained* but can only be *felt*. And as the writer/teacher here, I've come up against a thorny problem myself: how to explain the inexplicable. If you go back and read carefully some of the sentences I've written above, you'll notice that I've occasionally waxed a bit poetical: I've talked about "hidden worlds" and "mysteries." Hopefully, the connotations of these words have given you a feeling for what I mean. If I were playing *Silent Night* on a flute, you might get the point even better.

How Is the Plot Constructed?

Symbolist works are not primarily plot-driven. The action is often static, in that the characters spend most of their time reacting to something that's happened, revealing their inner feelings to one another, or dealing with one key crisis rather than a series of events. It would be more accurate to describe these plays as *mood-driven*, and because of this, they are typically one-acts, just long enough to establish and maintain a mood before it descends into boredom.

When symbolist plays actually tell stories, they often have a mythical core; many are based on ancient legends and appeal to an audience's sense of nostalgia and longing for some long-lost golden age. In this sense, they are very much in the tradition of Romanticism, tales in which a protagonist in some remote locale faces some personal crisis that tests his passion and that involves a loss of some sort. Maeterlinck's own *Pelleas and Melisande* is a sort of Romeo-and-Juliet love story set in a legendary kingdom by the sea.

Or these plays might be set in some vaguely distant past and tell stories of legendary heroes doing brave and daring things. Some of the one-act plays of William Butler Yeats deal with events in Ireland's history. His *At the Hawk's Well* is a verse play derived from ancient Irish legends about a hero named Cuchulain who tries to drink from a sacred well guarded by a hawk woman; the well contains the waters of immortality and wisdom. When he fails to do so, he gives up this vain search and goes off into the hills. We in the audience are meant to experience a range of emotions here: pride in our Irish history, awe in the presence of a hero, a bittersweet mixture of nostalgia and longing for an earlier, better, richer time.

As you can see, a sense of *smallness* and *quietude* tends to permeate these plays. Not surprisingly, they were often intended to be performed in very small spaces: theaters of no more than about nine hundred seats or, in Yeats's case, the living rooms of private homes.

What Is the Substance/Texture of the Characters?

For the same reasons that symbolist plays are not plot-driven, neither are they character-driven. The people in these plays are not meant to be lifelike in the sense that realistic characters are. They are not driven by their environment, nor are they psychologically motivated. While they certainly might have goals to pursue or fears that drive them, they are little more than representatives of types of people.

Often they do not even have names. For example, the cast list of Maeterlinck's *The Intruder* includes:

the Grandfather
the Father
the Uncle
the Three Daughters
the Sister of Charity
the Maid

You may recall that in chapter 4 we noted that characters in plays can be analyzed through three different lenses: the *literal*, which explains the kind of people they might be in real life; the *functional*, which explains how they help advance the plot; and the *symbolic*, which explains what they might suggest on a larger, more thematic, scale. Clearly, the characters in a symbolist play are meant to be seen through this third window: as personifications of emotional states or attitudes that have meaning below the surface.

What Is the Setting?

Remembering that symbolist dramas are typically small and quiet and often are designed to be performed in small spaces, it is easy to see that the settings are not meant to be realistic. In most cases, they are supposed to merely suggest a playing space that stands for another realm, creating—once again—not illusion but mood. Thus, the setting in *The Intruder* is "A dimly lit room in an ancient castle," a phrase evocative in itself. Little is called for but a few doors, one of which leads to a terrace outside. (Note the contrast between *inside* and a *door leading to a terrace*; what kind of mood does that already suggest?) The room is painted primarily in green. (Why that color? What mood does *green* evoke? What idea does it suggest? Earth? Grass? Living things? Does it feel right that a play about death coming to call should be set in a world of "living things"?) And it's dim—not easy to see into, just like the hidden world beneath.

This use of setting was enhanced in production because the emergence of this literary movement coincided with new developments in stagecraft. Important technological advances in electricity and stage machinery made settings more versatile and more complex. Designers such as Adolphe Appia, Edward Gordon Craig, and Max Reinhardt were not interested in replicating "real" places onstage; instead, they used platforms, curtains, steps, screens, and other structures to create not a "location" but a playing space for the actors—a space that because of its own line, mass, color, and arrangement conveyed a particular mood itself. The actor no longer performed in front of painted backdrops or went in and out of doors made of wood and cloth; instead, the body and movement of the actor became part of the visual, almost sculptural, look and feel of the environment. In addition, innovations in stage lighting made it possible to use color, texture, chiaroscuro (the blending of light and shadow), and intensity to help enhance the play's mood. Such things as fade outs, cross-dissolving, spots of light, and other devices that we now take for granted in a modern playhouse were first used as a revolt against realism.

How Is Language Used?

Language in a symbolist play tends to be more poetic than collo-quial, largely because the movement itself first emerged in the work of poets. The purpose of words was less to create meaning than it was to suggest the hidden world; again, the only way to do that was to create a mood.

In chapter 5, we examined the two primary ways in which language is evocative: first, by selecting words with the right *connotations*, and second, by *euphonics*; that is, stringing a series of words together according to their sounds. The symbolist writers made extensive use of these techniques and added several other as well.

Many plays were, in fact, written in verse. Therefore, the elements of rhythm and (occasionally) rhyme were called into play. Here's a passage from *On Baile's Strand*, another of Yeats's one-act plays about the Irish hero Cuchulain. Cuchulain is confronting a stranger who has entered his court. He draws his sword and speaks boldly:

> . . . you are in my house. Whatever man
> Would fight with you shall fight it out with me.
> They're dumb, they're dumb. How many of you would meet
> (He draws his sword)
> This mutterer, this old whistler, this sand-piper,
> This edge that's greyer than the tide, this mouse
> That's gnawing at the timbers of the world.

On the surface, he seems to be throwing a challenge to this intruder and his retinue. But there's something about the images he's using as well as the regularity of the rhythm within the lines that suggests—what? A martial sort of courage? A large sense of destiny? A conflict between man and the larger forces of nature? What do you make of the sound and sense of "this mouse / That's gnawing at the timbers of the world"? Maybe you can't explain it; maybe all you can do is thrill to the bigness and boldness of the image.

Many passages of dialogue do not move the play forward but rather express an emotion the character is feeling. It is generally agreed that, at least in well-made and realistic plays, dialogue is supposed to help reveal character and move the plot forward. However, many long passages in symbolist plays do neither. Rather, the play seems to stop and settle for a moment, as characters describe the mood they're feeling or the emotion the situation calls up in them. We might say that the play stops moving ahead and stays in one place for a moment while it moves "down," as in this passage from *The Intruder*. It's late in the play, and Grandfather has been restless and anxious all evening. He keeps insisting he hears things that nobody else does. His anxiety makes the family around him nervous.

GRANDFATHER: Is the window open?
DAUGHTER: Yes, Grandfather; I've told you.
GRANDFATHER: I can't believe you. It's so silent outside.
DAUGHTER: You're right, Grandfather, it's very quiet.
FATHER: More so than usual; it's very odd.
DAUGHTER: It's quiet enough to hear an angel flying past.
UNCLE: One more reason I hate the country.
GRANDFATHER: I need to hear some noise, some sound. Ursula, what time is it?
DAUGHTER: Midnight, Grandfather.
GRANDFATHER: Midnight!?

Notice how still but edgy everybody is, and also notice the slight sense of terror in Grandfather's last line: There's something ominous hovering just beyond the borders of our senses.

Some passages of dialogue are neither related to the plot nor help express an emotion but are like little lyric poems set in the middle of the action. An example comes from a play that is typically defined as belonging to the theater of the absurd but that shares many of the characteristics of a symbolist play, Samuel Beckett's *Waiting for Godot*. Vladimir and Estragon are two outcasts waiting in an empty field for a mysterious person named Godot to arrive. They exchange these lines:

ESTRAGON: All the dead voices.

VLADIMIR: Like leaves.

ESTRAGON: Like sand.

VLADIMIR: Like leaves.

(Silence)

ESTRAGON: They all speak at once.

VLADIMIR: Each one to itself.

(Silence)

ESTRAGON: Rather they whisper.

VLADIMIR: They rustle.

ESTRAGON: They murmur.

VLADIMIR: They rustle. (act 2)

Another device often used in symbolist dialogue appears in the example above, and technically speaking, it isn't "dialogue" at all: silence. Notice how Beckett calls for a moment of silence twice in the above passage. Before this little section of the play is over, he calls for silence at least three more times, creating a mood of stillness, mystery, and in part, expectation—which is what the play is all about anyhow.

Related to this is another device that's not literally "dialogue" but is part of what the audience hears and helps contribute to a mood: sound effects offstage. Many plays make use of noises in the distance that affect the characters onstage. In *The Intruder*, Grandfather reacts to the sounds of the wind, footsteps that he hears, something that sounds to him like a scythe being sharpened, the creaking of a door, and so forth. One of the most famous offstage symbolist "sounds" appears in the third act of Chekov's *The Cherry Orchard*: The family is having a quiet conversation outdoors, and they gradually stop talking and fall into a silence. Then, a strange sound is heard: Something that sounds like a breaking string or snapped wire seems to come from a vast distance. The characters onstage wonder what it is: Something breaking in a mine shaft? Some kind of bird? An owl? Nobody knows, and Chekov never explains; he simply lets the mysterious sound, along with the silence, add to the mood of impending disaster that falls over the whole family.

What Is the Form?

Most symbolist plays are typically representational. The action takes place behind the invisible "fourth wall," and we in the audience are merely spectators, standing outside and observing everything from an objective point of view.

How Does Symbolism Define the World?

For writers who adopt symbolist features, the world that we see is only a mask, covering a truer, hidden world beneath. This hidden world is made up of spiritual and abstract forces that are only personified by the world we see. These forces are active agents, affecting us in many ways. This hidden world can't be accessed intellectually; the way to experience these forces is through our emotions, using light and space, evocative language, personified characters, and a strong sense of mood.

Questioning the Play

1. When was the play written, and do the life and times of the author influence his choice of style? Is he writing during a time of literary experimentation? What, in other words, is the efficient cause?

2. Who—or what—seems to be the agent of action of the play? Is it a character we physically see, or is it some abstract concept or force, such as death, change, time, or something along these lines?

3. If it's a character we physically see, what might the connotative aspect of that character be?

4. To what degree is the play mood-driven, plot-driven, or character-driven? There may be elements of all three; which dominates? When? How? Why?

5. How does the setting of the play contribute to its mood?

6. How does language help evoke the play's mood? Where are there set pieces that operate like little poems? If the play's in verse, how does that contribute to the meaning and effect?

7. What use, if any, does the author make of sound effects to create mood? What particular examples stand out?

13

Expressionism

Background

Like other "isms," *expressionism* also emerged as a direct result of certain social influences, beginning as a specific movement in Germany during the 1920s and 1930s. The dominant culture of the times was severely repressive; within both the family unit and the state, rigid beliefs on conduct and morality were held. However, many young people of the time resisted social and paternal restrictions. In its way, the times were not unlike the 1960s in America, a time in which flower children, hippies, and militant political minorities protested against what they felt was an unfair social system, an unjust government, and a generally repressive older generation.

In 1914 in Germany, a play by Walter Hasenclever, *The Son*, was among the first of a wave of "counterculture" dramas. The young hero runs away from his stern, unforgiving father and has a series of adventures that liberate his spirit. When he finally returns home, he confronts his father, and as a result of an angry quarrel, shoots and kills him. This gunshot was a cry of defiance from the younger generation against the establishment.

In some ways, *The Son* has elements of symbolism: The characters are rudimentary abstractions at best, named only the Father, the Son, the Friend, and so on, and the play is written as a series of short scenes. Two things, however, make it unique: The first is its *tone*. Whereas a symbolist play would be moody and romantic, *The Son* has an overall tone of harshness and anger. If symbolist plays have the quality of a dream, this play has the feeling of a nightmare.

The second difference is the play's intense *one-sidedness*. The Son is absolutely in the right, and the Father, completely in the wrong. The play distorts the characters in order to express the author's own bias. Thus, the Son is righteous, noble, and sympathetic, while the

Father is an excessive martinet, stuffed-shirt, and villain. The writer is not trying to present the world as is to us; rather, he is trying to express his personal opinion about it; it's from this context that the term *expressionism* developed. This subjectivity would eventually emerge as one of expressionism's chief traits.

Plays that followed *The Son* borrowed and expanded upon these two important characteristics: tone and subjectivity. They took a harsh and almost revolutionary look at repressive elements of society and went further and further into distortion. Franz Wedekind's *Spring's Awakening* dealt with hypocritical attitudes toward sex and how it repressed and ruined young lives. The language was strident, unrealistic, and exaggerated. Wedekind broke away from the restrictions of both pedestrian, everyday language and almost incomprehensible verse drama and instead created dialogue that shocked his audience.

As this literary movement expanded, other writers enlarged upon these concerns and expanded the playing field. It wasn't just society that was dark and repressive, it was humankind as such and the whole world in general. The horrors caused by the destruction of Europe in World War I demonstrated that human beings were lunatics who used technology to destroy themselves. Freud said that people were like savage beasts, at the mercy of inner drives and hungers. Karl Marx taught that men and women were helpless creatures at the mercy of economic exploiters. Thus, plays took on increasingly angry tones: The German word *Schrei* came to be used to characterize them; the term translates into English as "scream."

Some of the characteristics of these plays began to appear more frequently in the first decades of the twentieth century. Later, Germans who adopted this style included Ernst Toller (*Man and the Masses*) and Georg Kaiser (*From Morn to Midnight*). Outside Germany, August Strindberg in Sweden and Eugene O'Neill in America wrote important works in this style.

After the 1920s, the expressionist movement began to fade. However, as with symbolism and other styles, writers have continued to adopt expressionist devices in various ways. Thus, a play like Arthur Miller's *Death of a Salesman* can be defined as realistic in some senses but clearly expressionist in others. Most of the play shows us Willy Loman's "real life" as he struggles with his job and family; however, Miller has written many scenes that take place "inside Willy's head" and makes the audience privy to his secret dreams and painful memories.

What Are the Concerns of the Author?

Writers of expressionist plays are almost always revolutionary in one sense or another; that is, they see very clearly what they feel is wrong with the world and want us in the audience to be aware of it. They look at the dark and repressive side of things. (In this sense, an expressionist play is a bit like naturalistic plays, which also reveal to us the underside of the rock.) Repression can come from many sources.

We can be our own worst enemies. We are plagued by deep feelings of guilt or evil, or trapped by historical patterns that we can't escape. *Spring's Awakening* shows how people are enslaved by their sexual desires. In O'Neill's *The Emperor Jones*, the title character is a black man who is running through a jungle for his life; we learn through the course of the play that he has been a killer, an escaped convict, and a brutal tyrant on this small tropical island. As he gets more and more lost in this jungle, his personal memories and nightmares come into his head and drive him insane, in the same way they do Willy Loman.

Some element of society traps us. In Georg Buchner's *Woyzeck*, the hero is a soldier trapped by the prisonlike structure and rules of army life, which is a clear metaphor for society in general. In Elmer Rice's *The Adding Machine*, the hero is a victim of technology: His job as a bookkeeper is destroyed when he is replaced by an adding machine, and this drives him to murder.

Sometimes what traps us is something larger and more metaphysical, such as the innate condition of humanity or the general abstract "way of the world." In one expressionist play by Strindberg, *The Ghost Sonata*, people are trapped by the vicious things they've done in the past. In another, *A Dream Play*, people are inherently trapped because they are by nature pitiable, sorrowful, and pathetic creatures with no hope for happiness.

What Is the Point of View of the Author?

Expressionism takes subjectivity as far as it can go. The author does more than simply take sides but actually takes us inside the mind of one person and shows us the world as that person would perceive it. If that person is rational, calm, and normal, the world will probably look fairly real. However, if that person is angry, insane, or perhaps even asleep, the world is bound to be distorted. Consider your classroom. To an objective outsider, the room reveals rows of chairs, the blackboard, and perhaps the figure of an adult standing in front, facing a group of younger people all sitting, listening, and taking notes. However, if we looked through the mind of a student who is failing the class, hates to be there, and is afraid of the instructor, the place might resemble a sort of prison. The students might be seen sitting in rigid, unthinking postures, suggesting machines—or perhaps they would be manacled to their desks like slaves. The windows—if there are any—would be covered by bars. The door would be made of steel six inches thick and firmly locked. The person standing at the front would be wearing, not a suit and tie, but a military uniform and carrying, not a piece of chalk, but an electric cattle prod. The outer world becomes, therefore, an *expression* of an inner state.

In his preface to *A Dream Play*, August Strindberg provides perhaps the best explanation for this intent:

> I have in this play sought to imitate the incoherent but ostensibly logical form of our dreams. Anything can happen; everything is possible and probable. Time and space do not exist. Working with some insignificant real events as a background, the imagination spins out its threads of thoughts and weaves them into new patterns—a mixture of memories, experiences, spontaneous ideas, impossibilities and improvisations. The characters split, double, multiply, dissolve, condense, float apart, coalesce. But one mind stands over and above them all, the mind of the dreamer; and for him there are no secrets, no inconsistencies, no scruples, no laws.

Another writer, Ernst Toller, put down his intentions in an essay entitled "Transfigurations," from which these key points emerge:

The expressionist wants to do more than take photographs. Realizing the artist's environment penetrates him and is reflected in the mirror of his soul, he wants to re-create this environment in its very essence. Reality [is] to be caught in the bright beam of an idea.

The world the dramatist shows is distorted, according to the point of view and vision of one central character. It will be helpful in understanding this concept if you label this character the *window character*; that is, the character through whose eyes we are looking at the world.

How Comprehensible Is the World?

For the expressionist writer, the world may be crazy, unfeeling, and destructive, but somehow, in a sort of topsy-turvy manner, it does have some sort of logic to it. Once you see the world through the subjective eye of the window character, your challenge is to understand what that attitude is. Early in O'Neill's *The Emperor Jones*, we learn that Brutus Jones has made himself "emperor" of this tropical island by force, cheating and killing his way to the top—he confesses several past crimes to a confidant—and he's made use of the natives' superstitious fears. We also see that he himself is superstitious, especially because he brags so hard that he is not. Then Jones spends the rest of that night running deeper and deeper into a jungle. It's not long before he begins to see visions: Some of the incidents of his past enact themselves before him; some of the men he's killed appear to taunt him. While all this may be confusing for a moment, it becomes clear when we realize that we are seeing these visions as Jones's own memories.

Many expressionist plays begin in what might be called the *normal*, or objective, world, in which we get enough clues about the central character to provide us with a sort of road map through his nightmare. When the character starts hallucinating, as it were, this road map provides keys to understanding the exact nature of the distortion.

In plays like *A Dream Play*, however, we aren't given a glimpse of the normal world; the whole play is a distortion. The challenge, in these instances, is to look for internal clues of the sort we've already met: Who seems to be the agent of action? Are there *raisonneur* characters? From what source does the inciting incident come? What is the nature of the antagonist? Looking at the connotative aspect of the characters, is there any consistent pattern of symbolic associations to them?

One other question makes interpreting these plays tricky: Is the window character actually in the play? As Strindberg seems to suggest, there is a "dreamer" who is dreaming this play, but the playwright never indicates who this dreamer actually is; he is, in fact, outside the world of the play. In a sense, the dreamer might be us—we might be dreaming the play. However, in *The Emperor Jones*, we see, in the first scene, the character of Brutus Jones depicted in a very realistic manner. When he begins to hallucinate, we see both him as a character and the figures in his imagination laid out before us. We are outside Brutus's mind at the same time we are inside it. A clue to the meaning of an expressionist play, therefore, lies in which of these approaches the playwright takes.

How Is the Plot Constructed?

As we suggested, the play sometimes begins in a normal world. Something happens to the character, in the nature of an inciting incident, that changes things drastically. In Georg Kaiser's *From Morn to Midnight*, the hero sees a beautiful girl and lusts after her; he robs and kills in order to get her. In *The Adding Machine*, the protagonist learns he is being replaced by an adding machine; in a fit of mad despair, he kills his boss and then enters a series of nightmares. Does this all sound a bit familiar? Does it sound like the basic pattern of a "green-world comedy"? In sense, this sort of expressionist play might very well be called a green-world comedy in which the green world is just not so green.

In these cases, the play may or may not return to the "normal" world at the end. In cases where it does, as in *The Emperor Jones*, the author gives us a chance to compare and contrast the normal world with the distortion, providing us additional clues to the play's meaning. In cases where it does not, as in *The Adding Machine*, the author's point may well be that the distorted world has overcome, beaten, and replaced the normal one.

Sometimes an expressionist play will bounce back and forth between a more normal world and a distorted one. Arthur Miller's *Death of a Salesman* is perhaps the most famous American example. In most of the play, we see Willy Loman struggling with life. But every time he faces a crisis, he retreats into his memories.

In general, here are some characteristics of an expressionistic plot:

Overall, the play is usually shorter than a realistic play might be. As is the case with symbolism, it is difficult to sustain an expressionist piece. A play like *Death of a Salesman*, as we've seen, is an interesting exception, but only because it's essentially a realistic play with some expressionist elements.

The play typically consists of a series of short scenes; its overall structure is episodic rather than extensive. Sometimes these scenes last several minutes, and sometimes they are as short as a line or two. The content of these scenes sometimes isn't as important as the speed with which they come and go and the sense they give us of a world that's fragmented and incoherent. It's as though the mind of the dreamer were tossing and turning in the throes of a kaleidoscopic nightmare.

The play's overall pattern is often that of a journey or a quest. The protagonist is trying to discover something that is unclear or missing (Meaning? Peace? Happiness?). In *A Dream Play*, Indra's Daughter, a minor goddess of Hindu mythology, descends to earth in order to more fully understand human beings and learn why they are always so unhappy. In Buchner's *Woyzeck*, the title character is trying to learn whether or not his wife has really been unfaithful and comes to see that the whole world is mocking him.

Sometimes the agent of action is trying to escape the consequences of a crime and to reach a place of safety. We've indicated two examples above: The tyrant in *The Emperor Jones* has been deposed and is now running through the jungle to escape retribution. The unnamed cashier in *From Morn to Midnight* is trying to avoid capture for his crime and finds himself in an ever more grotesque maze.

In some plays, this journey is not voluntary: It's been thrust upon the central character by repressive external forces, especially when these forces come from an inhumane social structure. The poor working girl in Sophie Treadwell's *Machinal* is just trying to get by; she is forced by circumstances to commit a murder, has no defense, and winds up being railroaded to the electric chair. She is very much like the poor bookkeeper in *The Adding Machine*, who is also driven to murder and squeezed through a merciless system.

A Walk Through O'Neill's *The Emperor Jones*

It might be useful to see in some detail just how an expressionist play works. *The Emperor Jones* begins in an objective, somewhat realistic world: the main room of the house that Jones has converted to his "castle." We learn several important things: He has made himself emperor; he once was a porter on a Pullman train; he is suspected of having murdered a white man; he spent time on a prison chain gang from which he escaped after killing a guard; and he has bullied his way "from stowaway to Emperor in two years!" However, the natives are now beginning to rebel. Jones is smart enough to see this and has made plans to escape: He has mapped out for himself a route through the dense jungle to a place where he's hidden a boat. As the first scene ends, just before nightfall, he begins his journey through the jungle.

The next six scenes show various stops on the way. Each is given a specific time of day:

nightfall
nine o'clock
eleven o'clock
one o'clock
three o'clock
dawn (which takes place outside the forest)

The scenes are two hours apart—why? The hours are odd numbers—why? Jones's journey takes him deeper and deeper into the night, the concept of *night* carrying all sorts of associations: darkness, moving downwards, mystery. The odd-numbered hours are somehow less stable than the even hours, since that's how we perceive numbers. He's moving closer and closer toward some "inner" state. As we'll see, this journey through time parallels another important journey.

You'll notice that O'Neill has caused the sound of drums to be heard throughout the play. They begin at a fairly steady beat, but as the play progresses, grow more intense, more rapid, more frightening. Again, there's a sort of journey expressed by these sounds: a journey from an emotional state of confidence and rationality (which is how Jones feels as he starts out) to an opposite emotional state of fear and panic (which is how we see Jones at the end).

You'll also notice that as the jungle scenes progress, Jones gradually sheds more and more of his clothing. His shoes pinch, and he tosses them away; he loses his hat; his coat and pants are torn into rags; and he eventually wears nothing but a ragged breechcloth. Again, a sort of journey is expressed by this loss of the "dressing" of civilization.

But the real heart of the expressionism in these scenes lies in the visions that Jones has. Each time he stops to rest, he sees images. Here's a list of what they are:

Scene 2: He sees what O'Neill describes as "Little Formless Fears. They are black, shapeless, only their glittering eyes can be seen." They look like "grubworms."

Scene 3: He sees Jeff, the man he thought he'd killed on the Pullman train. He shoots and kills him again.

Scene 4: He sees a line of prisoners on a chain gang, guarded by a prison guard. When he's forced to join the prisoners, he rebels and smashes a shovel on the man's head. He realizes it's an illusion and runs deeper into the jungle.

Scene 5: He sees a pre–Civil War slave auction in progress; he becomes one of the slaves for sale and is auctioned off. He shoots and kills two men and runs again into the jungle.

Scene 6: He becomes part of a crew on a slave ship, from which he runs away.

Scene 7: He is witness to a primitive savage ceremony that involves a witch doctor who demands that Jones offer himself up as a sacrifice to the Crocodile God; as a huge and frightening crocodile head appears from the riverbank, Jones again fires his gun and runs off.

In scene 8, we are back outside the forest, and we learn that Jones has been killed by the natives. What vision of the world is expressed by these hallucinations? How are they sequenced?

First, you'll notice that they all go backward in time, from the present, through Jones's life, the Civil War era, the earlier slave trade, and the even earlier time of primitive tribes. It's as though Jones were reliving his life in reverse.

Except that, when you think about it, it can't really be Jones's life. He could not possibly have been a slave auctioned off in 1850-something, nor could he have been on a slave ship coming over from Africa. He certainly could not have been a member of a primitive African tribe, at least fifty years before the Civil War. It's clearly not his own personal hell that provides the lens through which he see the distortions.

What, then, is Jones remembering? The question has been the subject of some critical thought. You may disagree, but many think that he is "remembering" partly his own experience and partly the experience of the black race in America. Many African Americans can trace their heritage back to its roots in a tribal culture, which was destroyed for them by the slave trade. The German psychiatrist Carl Jung theorized that there exists for all people a similar set of memories and experiences that we all share in some form or another. He calls this body of shared knowledge the *collective unconscious*. So the journey Jones makes takes him deeper and deeper into not just his own experience but the collective "soul" (if you will) of all African Americans, and by extension, all people.

In other words, the journey that Jones completes is a journey into the dark heart of his (and our) humanity. You can see, therefore, how the deepening hours of the night, the increasingly frightening drum beats, and the gradual shedding of clothing—along with the visions that we see through Jones's eye—all work to express this same journey.

What Is the Substance/Texture of the Characters?

As is the case in symbolist plays, the characters in expressionist plays are not meant to be lifelike. Rather, they are abstract qualities given a generic name: Father, Waitress, Cashier, Jurors, Woman, and so on. When they are given names, however, the names often have symbolic associations, as when Elmer Rice names the poor central character of *The Adding Machine* Mr. Zero. Essentially, all that we said about symbolist characters applies equally well to expressionist ones, with two additional points to mention.

Characters are more than abstractions: They are distortions. They are exaggerations taken to extreme limits. People, such as bosses, jurors, or policemen, who are uncaring or inhumane are often depicted as machines or robots—as stiff in their movements and manner of speaking as they are in their attitudes. Mrs. Zero is not just an uncaring wife, she is a monstrous, almost witchlike harridan who whines and berates her husband beyond belief.

The central character is almost always a victim of some sort. The central character, as we've noted, is trying to escape or trying to break free from excessive restraints. As we'll see below, a clue to the play's meaning lies in the nature of that restraint.

What Is the Setting?

In a sense, all expressionist plays have the same location: the inside of the central character's head. And they all share a common larger environment: They are all located in a world that is repressive and cruel. Therefore, what we see on the stage in the form of scenery is rarely intended to look normal; rather, it is intended to be part of the same distortion.

What's more important, however, than the stage setting is the larger world that the playwright defines. Some element in the outside world has driven the central character out of her mind and caused her to escape into hallucinations and distortions. Earlier, we noted that society can repress us in many ways—both external and internal.

The setting, therefore, of an expressionist play is thematically dominated by this repressive element, and we can use that dominance to understand the play: *The Emperor Jones* is a world dominated by collective fear and guilt; *A Dream Play* describes a world dominated by earthly pain and sorrow; *The Adding Machine* takes place in a cold, inhumane industrial world.

How Is Language Used?

As the world is distorted, so is the language the characters speak. While there may be passages of normal, that is, recognizable, dialogue, large sections of these plays use dialogue that is extremely stylized. This stylization takes several different forms.

Sometimes the speeches between characters are terse, short, staccato-like outbursts, sounding more like gunshots or machine noises than speech. This is partly because the central character's vision sees people as robotic, machinelike, or military figures, stiff and frozen in their attitudes. In Sophie Treadwell's *Machinal*, the protagonist (named, appropriately, Young Woman) comes to work and has the following exchange with her co-workers:

STENOGRAPHER: Why don't you get to work?

YOUNG WOMAN: What?

ADDING CLERK: Work.

YOUNG WOMAN: Can't.

ADDING CLERK: Can't?

YOUNG WOMAN: My machine's out of order.

STENOGRAPHER: Well, fix it.

YOUNG WOMAN: I can't. Got to get somebody. . . .

TELEPHONE GIRL: Don't let 'm get your goat, kid, tell 'em where to get off.

YOUNG WOMAN: What?

TELEPHONE GIRL: Ain't it all set?

YOUNG WOMAN: What?

TELEPHONE GIRL: You and Mr. J.

STENOGRAPHER: You and the boss.

FILING CLERK: You and the big chief.

ADDING CLERK: You and the big cheese.

YOUNG WOMAN: Did he tell you?

TELEPHONE GIRL: I told you!

ADDING CLERK: I told you!

STENOGRAPHER: I don't believe it. (act 1)

Sometimes the dialogue is stalled by long and extravagantly lyrical passages that are often so subjective the audience has trouble following the character's train of thought, most likely because the train of thought is derailed by madness. Here's a brief section of a monologue the Young Woman has at the end of the scene we just quoted. She speaks her thoughts:

Marry me—wants to marry me—George H. Jones—Mrs. George H. Jones.—Mrs George H. Jones—Dear Madame—marry—do you take this man to be your wedded husband—I do—to love honor and to love—kisses—no—I can't—George H. Jones— . . . Why Mr Jones—I—let me look at your hands—you have such pretty little hands— . . . George H. Jones—fat hands—flabby hands—don't touch me please—fat hands are never weary—George H. Jones—please don't—married—babies—a baby—curls—curls all over its head—George H. Jones—

The speech goes on like this for about three solid minutes, running the gamut from babies to work, to her mother, to sleeping, to not working, to a section of short, babbling words from all over these subjects, and finally ends with a plea for sanity, "Tell me, ma—something—somebody!" as the scene blacks out.

Often, the characters' speech may have hidden and personal references that relate to some aspect of the author's life and times, or to some metaphysical or spiritual canon the author subscribes to. Many passages in Strindberg's plays are of this nature: It has been suggested that the characters in *A Dream Play* are all manifestations of Strindberg's view of his own fragmented personality, many of the settings reflecting places in his house and his homeland, while certain phrases are misquotes from books he himself was familiar with. Therefore, understanding the efficient cause may be doubly important.

What Is the Form?

As always, it's dangerous to generalize, but expressionist plays are typically representational, not drawing the audience into their frame of reference.

How Does Expressionism Define the World?

For writers who use expressionist techniques, the world is the subjective experience of a window character. It's an outer manifestation of this one person's inner perceptions; the world is how she makes it. The world is often an angry, harsh, and repressive place, in which people are distortions; their behavior, their speech, their reactions are often more like those of robots than of human beings. This world is a place to escape from if at all possible.

Questioning the Play

1. When was the play written, and do the life and times of the author influence his choice of style? Is he writing during a time of social change? To what extent might the author be considered a revolutionary thinker in his time? What, in other words, is the efficient cause?

2. What institution, if any, seems to be a repressive force, acting to imprison the characters?

3. Who is the window character? Does she seem to be outside the play or a character in the play?

4. What is this window character's psychology? Her status in life? What do we learn about her by seeing her in the "normal world"— if we do?

5. How do any of these traits help us understand the distortion she places on the world of the play? What is the nature of that distortion? What larger idea might that suggest? How does it help you understand the play?

6. To what extent is the play a journey or a quest? What is the agent of action trying to discover? To what extent is this a willing journey or an unwilling one? If the latter, what is forcing him to undertake this journey?

7. How are the play's scenes arranged? What symbolic association can you see in this arrangement? How do the various scenes help contribute to the journey of the character?

8. What unique features of the language do you notice? How does the language help convey the play's distortion?

9. Are there any *raisonneur* characters in the play? What speeches do they have that shed light on the play's meaning?

14

Theater of the Absurd

Background

The term *theater of the absurd* applies to the works of certain key writers of the 1950s and early 1960s. Unlike those writers working in realism, symbolism, or expressionism, these writers were not part of a conscious or deliberate movement rebelling against earlier conventions. Rather, they were expressing, in their own ways, a view of life that they all shared: a sense that the universe is cold, hostile, and irrational and that humankind's position in it is helpless, comic, futile, and—in a word—*absurd*.

Among these writers, the most important include Eugene Ionesco, Samuel Beckett, and Harold Pinter, and we could add Edward Albee and Arthur Kopit, especially for some of their early work. However, you can find trace elements of theater of the absurd all through the history of drama, beginning with Euripides and Aristophanes, passing through Shakespeare, and all the way up to and beyond Chekov. You can also find trace elements in popular theater as well, especially in the world of commedia dell'arte, clowns, puppet shows, music halls, and carnivals. Many early silent movie comedies—the work of Charlie Chaplin or Harold Lloyd—also are, in their way, works of the absurdist school.

What brought these various threads together in the middle years of the twentieth century was a nihilistic view of the world that emerged as a result of the grotesqueries and horrors of World War II and the despair that followed. The coming to power of the Soviet Union and the Cold War that arose between it and the West created a Manichaean split between "good guys" and "bad guys" that had more basis in manufactured belief than in reality. In addition, the bizarre practices of various government agencies—notably Senator Joe McCarthy and his communist witch hunts—created an atmosphere in which nothing was secure, nobody was to be trusted, and things were never what they seemed to be. People were at the mercy of leaders beyond their control, armies without minds, technology they didn't understand, and social movements that seemed to shut down progress and individualism.

In a sense, this thinking was not completely unlike the attitudes that gave rise to expressionism. In both styles, the common people are at the mercy of powers, structures, and attitudes that overpower them. However, expressionism seems to suggest that these factors are somehow temporary and changeable. If society has repressive laws, or if a man's conscience is tormenting him, these laws can be altered and this conscience can be appeased. This prospect gives plays like Elmer Rice's *The Adding Machine* and Eugene O'Neill's *The Emperor Jones* something close to an optimistic attitude. In this sense, expressionism is similar to classic comedy: It involves a flawed society.

In absurdism, however, the fault is irreparable: It is not anything temporary that plagues us; rather, it is the universe itself. The very nature of being is illogical and indifferent. And there is no way out. In this respect, theater of the absurd is also a bit like classic tragedy: The playing field is the nature of existence itself.

Many of these ideas are expressed in an essay by Eugene Ionesco:

Each of us has surely felt at moments that the substance of the world is dreamlike, that the walls are no longer solid, that we seem to be able to see through everything into a spaceless universe made up of pure light and color; at such a moment, the whole of life, the whole of history of the world, becomes useless, senseless and impossible. . . . [We are] in a world that now seems all illusion and pretense, in which all human behavior tells of Absurdity and all history of absolute futility; all reality and all language appear to lose their articulation, to disintegrate and collapse, so what possible reaction is there left, when everything has ceased to matter, but to laugh at it all? . . . Language breaks down . . . and words drop like stones or dead bodies; I feel I am invaded by heavy forces, against which I can only fight a losing battle. . . . I have tried [in my plays] to give some indication of what emotional material went into their making, of what was their source: a mood and not an ideology, an impulse not a program; not submission to some predetermined action, but the exteriorization of a psychic dynamism, a projection onto the stage of internal conflict, of the universe that lies within.

This quote contains, essentially, all the ingredients of theater of the absurd, and we'll refer back to it occasionally in this chapter.

What Are the Concerns of the Author?

As Ionesco points out, writers of absurdist plays have no specific agenda or ideology. They are overwhelmed by feelings of helplessness and terror that come from living in a world devoid of rational meaning. The purpose of writing, therefore, is simply to express their despair and perhaps to share it with others: to find, in a sense, comfort in knowing that they are not alone in realizing that they are, in fact, completely alone.

In Ionesco's *The Lesson*, a girl has come for a private lesson from a professor. The underlying assumption of "taking lessons," of course, is that gaining knowledge gives us some measure of control over the universe. However, bit by bit, the lesson disintegrates, becoming more and more abstract and irrational, so that what the professor really communicates is just incomprehensible nonsense.

During all this, the young girl begins to complain of a toothache, which the professor insists that she ignore. It grows worse and worse, until he screams at her in despair. Then he picks up a knife and tries to get her to understand how to pronounce the word *knife*. When she can't, he loses control and stabs her.

The play is absurdist in several important ways.

Numbers cease to have meaning. There is no connection between the word we use and the actual thing itself. At one point, the professor tries to teach subtraction. He invites her to assume that she has three ears. If he takes one away, how many will she have? She answers "two." And if he takes one away again, how many now? She answers "two"—because that's the reality of her ears, no matter what word is used to mean some number.

Think about how we use numbers to record time, dividing this abstract concept into measurable units. From sundown to sunup is *night*; from sunup to sundown is *day*. Furthermore, we've subdivided night and day into *hours*, and we assign numbers to these hours in order to keep track of our progress through them: Thus, four o'clock is one hour later than three o'clock.

However, Ionesco reminds us that numbers themselves have no intrinsic meaning. Therefore, if we don't all understand and agree upon these units (if we don't all assign to them the same meaning), how do we count? How do we add? How do we relate one concept to another? What is *more*? What is *less*? What is *sooner*? What is *later*? These basic foundations of our very existence, in other words, don't really have any solidity or meaning at all. And for us to rely for our sustenance, our health, our very lives, on such puny, unreal "things" is foolish, dangerous, and absurd.

Language has become devalued. As suggested in the above paragraph, a word is just an arbitrary arrangement of sounds that in themselves have no meaning. It doesn't much matter what language influenced what other language, because the sounds only have the meaning we agree that they will have. And if we don't understand the meaning, the sound is useless. There is, at bottom, no real connection between them, so it really doesn't matter what word we use after all.

Numbers don't matter. Words don't have meanings. The connection between things has disappeared. This is what Ionesco means in the passage quoted above: "the world . . . becomes useless, senseless and impossible. . . . all reality and all language appear to lose their articulation, to disintegrate and collapse."

Please note that Ionesco's use of the term *articulation* in this quote is important. He doesn't use the word in the sense of "speaking clearly and distinctly," but rather in the sense of "a thing having connections," as bones articulate at their joints.

There is a chilling difference between abstractions and reality. All the while the professor is babbling away, the girl suffers from her growing toothache. All that matters to her is this pain, which grows more and more severe and which the professor completely disregards. The universe doesn't care how much we hurt.

And when he tries to get her to pronounce the word that defines this short, sharp, pointed object, and she can't, the short, sharp, pointed object ceases to be only an abstract thought and becomes a reality—a real thing—that proves fatal. Abstractions fail us. But reality kills us.

At the end of the play, we learn that this has happened before. Every one of the professor's young pupils has met the same fate: He has lost control and stabbed them all. As the curtain falls, he is preparing to meet yet another girl, to go through the process all over again. Nothing is learned; nothing is changed; nothing has made any difference. To repeat the above, Ionesco has told us: "[We are] in a world that now seems all illusion and pretense, in which all human behavior tells of Absurdity and all history of absolute futility."

You may recall that we met something like this when we examined symbolism. That style posits that the surface we see is only arbitrary, in the same way that the absurdists do, and that the world beneath or behind the surface is the true and real world. However, in a symbolist play, there is something profound, everlasting, and spiritual hiding out of sight, some truth we must discover through our emotions. In an absurdist play, on the other hand, there's nothing there.

How should people behave, therefore, in a world like this? Ionesco's essay gives us a clue: "What possible reaction is there left . . . but to laugh at it all?" But what could possibly be funny about such a world? Your hopes are going to be frustrated; your expectations are not going to come to fruition. There's no logic to the universe; causes do not necessarily result in effects: You can plan your life very carefully, eat well, stop smoking, go to bed early in expectations of a long life—and get hit by a bus whose driver lost control because he was trying to swat at a fly buzzing around his head. But why is that funny?

To find an answer, look back at the various causes of laughter we explored in chapter 7. Some of the theories explaining why people laugh have a direct bearing here.

We seem to be meeting Henri Bergson's theory again. You'll recall that he wrote that we laugh when we see humankind reduced to machines, at the mercy of things or forces beyond their control—whether that thing be a loose banana peel that we step on or a "professor" gone cuckoo. Human beings are not in control. It's in this sense that *The Importance of Being Earnest* or even *The Cherry Orchard* might be considered absurdist.

We seem to be juxtaposing things that don't belong together. We live in an illogical universe. It's in this sense also that *The Importance of Being Earnest* becomes absurdist; after all, what could be more il-logical or irrational than marrying somebody only because his name happens to be Earnest, joining such an important decision to such a silly reason?

We often seem to be in the world of farce. Things happen at a break-neck speed; objects (such as knives, or letters, or fans) often show up in the wrong place at the wrong time; and people are at the mercy of the malevolence of things. Consider all the Roadrunner cartoons you've ever seen, in which the coyote is always falling down a cliff, getting socked in the head, running into brick walls, or tripping himself up—clearly a sentient being pummeled by a hostile and dangerous world.

In short, theater of the absurd is concerned with a universe that's gone crazy—or that always was.

What Is the Point of View of the Author?

The author, while expressing a unique personal philosophy, is giv-ing us an objective view of the world. We'll discuss this a little more fully in conjunction with the next component.

How Comprehensible Is the World?

At first glance, an absurdist play is somewhat like an expressionist play: The series of events doesn't seem to have a clear meaning. In Ionesco's *The Bald Soprano*, a group of people sit around convers-ing, and most of what they say appears to be nonsense. One couple spends about five minutes trying to discover where they've seen each other before and are amazed to realize they both live in the same house, share the same bedroom, and have the same children, and therefore—eureka!—they must be married! A fireman comes in, trying to determine whether there's a fire in the house or not (since he's been sent to extinguish all the fires in the city); they de-bate whether or not that glowing thing in the fireplace is or is not a fire. The maid enters and recites a poem. The characters begin to quote proverbs at each other and to babble ever-increasing nonsense. The lights go out. They come up again, and the play starts all over—the last moment exactly replicating the first.

If this were an expressionist play, we would first try to identify the window character through whose mind we are watching the play. Is he insane? What has repressed him? Is he only dreaming? Once we had that key, we could hopefully fathom this madness, and the world would be comprehensible.

In the absurdist play, there is no such clue. Our lens is not distorted; the world is exactly as insane as it appears to be. The madness is not, therefore, subjective, but objective.

How Is the Plot Constructed?

In theater of the absurd, as in symbolism, plot is of less concern than is *mood*. After all, how can there be a plot in an absurd world? *Plot* is, by definition, a selection and arrangement of events that, taken together, add up to some meaning. But the absurdists claim there is neither meaning nor connection. Thus, the very idea of a linear narrative is useless. Therefore, the plays are often a series of extremely episodic, random, disconnected scenes.

However, there are exceptions. Events might seem to follow other events with some sense of causality; but this causality is deceptive. We are often led to anticipate a particular ending. We might well assume that certain expectations will be satisfied. But we're almost always proven wrong.

Beckett's *Waiting for Godot* supplies a classic example of such failed expectations. Two bums come to the same place every day (or what they assume to be the same place; they're never really sure). They pass the time in a variety of ways: debating metaphysics with each other, dealing with hunger and deprivation, encountering a mysterious stranger and his servant, and trying to keep their spirits up. At the end of each act, a young boy comes to tell them that Godot will not come today but will surely come tomorrow. They continue to wait. He never comes. Never. Never.

Never.

What Is the Substance/Texture of the Characters?

Characters in absurdist plays share many of the same characteristics as those in symbolist or expressionist plays. They are rarely if ever well-rounded human beings who look, sound, or behave like real people in our lives. They are often abstract qualities brought to life; thus, the characters in *The Lesson* are described as a Professor, a Young Girl, and a Maidservant. Characters often don't have names per se, but simply designations: Mommy, Daddy, Mr. and Mrs. Smith, Mr. and Mrs. Jones, and so on.

Some plays, however, do make some attempt to give their characters individual personalities. The two bums in *Waiting for Godot* are distinct people, with unique names: Vladimir and Estragon. One emerges as leader, the other as follower. However, in such plays, these characters become almost expressionistic: That is, they are victims of objects, circumstances, bullies, or simply a world that doesn't care.

What Is the Setting?

We've already noted that geography has little meaning in an absurd universe. Therefore, locations can be vague and superficially unspecific; in this respect, absurdist settings are like symbolist settings: They provide hints about the world behind appearances. However, the world behind the curtain, remember, is illogical and overwhelming.

Some settings clearly reflect this point of view. The two tramps in *Waiting for Godot* are in a large open field, bare except for a single tree. In other plays, the setting comments ironically on the supposed symbolism. *The Lesson*, as we've noted, takes place in the professor's home—supposedly a place of learning and knowledge. But we've seen what sort of learning takes place and how little real knowledge is communicated.

There are also plays in which the playwright dispenses with the illusion of setting completely and sets the play in the theater itself. This is the case with Edward Albee's *The Sandbox*. We are constantly reminded we're in a playhouse: Characters refer to the wings, one of the characters is clearly an actor playing a role, and Grandma even addresses the audience.

In any case, the absurdist setting reinforces the contention that the universe is a void: No matter where you are, you really aren't anywhere at all.

How Is Language Used?

Most often, the language in an absurdist play is similar to the language used in realist plays. People speak in recognizable sentences, using conventional syntax and grammar; the playwright has made use of both literal and connotative meanings; and some attention has been paid to euphonics. Reading *Waiting for Godot* or *The Lesson*, therefore, is not too different from reading *The Glass Menagerie*.

Occasionally, absurdist dialogue also shares some features with symbolist, in that it calls up a mood. Remember that passage from *Waiting for Godot*, which could almost have been written by Maeterlinck.

ESTRAGON: All the dead voices.
VLADIMIR: Like leaves.
ESTRAGON: Like sand.
VLADIMIR: Like leaves.
(Silence)
ESTRAGON: They all speak at once.
VLADIMIR: Each one to itself.
(Silence)
ESTRAGON: Rather they whisper.
VLADIMIR: They rustle.
ESTRAGON: They murmur.
VLADIMIR: They rustle. (act 2)

At other times, the mood created by absurdist language is frenetic and ridiculous. After all, words are not things. The relationship between words doesn't always carry meaning. Therefore, language is often filled with non sequiturs, incongruities, analogies that don't make sense, logic that falls apart in the middle, and extremely exaggerated distortions of what should be familiar references. A prime example of this feature comes from Ionesco's *The Bald Soprano*.

MRS. MARTIN: I can buy a pocketknife for my brother, but you can't buy Ireland for your grandfather.

MR. SMITH: One walks on his feet, but one heats with electricity or coal.

MR. MARTIN: He who sells an ox today will have an egg tomorrow.

MRS. SMITH: In real life, one must look out of the window.

MRS. MARTIN: One can sit down on a chair, when the chair doesn't have any.

MR. SMITH: One must always think of everything.

They go on and on like this for five minutes or so. The pace becomes quicker, the sentences shorter, the meaning ever more ridiculous. Here are the final minutes of the play:

MR. MARTIN: Marietta, spot the pot!

MRS. SMITH: Krishnamurti, Krishnamurti, Krishnamurti!

MR. SMITH: The pope elopes! The pope's got no horoscope. The horoscope bespoke!

MRS. MARTIN: Bazaar, Balzac, bazooka!

MR. MARTIN: Bizarre, beaux-arts, brassieres!

MR. SMITH: A,e,i,o,u,a,e,i,o,u,a,e,i,o,u!

MRS. MARTIN: B,c,d,f,g,l,m,n,p,r,s,t,v,w,x,y,z!

MR. MARTIN: From sage to stooge, from stage to serge!

MRS. SMITH: Choo, choo, choo, choo, choo, choo, . . .

MR. SMITH: It's!

MRS. MARTIN: Not!

MR. MARTIN: That!

MRS. SMITH: Way!

MR. SMITH: It's!

MRS. MARTIN: O!

MR. MARTIN: Ver!

MRS. SMITH: Here!

All together, completely infuriated, they are screaming in each other's ears. The light is extinguished. In the darkness, we hear

ALL: It's not that way, it's over here, it's not that way, it's over here, it's not that way, it's over here, it's not that way, it's over here!

The words cease abruptly. Again, the lights come on. Mr. and Mrs. Martin are seated like the Smiths at the beginning of the play. The play begins again, with the Martins saying exactly the same lines that the Smiths said, while the curtain softly falls.

Is there any meaning to this at all? Perhaps there might be some significance to the last repeated line ("It's not that way, it's over here,") as a sort of signpost to our place in the universe, but who knows? It all just disintegrates and then, horror of horrors, it starts all over again!

What Is the Form?

In its purest sense, theater of the absurd winds up being representational. The audience is not an active part of the event. Even in those plays, such as Albee's *The Sandbox*, that are set in the theater where the play is being performed, the audience typically remains outside the fourth wall.

How Does Theater of the Absurd Define the World?

For writers who use absurdist techniques, the world is incoherent, illogical, nonlinear, and irrational. The laws of cause and effect don't operate, language ceases to have any inherent meaning, numbers and places are only arbitrary, and it all winds up being so horrible you can only survive by laughing at the absurdity of trying to find meaning where there is none.

Questioning the Play

1. When was the play written, and do the life and times of the author influence her choice of style? Are there current philosophies that shed light on the thinking of this era? In other words, what is the efficient cause?

2. In what sense does the play illustrate what Ionesco means when he speaks of a "loss of articulation"? Where in the play are connections made or missed or ignored?

3. What instances, if any, do you find in the play wherein reality is juxtaposed with abstractions? Do people talk about something in one way, but behave in a different way, as in the examples from *The Lesson*?

4. How does language fail in the play?

5. What sources of laughter do you find in the play?

6. What sort of plot structure does the playwright choose? Is it episodic? Linear? Does it lead anywhere? How does the ending flow from the rest of the play—logically, illogically, or with failed expectations?

7. How do the characters function, especially on the connotative level? What abstractions might be personified here?

8. What influence does the setting have on the action? How does the setting function as a symbolic representation of the absurd world?

9. Examine the language used. Where does it function as true and useful communication? Where does it cease to have this function? Does language become a series of words for their own sake, and if so, where? How does the logicality, or lack of it, contribute to the play's meaning?

15

Epic Theater

Background

Epic theater, as we'll describe it in this chapter, came about through the work of one major dramatist, Bertolt Brecht; therefore, most of this chapter centers on his work. However, traces of its characteristics can be found in works of his contemporaries, and it is still very much a major style today.

Its origins are partly in Germany, during the years between the First and Second World Wars, and partly in America during the years of the Great Depression, when many theorists and critics began to see drama as an important resource for bringing about social change. The world was suffering a financial depression; jobs were scarce; inequities in civil rights were blatant; hard-core manufacturers of munitions, oil products, heavy industries, and the like were earning large fortunes over the sweat of the oppressed poor. Among many who thought seriously about these problems, there developed a great concern that art should provide much more than entertainment. They believed that art—specifically theater—should be used as a weapon.

We saw a bit of this in the origins of expressionism, in that many plays of that style were characterized by a harsh tone, a political point of view, and a sense of crying out against repression. However, while expressionism sought to disguise its agenda in the form of representational plays, this new style wanted to present its arguments to its audience in bold presentational terms.

This agenda gave rise to several forms of theater. One was a form of play called *agit-prop*. This term abbreviates the words *agitation*—"arousing anger"—and *propaganda*—"putting forward a political agenda." One of the most famous examples of this is an American play by Clifford Odets called *Waiting for Lefty*, written in the mid-

1930s, during a time when union organizing was controversial. The play's purpose was to urge workers to step forward and sign up.

The scene is a labor union meeting; the audience is supposed to assume they are members of the union at that meeting. The characters are leaders of a taxi-drivers' organization trying to recruit new members. They are waiting for a man named Lefty to come from a meeting with managers. While they wait, various workers tell us why they joined this union; short scenes show us their moments of decision. At the end of the play, word comes that Lefty has been killed. The leaders are outraged. They raise their fists and call for a strike. They keep calling; members of the audience (real and imaginary) are urged to join in. The play ends with everybody in the theater supposedly calling out, "Strike! Strike!" And then, according to the premise of agit-prop theater, the real audience is supposed to march out of the theater and into the streets or real union halls and really vote to become union members themselves.

A second form of political-based theater first appeared in Berlin during the 1920s and 1930s. Places of entertainment called cabarets emerged, featuring political poems, songs, and short sketches. If you've ever seen the musical *Cabaret*, you'll remember that its central female character, Sally Bowles, works in such a club.

A third form to appear at about this time was street theater: Actors would gather in outdoor public places and perform short, satirical farces. Characters were labeled "Manager," "Starving Worker," "Rich Capitalist," and the like. These short sketches often ended with somebody making a speech, advocating one political agenda or another. Then the group would disperse, go somewhere else, and do it again.

All of these trends gradually coalesced in the work of Bertolt Brecht into what we now call *epic theater*. He first began in the more popular cabarets in Berlin during the 1930s with agit-prop pieces and political songs. At the same time, he began to write theoretical works, explaining what theater should do, why, and how. Over the years, he wrote important plays to demonstrate his ideas and also created his own theater company in order to put his theories into practice.

What Are the Concerns of the Author?

Brecht's theories are explained in several important essays: "The Modern Theater Is the Epic Theater" (1930), "A Short Organum for the Theater," (1948), "A Model for Epic Theater" (1949), and "An Experimental Theater" (1959). Taking them collectively, his line of reasoning goes as follows.

Why Do We Go to the Theater?

The purpose of theater is, first and foremost, to give pleasure; that is, to have a good time. However, what constitutes *pleasure* and what makes up a *good time* are always relative.

We now live in a scientific age: a time of inquiry, of intellectual ideas and research. We are not bound by tyrannies or censorship; we are free to think, to study, to experiment, and to learn continuously. Therefore, what gives us pleasure in this scientific age is the joy that comes from this intellectual inquiry. It's fun to learn. To that end, the theater ought to be a place in which this freedom of thought and this ability to rationalize are exercised.

The *final cause* of a play, therefore, is to make us question the world and make changes. However, when we look at the conventions of today's theater, we find this is not being done.

The Problem of Empathy

When we go into a typical playhouse to watch a typical play, we find ourselves in the grips of *empathy*. This term means that we "identify" with the characters in the play; becoming involved in their situation and subconsciously putting ourselves in their places. We hope, as does the agent of action, that things will turn out fine; we laugh and cry as he does, and we are afraid, as he is, when things get too tense. In effect, we lose ourselves to become somebody else.

What causes this sense of empathy? Two important things: the *conditions of performance* and the *text of the play*.

In regard to the conditions of performance, recall your experiences at a typical performance. You sit in a darkened room with many others. You have become part of a collective mass of people all doing the same thing: staring at the other end of the room in which actors walk around saying lines and doing business in such a way as to convince you that you're watching real life take place before your eyes.

The room is dark, the stage is lit—so all your attention is focused on one place. You don't have to decide where to look; that decision is made for you. If there's scenery, it's designed to look like a real place—there are doors that open and close like real doors, there's furniture to sit on, there's a view out the window. You don't have to figure out where you are; that decision also is made for you.

If the stage is well lit, all the instruments are hidden so the light gives you the feel of real light. If the costumer has done a good job, you see the people in appropriate clothes that add to the illusion. The gowns are in period, the working clothes are distressed, the fashionable rich are wearing today's latest trends. You can believe these are real people in real clothes.

If the acting is good, you forget that you're watching a pretense. You ignore the fact that this is your classmate Sally, and all she's doing is pretending really well. Instead, you feel somehow that Sally is no longer there but has "become" Lady Bracknell.

In short, everything supports the illusion of real life. And almost all of the key decisions have been made for you. All you in the audience have to do, therefore, is relax, lean back, accept it all, and watch to see how it all turns out. You have—along with the rest of the waking dead—become passive. Brecht has described this room as a crowd of sleepers staring blankly ahead, eyes glazed over, mouths slightly agape, looking for all the world like zombies.

The text of the play reinforces this feeling of empathy. The playwright has very skillfully made us believe that the hero is psychologically accurate and very understandable. He's exactly like us. Certainly, we might not ever actually kill our own fathers and marry our own mothers, but we can fully understand the conditions in which Oedipus did these things. He was confused; we're often confused. He's shocked and terrified at the truth; we would be too, because the truth is just horrible, no matter whom it happens to.

In short, empathy tells us that things are the same everywhere. People are the same throughout history. Nothing important really changes. We've met this concept way back in the introduction, when we discussed Aristotle's idea of *purgation*, or catharsis. He said the purpose of plays was to provide us with a feeling of emotional release; that is, we cry with the characters, and when we're done having a good cry, somehow we feel better.

The Universal Versus the Particular

However, Brecht claims that this effect is dangerous. If we watch a play and say to ourselves, "Ah, yes, that's the way it is," we somehow accept the lack of change as inevitable because we see events as being universal, rather than rooted in a specific time and place. We take life to be constant, not relative.

The reason this is dangerous is that once we begin to accept the sameness and the inevitability of things, we no longer question them. We give in to the way things are, believe the same set of ideas, and abide by the same set of laws as always. But what we don't do—and this is the heart of the matter for Brecht—is question them. Rather than show us things as they always have been—which makes them seem permanent—Brecht says plays should instead show us things as they once happened in a particular time and place—which makes them relative. This process is called *historicizing*: placing events in a specific time and place. Then, once we historicize an event, we see that things are not always the same. And once we see that things are relative, we see they are changeable. And once we realize that things are changeable, we leap to the delightful conclusion that we can change them. And once we realize that we can change them, the next logical step is indeed to go right out and actually do it.

Again, think of Oedipus. Normally, we perceive how the gods forced him into his blind alley; he had no recourse but to obey and suffer the consequences. It is the way things are, and we come away thinking, "fate is a terrible thing."

But suppose we historicize the play. Suppose we compare in our minds the world Oedipus lived in with the world, say, of the Reformation, or the Renaissance, or the 1920s, or the 1960s, or the world of your own generation—all periods in which people called into question the "power of the gods" or did not believe in them at all. We realize, then, that gods are not inevitable. Therefore, Oedipus did not have to believe in them; he did not have to obey something he didn't want to; he did not have to put out his eyes. And—wonderful conclusion, this: Perhaps we don't have to either.

To repeat: It's getting to that conclusion—"perhaps we don't have to either"—that's the purpose of Brecht's theater.

Alienation

Because the theater should be a place of intellectual inquiry, it is counterproductive for the audience to sit passively in the dark. Rather, we must be kept wide awake and detached so that we can constantly evaluate what we see and hear. We must be kept *alienated*—in the sense of being separate and removed. The German word for this concept is *verfremdung*. One of the aims, therefore, of Brecht's theater, is to jolt you out of passivity and get you to see things in a new way.

There are many instances in our real lives in which this sort of alienating jolt occurs: If you were a teenager, for instance, and your parents suddenly told you they were getting divorced because your father was cheating on your mother, you would probably never look at your father in the same way after that. If you read the newspapers and learned that the president of the United States was guilty of sexual indiscretions or secret insider-trading, you might call into question everything else about him and perhaps the system that elected him, and that in turn might make you question whether democracy itself works. Your new line of reasoning might become very long indeed.

How do we bring about this jolt in the theater? By casting aside all the conventions of production and all the typical devices of the well-made play. Brecht recommends several specific techniques, which he calls *verfremdungseffects*—which translates as "alienation effects." The rest of this chapter describes these.

However, unlike the organizational method we used in other chapters of this section, we're not going to examine these effects through the lenses of plot, characters, or language. For one thing, it's easier and clearer to look at them in a different way. For another, changing our approach this late in the game is itself a sort of *alienation effect* of its own. You'll have to understand what these devices are and then decide for yourself which category they fit into. Welcome to the world of epic theater.

What Are the Alienation Effects of Production?

Clearly, Brecht is an advocate for highly presentational theater. He wants to remove all those devices that create the illusion of reality.

We don't necessarily have to lower the house lights; people should understand that they're in a public place with other people. The audience has become a group of individuals who have come to hear a story, and we need to tell this story in the simplest, most direct way possible. For instance, if a character has to open a door and go into the kitchen, we do not need to see this happen before our eyes. All we need is to be told that she does. If the character goes into a forest, we don't need to see the woods. We just need to be told "this part of the story takes place in a dark forest."

Thus, we don't need any more scenery than absolutely necessary: perhaps one make-believe tree on the stage, or a sign by the proscenium that says, "This scene takes place in a forest"; or even, as it was in Shakespeare's theater, just the reference one character makes in a speech, "Hey, this forest is scary!" will be plenty for us. Extensive scenery only lulls us into empathy.

We don't need to hide the backstage area. No need to put up masking pieces that prevent the audience from seeing into the wings. After all, we *are* in a theater, and theaters have wings. The space isn't important; the story is. We don't need to hide the lighting instruments, for the same reason.

We don't need elaborate or realistic costumes. All an actor has to do is say, "I'm a poor immigrant from China," and we'll accept the fact. We don't need a realistic style of acting either. If the character that Sally is portraying suddenly breaks into tears, we don't have to see Sally, our friend, struggle to pretend to shed real tears. All we need to hear is that at this point of the tale, the woman is sad; Sally could simply say, "I'm so sad about this that I just have to cry," and we'll take it from there.

In all these instances, you see, Brecht has removed all pretense from the experience. The point is, the more alienated we are, the better we're in a position to critically think about what we're being told.

A great deal of contemporary stagecraft borrows heavily from Brecht's theories. Modern designers often use minimal scenery, suggested costume pieces, and even revealed lighting to enhance the theatricality of their productions.

What Alienation Effects Appear in the Text?

Please note that the eight devices we'll discuss are part of Brecht's mature theory. Not all of his plays use them. Many of his early and later works fall into styles that are in many ways like realism or expressionism. The "purest" examples of his true epic theater appear in such plays as *Mother Courage and Her Children*, *The Caucasian Chalk Circle*, *Galileo*, and the one we will use for a detailed example, *The Good-person of Setzuan*.

This play was written in 1939, some years after Brecht had escaped Nazi Germany and was living in Hollywood. It is set in a mythical Chinese village. Three gods have descended from heaven in search of a good person. They attempt to find lodgings for the night, and the only person who will take them in is a young prostitute, Shen Te. The gods don't know her real occupation: They only see what they want to—that she is a "good person." To reward her, they give her a generous sum of money, which she uses to set up a tobacco shop. However, the cruelties of life complicate her story. Try as she may, she has trouble holding onto her money. Clever thieves try to trick her out of it. Poor relatives come and demand help. She finds herself falling in love with a no-account flier who needs money to buy himself a job. In order to protect herself from these demands, she goes into disguise: She dons men's clothing and calls herself "Shui Ta"—ostensibly a clever relative of Shen Te's. Once she's in this persona, she can be hard, calculating, cold—and successful.

Events become rather complicated: She becomes pregnant by the flier. In order to save her reputation, she agrees to marry a wealthy butcher. As she grows closer to term, she must work harder to disguise her twin identities. She is forced at one point to "dispose" of Shen Te—but then, as Shui Ta, is charged with her murder.

At the end, Shui Ta is put on trial. She removes the disguise and tells the court—the judges of which are the three gods—the truth: When she tried to be good, she was poor and met disaster. It was only by being bad that she could get rich and survive. It all came down to the question of, What do people require in order to be good? How much of our energies can be spent on good works when we have to earn a living and stay afloat?

This theme is typical of many of Brecht's greatest works. As a Marxist, he saw many of the evils of a capitalistic society and despaired at the lengths people would have to go to in order to survive. Therefore, he wanted his audiences to see how money brings out the worst in us, often forcing us into prostitution, theft, betrayal, or deception. He used many of the following alienation effects, therefore, to keep us thinking as we watch the events unfold.

Plot

When you first hear the word *epic*, what probably comes to mind is an "epic adventure" that you see in a contemporary big-budget film. A superhero gets involved in hair-raising adventures because he has to save the world. He travels from place to place, doing daring deeds and struggling with monumental foes. The story ranges over time and location. It has size and scope; it has romance; it has, finally, a happy ending.

This is only partly what Brecht has in mind. He uses the term *epic* in its more classic context: a story told in verse by a storyteller, who narrates a series of adventures involving a great deed of historical importance. In this sense, *The Iliad* and *The Odyssey* are epics, as is the tale of Moses in the Pentateuch, or the *Epic of Gilgamesh*, or *Beowulf*, and—in some respects—the story of Jesus in the New Testament. In Brecht's world, this struggle is against repressions imposed by social codes, politics, or—most often—economic necessities. A typical issue in his works is how a character balances morality with survival.

To that end, *Goodperson* shows Shen Te trying to survive despite the machinations of her neighbors; she has to find a way to be good in a society that's run by dollars and cents. *Mother Courage* is about a woman who tries to earn a living by peddling goods during the Thirty Years War; the play shows us the kinds of sacrifices she has to make. The plots, therefore, are epic in the sense of involving great social forces.

Structure

An epic play takes place over a long period of time, often travels through a variety of locations, and involves many activities. That the story should be large makes sense, since the forces that oppose the central character are large and his journey is huge. However, Brecht never tries to put the whole story onstage; he only shows us certain key scenes in which particularly important crises occur. These crises may be days, weeks, or even years apart.

Therefore, the play often will have a somewhat disjointed feeling to it as it progresses through a series of typically short scenes. In *Goodperson*, for example, we can list the scenes as follows:

Prologue: the gates of the city
Scene 1: a tobacco shop, three days later
Scene 1-a: inside a den made in a sewer pipe, belonging to
   Wong, a water seller, four days later
Scene 2: the shop, some days later
Scene 3: a city park, some time later
Scene 4: the square in front of the shop, some days later
Scene 4-a: in front of a curtain
Scene 5: inside the shop, some time later
Scene 5-a: in front of the curtain, some time later
Scene 6: a private dining room in a restaurant, some time
   later
Scene 6-a: Wong's den, some time later
Scene 7: the yard behind the shop, some time later
Scene 7-a: inside Wong's dream while he's sleeping
Scene 8: Shui Ta's factory; the scene bounces around in time
   and space, covering several months
Scene 9: the shop, now become a fancy office, much later
Scene 9-a: Wong's den, some time later
Scene 10: a courtroom, some time later

Because so much territory has to be covered, Brecht does not spend much time in any one scene. He shows us only the important parts of the story—that is, the parts that will best express his meaning—and leaves the rest out. Notice one more thing about the list above: Only in a few instances does Brecht ever tell us exactly how much time has passed. In most cases, we just know that we've moved to a different time, but exactly when something happens is not usually as important as the fact that it did happen.

Compare this somewhat choppy structure to a play like Chekov's *The Cherry Orchard*. Each of its four acts takes place in one (albeit different) location. People come and go, but we're always in the same place. We spend time with these people in the same atmosphere. The characters have long conversations, or become involved in emotional crises, or work out their relationships. Things seem more or less "stable"; and this stability in turn creates a mood that weaves a spell around us and makes us feel deeply for the characters. The consequence, of course, is that we don't stop and think how very silly these people are! We don't evaluate them or criticize how they've conducted their lives or what kind of world they have allowed themselves to live in.

You will not find this mood in Brecht. The choppiness of the structure works to alienate you and make you think.

Storytelling: Drama Versus Narrative

Since we only see the key scenes in the story, the audience often has to be brought up-to-date. Brecht needs to find ways to bridge the gaps. He does this often by sending a character to the edge of the stage to tell us. These narrative passages describe for us what other writers might have felt it necessary to show us. They also give us a chance to step out of the action briefly, detaching our emotions from the scene that we've just seen and removing us once again from empathy.

Thus, at the beginning of scene 1, Shen Te steps forward to tell us that three days have passed, the gods have given her money, and she's bought a tobacco shop. At the beginning of scene 5-a, she again steps forward and now reveals intense and emotional information: about how the old people have turned sick with worry over money they've lent her, how her boyfriend refused to care about it, how she fell into his arms and forgot about her debt, and so forth. Clearly, some very important story points took place offstage, and obviously more than one very emotional scene must have occurred. However, we don't need to see any of it. It would only get us too emotionally involved.

The narrative elements keep the bare story moving. Furthermore, since classical epic poems were always narrated, this is one additional reason for Brecht's naming his theory *epic theater*.

Telling What's Coming

Suspense is a story element, not an intellectual argument, and Brecht would much rather present us with the intellectual argument. Thus, time after time, he finds some way of letting the audience know at the beginning or in the middle of a scene exactly what's going to happen next. Therefore, we can stop worrying about what will happen and can instead pay attention to why or how it happens. We can study the situation as though we were studying a scientific experiment or listening to a legal brief.

Sometimes these advance notices are given to us directly by a character in the play. In some plays, as in *Mother Courage*, Brecht calls for a screen to drop down, displaying a text that tells us what's going to happen in the forthcoming scene. In *Goodperson*, in her speech at the beginning of scene 1, not only does Shen Te tell us how she got the money but also that she intends to start doing a lot of good with it. She mentions, in particular, that she hopes to help Mrs. Shin, the poor woman who sold her the store. When the scene begins, however, what happens? Mrs. Shin comes in and, jealous of Shen Te's luck and suspicious of her motives, begins to attack her, demanding payment. Following that, many of Shen Te's relatives, having heard of her success, come around to get some of her money. More and more, they pile into the shop, demanding she help them. She finds herself sinking under this greed. At the end of the scene, she steps forward and speaks a small epigram to the audience that says, essentially, When too many people try to climb aboard the lifeboat, watch how quickly it sinks and they drown!

The content and the ending of this scene are certainly clear and powerful. But Brecht has made it harsher because he has already had Shen Te tell us how much good she had hoped to do. As we watch her sink under the demands of her greedy kin, we keep in mind this earlier hope, and the scene becomes doubly ironic. And the point is made more painfully clear.

Interruptions Within the Scene

This is one of Brecht's more unusual innovations. We've seen how a character will speak directly to the audience at the beginning of a scene, bridging the narrative gaps and foreshadowing what's ahead. But Brecht sometimes has the character do this in the middle of a scene as well. Just as the action seems to be going hot and heavy, Brecht will insert some alienation effect that once again jolts us out of empathy. A character may step forward and deliver a line or a short speech about what's happening and what it means. A character may suddenly sing a song, the subject of which makes some ironic commentary on what's going on in the scene. Or a character may recite a short poem or deliver an epigram that sums up the point.

To illustrate, let's examine scene 3, which takes place in a city park. It's a spring evening. Yang Sun enters; he's the young man who wants to be a flier, and Shen Te will fall in love with him. This is the scene in which they first meet.

He first encounters two prostitutes, who will have nothing to do with him, since they know he's too poor to buy their services. (Knowing that prostitutes earn money through sex, can we see in this little exchange a Brechtian comment on capitalism?)

Shen Te enters, and the prostitutes ask her bluntly if the rumor is true that she's going to marry a rich man for his money. She admits that she's on her way to see him, when Yang Sun angrily interrupts their conversation and tells them to leave. He tells them this isn't a brothel, it's a park! (It's interesting that Brecht would conflate those two ideas: making a park a place where whores go to earn money, rather than a place of innocent enjoyment. Is this another comment on capitalism? And you certainly have noticed how Shen Te, who had thought she was through being a prostitute, is about to go and prostitute herself once again by marrying for money. What price goodness?)

The prostitutes leave, and Shen Te sees the bit of rope that Yang Sun has with him; she understands he's going to commit suicide. She tries to talk him out of it. As she does, it begins to rain, and they take shelter under a tree. Standing there, he confesses his failed dream and bitterness to her. They are clearly falling in love.

Imagine such a scene in a romantic comedy and how filmmakers might make this tender and beautiful. We'd have soft lighting, with gentle rain in the background. We'd have lush romantic music playing underneath. We'd have close-ups of the handsome leading man and the gorgeous leading lady. We'd soon find ourselves becoming caught up in the emotion. Maybe we'd cry a little bit?

But Brecht won't have any of that. Suddenly, Shen Te steps to the front of the stage and delivers a short poem to the audience. She tells us that such evenings are dangerous, because in the grip of the emotion of the moment, a miserable man might give in to his mood and commit suicide—which is, of course, exactly what's happening. In other words, Brecht, through Shen Te's poem, is telling us, watch out for the power of emotions; they'll cloud your reason (which is what his epic theater itself is all about).

Shen Te steps back into the scene, and the two continue to fall in love. She explains that she's conflicted about her upcoming marriage, and he confesses that he's very thirsty and tired: He couldn't make love to her even if he wanted to. All very tender and lovely again.

But now Wong enters. Wong is a poor man who earns his living by selling water. He steps forward and sings a song to the audience, "The Song of the Water Seller in the Rain." In what sort of realistic play would you ever find somebody entering from nowhere in the middle of a scene and start to sing? And notice what the song says: He bemoans the fact that nobody is going to buy water, especially when it's raining, and they can get it for free. He imagines how his life would be better if there were a severe drought; then the people who ignore him now would come pleading for his wares, and he would be a rich man. (Another sly, ironic, and subtle attack on capitalism.)

As he finishes his song, the rain stops. Shen Te runs to Wong and buys a cup of water from him to give to the flier. She doesn't just ask him, however; she recites another little poem, in which she tells Wong that she would rather buy water from him anyhow because, as the title ironically tells us, she wants to be a good person.

The scene ends as she runs to give the water to Yang Sun, only to find that he's fallen asleep.

The scene is loaded with emotional undercurrents: young people falling in love, a woman coming to a decision about her life, the bitterness of a ruined salesman. At the same time, the scene is rich with symbolic and thematic material: water as a symbol of life, renewal, baptism, and health, on the one hand, contrasted with water as an image representing tears, merchandise, obstacles, and danger, on the other hand. And through it all, Brecht continues to jolt us out of empathy, pointing out to us exactly what the scene is trying to say and providing ironic ways to make sure we hear it.

Topsy-Turvy Elements

Remember that topsy-turvy elements are a major comic device that turns things upside down, reversing our usual expectations. Brecht loves the irony provided by this device. Who is considered by the gods to be the one "good person" in the province? A prostitute. What sort of gods are these anyway? Stupid, fallible, and weak; they can't see the truth, they get beaten up by robbers, they refuse to listen to Wong when he asks for help, and at the end, they pay no heed at all to Shen Te's impassioned confession. And what topsy-turvy element forms the basis of the play itself? The idea that in order to do good works, you must resort to lies, betrayals, deception, and sometimes even robbery.

Raisonneur Moments

To make perfectly sure we get the message, Brecht often has characters step forward and tell us exactly what the message is, becoming the unmistakable voice of the author. *Goodperson* has many examples. Here are a few:

In scene 4-a, Shen Te steps forward and sings "The Song of Defenselessness," in which she says, without any subtlety, "You can only help one of your unfortunate brothers / By ruining a dozen others."

In scene 5, when she realizes that her flier has betrayed her, she turns to Mrs. Shin and tells her, essentially, that times are hard and the city is cruel, but we must cut each other's throats in order to survive, and we must especially do without the confusing treachery of love.

Brecht writes an epilogue to be spoken directly to the audience. The speaker says, essentially, Yes, we know we've failed to provide a happy ending to this play, but this is how the world is. If you want a happy ending, you have to help us write it. You have to find a way to create a world in which good people can *be* good. *You* must find a better way.

Social Dilemmas

Time and again, Brecht arranges his story so that his central character is faced with a terrible dilemma, having to choose between what she wants to do and what she is forced by society to do in order to survive. Sometimes he will tell us in advance that the decision is coming, so that we can see how the historicized scene plays out. Often he will interrupt the action within the scene to have somebody come forward, spell out the dilemma, and ask us, What would we do in that situation? At other times, he will allow the scene to play itself out and only make us wonder about it later.

One extremely important example of such a dilemma involves Shen Te and her friend Wong, the water seller. At one point, there is an altercation in the street: a quarrel between Wong and a Mr. Shu Fu, a wealthy barber. The barber jabs Wong with a hot curling iron, giving him a nasty burn. Wong wants to press charges and calls out for a witness. Nobody steps forward, until Shen Te herself volunteers to say that she saw the event, although she didn't. She's prepared to commit perjury to help her friend—once again, showing that sometimes a good thing can only happen through bad ends.

Later in the play, it happens that the wealthy barber has wooed Shen Te and is willing to marry her. Just then, Wong comes on the scene, looking for Shen Te to keep her promise and testify against the barber. In the scene, Shen Te is in her disguise as Shui Ta. When Wong asks for Shen Te, "Shui Ta" tells him that he was mistaken: Shen Te did *not* see the event and will not help. Wong is left hanging in the wind. Shen Te has been forced by circumstances to choose between doing the right thing or the economically necessary one;

she has no choice but to adopt the survival mode. Indirectly, Brecht is asking us, What would you do?

Brecht applies these eight textual devices to alienate the audience from the story on the stage. By using these techniques, and by deciding not to hide the elements of production, he has found ways to remove us from becoming emotionally connected to the characters. In our objective, uninvolved state, we are the better able, therefore, to understand what the message is and to apply that message to social change.

However, an interesting question often emerges. Do they work in actual practice? As much as Brecht wants us to remain detached, do we in truth actually do so, or do we rather find ourselves getting empathic in spite of ourselves? How detached are you? The question is quite controversial, and for each production and each audience member, there will no doubt be a different answer.

How Does Epic Theater Define the World?

For writers such as Brecht and those who adopt his theories, the so-called world is merely a particular, historicized, society. It has been organized and founded on some assumed premises—such as "the gods are powerful," "money is the most important thing to have," "certain people should have certain powers while others have none," or any number of other ideals. For Brecht in his major works, the basic premise comes from his Marxist thinking: that capitalism creates more evil than it alleviates.

In this way, these writers view the world as though it were the flawed society of a classic comedy. And like that flawed society, it exists only so long as people put up with it by believing in its assumptions and accepting them as eternal. Therefore, in this view, the "world" is an ever-changeable social contract that exists as it does only because people allow it to.

Questioning the Play

1. What is there in the life and times of the author that helps give the play meaning? What is its efficient cause?

2. What *raisonneur* characters and speeches seem most important? What do they all say in common?

3. What do the lyrics of the songs, if there are any, tell you about the author's message?

4. What particular social dilemmas are the characters placed in? Why do they make the choices they do? Are they right or wrong? How are they influenced by the assumptions of their societies?

5. What unique topsy-turvy elements help reinforce the play's ideas?

16

Postmodernism

Background

Like tragedy, *postmodernism* had one specific meaning when it first appeared but gradually became a catch-all phrase describing a wide range of styles. It was first used in the 1940s to describe the innovative style of architects like I. M. Pei; in the 1950s and 1960s, it described the work of novelists such as Thomas Pynchon and Jorge Luis Borges; it also described the work of painters like Andy Warhol, Roy Lichtenstein, and Robert Rauschenberg, who took for their subject matter popular commercial icons, comic strips, everyday objects, and collages.

Many of these artists were influenced by the ideas of contemporary philosophers who conceived innovative theories about the nature of our world. These theories gave rise to a variety of literary movements, such as modernism, structuralism, and poststructuralism. If you took a course in modern critical theory, you would study them in detail. Rather than try to examine each, this chapter will look at some assumptions they have in common and will use the term *postmodernism* to refer to any avant-garde writing style that rejects traditional assumptions and seeks to define the world in new ways.

The Assumptions of Liberal Humanism

In order to fully understand these "new" assumptions, we need to first review the old ones. Scholars have used the term *liberal humanism* to categorize six basic ideas.

Literature Has Meaning for Us: The Concept of Essentialism

We read a book or see a play because it is supposed to speak to us; it is supposed to have meaning. However, this assumes that there exists such a thing as *meaning* in the first place. In other words, you and I and everybody else are supposed to be able to perceive the same thing when we examine the work: We can all agree upon some basic element it contains. We came across this theory when we spoke of *denotation* and saw, for instance, that all chairs—no matter what kind they might be—share the common attribute of "sittability." This attribute is its essence, that common, basic thing at its core. Thus, the essence of air (foul, fresh, smoky, or clear) might be what: Its breathability? (Maybe not.) Its being lighter than earth? Its oxygen content? What can we all agree is its "essential" quality?

Reducing a complex phenomenon to its basic core is known in literary and cultural criticism as *essentialism*, and this basic attribute is the matter that allows a bridge of understanding between you and me.

To ascertain the essence of a work of literature, we have to first agree on two qualifying premises:

First, we are all alike. Somehow we agree on something that affects us all in the same way. (We all know what it means to *sit*, or if we don't know, we could learn; that is, we could eventually reach a common ground.)

Second, objects do, in truth, possess essential qualities. There really does exist something at the core of things, and if we can only reach it and share it, we can safely talk about them without entering the world of the absurd.

Thus, when we look for the meaning in *A Glass Menagerie*, we assume that there is something at its core that you and I can see the same way because we are alike in some way. (Whether or not this assumption is right is a question we'll raise a little later.)

Language Functions as a Way of Describing Reality

Words are our trusty servants; they help us understand each other. We saw how important this idea was in our discussion of language; but we also learned, in our discussion of absurdism, how dangerous words can be.

Literature Has a Purpose

The purpose of literature is to communicate to us something the author has in mind. It is a vehicle for connecting us to each other.

There Exists an Author of the Piece Who Is Removed from Us

Somebody with an intelligence sat down and created this work. However, that person is not here; she exists or existed in another time or place. And even if that person were in the same room with us, she'd still be separated from us because, at bottom, we are all living inside our own minds and can never truly be connected.

The Work Consists of an Idea That Began in the Author's Mind

The work we read or hear was created by someone, and in some way, that person is reflected in the work. We say that there exists an "author's voice" at the bottom of the work. When we read *Hamlet*, we are somehow hearing Shakespeare's voice.

The Author Holds a Position of Authority over Us

The author has the idea; we have to learn it. The author sent the message out; our job is to receive it. Communication is a one-way street.

In summary, liberal humanism distinguishes between *author* and *audience* but assumes that the two can connect with each other through a work of art that uses language effectively to convey meaning.

The Assumptions of Postmodernism

Postmodernism contradicts or rejects all of these assumptions and offers some of its own.

Essentialism Does Not Work

The nature of reality is not found in the substance of things. There are no essentials; a chair can never be the same for all of us because we are different people. We can never truly remove connotations. Furthermore, trying to find the essence of some ideas is to cheat them: What, for instance, would you label as the essence of *woman*, or *truth*, or *beauty*? It can't be done.

Signs and Signifiers

Therefore, the nature of reality is not within the object itself. True reality is formed by the *relationships* between things and the *vehicles* we use to describe them. This is true for words, people, and events. The reality of a chair exists through the dynamic of three concepts:

- *signifier*—the sound or image that forms the word we use; the squiggly lines on a page or the waves in the air that reach our eardrums
- *signified*—the object that the word refers to; the physical thing with four legs that we sit on
- *sign*—the sound/image itself that combines the two concepts above; the piece of language that is the thing we call a "word"—in this case, *chair* or *silla* or *chaise*

Our reality, therefore, consists not of things but of the signs we use to talk about things and the assumption that we all translate the signs into the same signifieds.

However, there is another tricky quality of signs. While part of what makes up their signifiers are those objects or ideas for which they stand, another and equally important part are those things that the object is *not*. Thus, a chair is what it is partly because it is a thing to sit on; but it's also not a bed, or a ladder, or a floor, or a table. Light is what it is partly because it is not dark; and truth is what it is partly because it is not a lie.

When we use any word, we are constantly implying this relationship between what a thing is and what it is not. As we interact with the world around us, looking at things and examining concepts, we are continually categorizing and labeling them by their separateness.

How does this relate to analyzing plays? It means, simply, that from the postmodernist standpoint, it might not be so important to examine the total play as we've been doing. It's useless to search for "how the end differs from the beginning" or to seek meaning in the "pattern." What does matter is how any one section relates to those sections immediately surrounding it. Is it like those sections? Is it different? Is one funny and the next sad? And what feelings, ideas, or associations emerge from this relationship? In short, is the part more important than the whole?

Grand Narratives and Small

In the same way that we assign meaning to words, we also assign meaning to certain concepts. We agree that certain kinds of attitudes and behaviors all represent the same thing. Thus, we see an American flag, which immediately becomes a symbol for us (i.e., a sign). It represents our American way of life (signified), which itself stands for certain assumptions we make about that way of life—such as "it's a free country," "every vote counts," and so on (signifiers). We don't question such ingrained beliefs but take it for granted that "America leads the way in the world," "Abe Lincoln was a hero," or "marriage must involve a man and a woman." We call such large assumptions *grand narratives*, and when we accept them, we are actually subscribing to essentialism.

However, these assumptions aren't always true. There might be times when America does not lead the way but in fact follows; or instances in which old Abe was less than heroic, perhaps even cowardly; or where two men form a long-lasting and loving bond. Therefore, when we think in essentialist terms, we run the risk of making mistakes; it is more important to see any event in its own context. Once again, the part is more important than the whole.

Language Forms the Bedrock of Our Existence

We noted in an earlier chapter that words are not real things but only symbols. Language, therefore, only represents or suggests reality. Some philosophers take this relationship between words and reality even further and believe that words actually create reality. As we gradually learn what a word is, we often subconsciously alter our behavior to fit the definition (rather than the other way around). When you were a child, you were taught that *daddy* meant one person and *mommy* another, and then, as these people behaved in certain ways, you learned to define what we might call "daddyhood" and "mommyhood" by these behaviors. Then you learned daddy was a *man*, and mommy was a *woman*. Perhaps one day, when you were crying, somebody said to you, "Stop crying. Act like a man!" In your head, you figured out that meant, "Adapt your behavior so you fit the mold established by that person you call *father*." In a way, therefore, the definition created you. The same applies to ideas such as *fair, good student,* or *American citizen.* In such cases, the word comes first, and we adjust our reality to fit.

The Purpose of Literature Is Not to Show Us Anything but Rather to Engage Us

Plays aren't about *communicating* at all; rather, they should be occasions for bringing us together and challenging each other. Bertolt Brecht's idea of alienation follows from this premise. Other writers create works that are often confusing and obscure, inviting the audience to make its own sense of the piece; that is, to meet the writer halfway and together create what it means. We in the audience should have a sort of "dialogue" with those on the stage. The moment should be interactive, not one-way.

There Really Is No "Author"

There is no true author, in the sense of someone who controls the meaning of the work, because every moment in literature or in the theater is really an interaction between somebody sending and somebody receiving. The true meaning of any work is the relationship. The truth of, say, *David Copperfield* stems from how the reader perceives and reacts to what Dickens wrote. If the reader thinks Davey's an idiot, then *idiocy* forms part of the meaning for her. If people in the audience have to struggle to understand what a character is saying or violently disagree with something that happens, that struggle and that disagreement form the true meaning.

The Author Is No Longer "Privileged"

It follows logically from the above that the "author" has no privileged position as creator. It further suggests that what the author says is of less account than our *perceptions* of it.

Characteristics of Postmodern Plays

Given these basic assumptions, plays that we'll broadly categorize as *postmodern* will typically have one or more of the following characteristics. Please keep in mind, however, that we are reducing a complex subject to some very basic points in order to help understand very unusual plays.

The Idea of Meaning Is Greatly Altered

Whereas a liberal humanist writer wanted to show us the world as she conceived it and therefore "put" meaning into the work, the postmodern writer wants to engage us in a collective activity. Only part of the meaning in a piece is provided by the playwright. You supply the rest. So, it's true now more than ever: There are no right or wrong answers in play analysis.

The Structure Departs from the Conventional Well-Made Play Pattern as We Know It

The playwright is more interested in how one scene relates to another than in how they contribute to an overall unity. The idea of *beginning, middle, and ending* ceases to have importance. A play-wright may completely disregard chronology and causality and bounce all around in time and space, so that she juxtaposes scenes that are all alike or completely different in their emotional quality, their rhythm, how they contrast one aspect of a situation with another, or how they look at the same situation from several different angles.

Paula Vogel's play *How I Learned to Drive* provides an example. The story is about how a girl named "Li'l Bit" grew up to be the hard woman she is. As she narrates, we gradually learn that her uncle abused her. However, we don't see the story unfold as a well-made play. Vogel connects the scenes according to their thematic or emotional relationship. A scene with the family leads to a scene with the uncle as he teaches her to drive, which contrasts with a scene in her high school, which contrasts with scenes of her gradually learning about dating and sex from parents and peers, and so forth. Running through the whole play is a voice-over announcing the rules of "safe driving." After a while it becomes clear in the scenes that follow how these "rules" are broken—in a symbolic sense, of course.

There May Be Multiple Narratives Interacting with Each Other

While the well-made play structure disappears, writers have not given up on stories per se. Mac Wellman, Charles L. Mee, Suzan-Lori Parks, and other writers just look for different ways of telling them.

In some plays, there may be several stories going on, and the play bounces back and forth between them. Len Jenkin's *American Notes* takes place, supposedly, on one night in a small town. Over the course of the evening, we become engaged in the activities of five different people, none of whom are connected to each other, except geographically or emotionally. A scene of hope contrasts with one of despair; a scene of "normalcy" contrasts with one that's a little bizarre; while a scene of two people falling in love contrasts with one in which a woman realizes she's been deserted.

As is the case with language and myth, the parts are more important than the whole.

The Plays Are Characteristically Fragmented

Realizing, again, that meaning comes from the relationship of parts, we see that fragmentation appears in several ways:

Plays Operate on Many Levels of "Reality"

An outstanding example of this multilayered structure is Len Jenkin's play *A Dark Ride*. One almost needs a tour guide to travel its labyrinthine twists. Here's a brief description.

We begin with a translator describing the problems he's having with a document about a woman named Margo. We then see Margo herself in her story, as she reads aloud to herself a book she's reading, about a jeweler in a mental hospital. As she reads, we see some of the events she reads about. But then she puts her book away and reads a postcard from a friend who's a thief.

We then see the adventure the thief is describing on the postcard, as he goes into a restaurant and meets Ed, with whom he gossips; meanwhile, a television set shows us a news broadcast about a general, and then suddenly we are with the general as he tells us his story.

So far, we've gone down five different levels of story. As the play continues, one keeps melting into the other. The translator and the thief wind up being in the same story; the jeweler and the general likewise; the folks in the restaurant wind up chasing the folks in the other stories. Along the way, Jenkin tosses in another two levels, and the whole cast winds up in the same story, dancing in a hotel room in Mexico.

(A hint as to Jenkin's purpose here is that the object the jeweler is working on is the object that the thief steals and that the general wants: a brilliant diamond. Thus, Jenkin is writing a play of many surfaces, as a well-cut diamond has many facets.)

The Plays Are Often Pastiches

Pastiche means a collection of things from a variety of sources, all tied together randomly, as in a collage. Such plays are an assortment of various moments, images, speeches, or interactions, all of which provide the audience an overall impression of something, while at the same time inviting them to figure out for themselves just what the overall connection is.

A useful example is Charles L. Mee's play *Bobrauschenbergamerica*. The play is a motley assortment of scenes that supposedly reflect typical American myths: a birthday party on the back porch, a trucker musing on his life, teenagers falling in love, a couple in marital difficulties, a guy making a home movie, his movie, a small-town murder, and so forth and so on. As does Vogel, Mee juxtaposes one image after another; and it helps to know that Robert Rauschenberg is an important postmodern artist whose paintings are also collages—images juxtaposed.

For Mee, an important part of the work is not the text itself but the process by which it has been created. Another important part is the active effort the audience has to expend to "understand" it. It was not written as plays usually are—one man sitting at his desk and speaking through his "voice." Rather, it was developed in a workshop with other actors, all of whom—along with others—contributed to the piece. He credits many artists whose work he has incorporated into his text, including Rauschenberg, Walt Whitman, William S. Burroughs, John Cage, Merce Cunningham, and Allen Ginsberg. The "author" has effectively disappeared from the picture altogether.

The opening of the piece provides further insight into its pastiche nature.

An empty stage covered by a blank canvas. The actors come out to remove the canvas as music starts. A chicken slowly descends

from the flies on a string. It has a sign around its neck that
says: bobrauschenbergamerica. A voiceover is heard:
. . .
What I like to do is . . .
I start with anything,
a picture,
these colors,
. . .
I like these colors,
. . .
or I might have an idea about something I'd like to try with a
    shoe,
or maybe I just feel
happy.
. . .
Look,
everything overlaps doesn't it?
Is connected in some kind of way . . . ?

In Some Plays, There Are No "Scenes" or "Stories" at All

Beginning in the 1960s, several important theater practitioners and
companies emerged that attempted to do away with narrative.
Rather, they created events that bonded performers and audience
into one collective experience. They used ritual, poetry, mixed-
media, dance, and other nontextual elements to create what was
then called a "happening"—an event whose meaning was the event
itself. Some of these groups included Richard Foreman and his
Ontological-Hysteric Theater, which produced works that were
basically a series of tableaux and moments that illustrated Foreman's
own meditations on life—with no narrative connection at all. He
was inviting the audience into his own mind and encouraged them
to meet him halfway.

Richard Schechner formed a group called the Open Theater,
in which he and an ensemble collective created pieces that were
closer to dance and ritual than to drama. These pieces explored the
various ideas, attitudes, emotional responses, and moods that were

associated with one central subject. *Viet Rock* mused on the war; *The Serpent* was a series of near-ballet sequences centered on the Book of Genesis; and *Terminal* was a collage of scenes, sketches, monologues, dances, and spoken verse, all of which explored some aspect of death and dying. None of the works would be classified as "plays" as we've defined them; all of them require the audience to put together for itself a connective thread between a series of moments. The fact that they were prepared by an ensemble, rather than written by one author, is symptomatic of their breaking away from convention.

In Many Plays, "Characters" as We Know Them Do Not Appear

In chapter 4, we noted that one way to look at characters is to see them as though they were "real" people. However, if you review the previous chapters on styles, you'll note that there's been a gradual shift: Characters in plays have become less and less lifelike. They are either distortions of real people, symbols of dreamlike or spiritual forces, incoherent nobodies buffeted around by an absurd world, or simply *raisonneurs* for one political agenda or another.

This gradual shift away from characters as "people" continues in postmodernism in several ways:

They may be parodies of characters in other plays or genres. In this sense, the characters are often comic exaggerations, recalling to mind the original ones and making a comment on them, as are the characters in Eric Overmyer's *Dark Rapture* and *In Perpetuity Throughout the Universe*. Among the clichés that Overmyer pokes fun at are hard-boiled detectives from novels, mysterious oriental figures from 1940s movies, sinister women, and nefarious gangsters.

They may be puppetlike figures. The characters may be moved around by the author from one scene to another, showing different sides of a mood, an issue, an idea, or an attitude, as do the characters who serve as political symbols of African American culture in Suzan-Lori Parks's *The America Play*.

They may be only animate bodies or part of a visual tableau. We saw examples of this in Charles L. Mee's play *Bobrauschenbergamerica*, described above.

They may be part of an ensemble, performing a balletlike ritual. Instead of speaking and interacting, the characters may simply move, chant, dance, pose, and so forth.

The Plays Are "Language-Based": Their Primary Focus Is on the Words, Rather than on the Story or the Characters

We noted earlier that one of postmodernism's basic philosophical assumptions is that we define our existence by the words we learn. Language is also the only vehicle we have for connecting with one another. What we didn't indicate previously is that many writers see an important difference between spoken and written language. We need to say a little more about this difference in order to appreciate why the work of writers like Mac Wellman seems so dense.

Between the two forms, spoken and written, only one is alive and the other dead. When we read what's been written down, we are forcing ourselves, in a sense, to enter into an impossible dialogue with a mind that isn't there. However, when we speak and listen, we are alive, fully engaged, in the present, creating an event, interfacing with another living creature, and making reality happen.

Writers of language-based plays are interested in creating vehicles for this kind of event to happen. They don't want their language to be "frozen" as part of a one-way event but rather to serve as an invitation for the audience to participate in the moment. To that end, writers such as Wellman like to spin elaborate riffs on language, to have their characters invent their own language, to play with slang and dialects, or to have different kinds of language intermix in different parts of the same play.

In one of his plays, *Whirligig,* Wellman uses language to create a strange reality, one that may or may not exist. A girl is talking to a man, and they are each trying to ascertain who the other is and where the other is from.

MAN: My world is sand world of Plinth.
GIRL: Yeah, and I'm Madonna.
MAN: What is "Madonna?"
GIRL: What's "Plinth"?

MAN: Sand world of Plinth. Far away. Very old place filled with stuff. Colorful tents, gasbags, flying sandwiches, as you say. Slight accident. Advanced nuclear fusion project. We call it "the big boo-boo." Gizmo out of control on thirty-seventh level. Kablooey. No more jamboree on Plinth. No more Plinth. Sadness. We are scattered among the planetoids. Thousands, thousands upon thousands. Most dead. No more rock 'n' roll. . . . Hop from one planetoid to next, as for instance, Mitake mura, Dikan'ka, Elmer.

GIRL: What's Elmer?

MAN: Elmer is a small world in the local argot, of where I am from. Name of Elmer is different. I am Xuthus.

GIRL: Funny name, Xuphus.

MAN: Not Xuphus. Xuthus.

GIRL: I won't tell you my name.

MAN: So be it. *(Pause)* The surface of things is obscure. (act 1, scene 1)

The man might very well *be* an alien; his reality is defined by words the same way ours is.

At the same time, these writers are aware of the pitfalls of language that we've described elsewhere. But they like to skirt the dangers of language, to point out the absurdities of it, and to call our attention to the effects it has on us. Overmyer sprinkles his plays with wordplay. In *On the Verge*, the ladies who are bushwhacking their way through the jungle talk about "whacking the bush." One woman continually falls into malapropisms, saying, "I am delicious. I mean delirious. Not delicious."

Writers also take advantage of a little-considered part of language: silence. When actors do not speak, they are still engaged in communication; they are inviting the audience to sit with them in the moment, being present with the actors in the same event. Suzan-Lori Parks has invented a whole vocabulary of silences. She calls for her actors to pause and just "be" for a moment and writes into her text such directions as this:

LINCOLN
BOOTH

LINCOLN

BOOTH

BOOTH

And she explains:

> This is a place where the figures experience their pure true simple state. While no "action" or "stage business" is necessary, directors should fill this moment as they best see fit.

The Plays Involve Metadrama or Metatheater

The terms *metadrama* and *metatheater* mean that the art form (i.e., the play or the theatrical production) makes comments on itself. In a spirit of fun and self-parody, the work seems to be saying, "Look, I know I'm all make-believe; so do you. So let's not pretend but just have a good time." The playwright will make specific reference to things that are actually happening, pointing out to us their artifice and engaging us as fellow-conspirators, all working together to find some meaning in this abstract piece. Thornton Wilder's work does this often. In the beginning of his classic *Our Town*, he has a character called the Stage Manager (a very theater-based person, indeed) announce right at the top, "The name of this play is 'Our Town.' It was written by Thornton Wilder; produced and directed by . . . In it you will see . . ." The actor is supposed to fill in the gaps with the names of the actual personnel involved in this particular production.

Plays Often Make Reference to Other Genres or Other Plays

Fitting in with the postmodern characteristic of pastiche, writers often parody or pay homage to other kinds of literature or even to specific works. One reason for this is to debunk old-fashioned literary conventions, to mix (as in collage) elements of one idea, culture, form of art, or language with those of others—all in order to rearrange our thinking about things we take for granted.

One form of literature often parodied is the detective story, primarily as seen in such hard-boiled novels as the work of Dashiell Hammett and in such film noir classics as *The Maltese Falcon*. There is something about the struggle between good and evil that intrigues writers. We've seen a trace of this in Jenkin's *A Dark Ride*, which centers on a jewel thief. Eric Overmyer builds an entire play, *Dark Rapture*, as a mock detective story. In another of his works, *In Perpetuity Throughout the Universe*, he combines several influences: It's a play about some weird characters involved in writing and publishing a sort of crime novel, while at the same time, it's the crime novel itself.

Plays Are Often Concerned with Reevaluating a Grand Narrative

Remember that a grand narrative is a sort of national myth that we take for granted. We assume it has universal meaning. Postmodern writers invite us to question these "meanings" by debunking these myths, showing them to be untrue in one case or another. Again, it's a matter of looking more closely at the part than at the whole.

In several of her plays, Suzan-Lori Parks does this with the figure of Abraham Lincoln. She uses his historical association with slavery and the plight of the African American to comment on the position of blacks in America today. In both *The America Play* and *Topdog/Underdog*, a black man takes a job impersonating Lincoln in a sideshow, reenacting his assassination for the delight of white people. In the first-mentioned play, she refers to Lincoln as "The Greater Known," and the black man as "The Lesser Known," thus commenting on the myth of Lincoln as a "savior," whose myth is stronger than his reality.

In his play *American Notes*, Len Jenkin writes what's almost a parody of *Our Town* and the mythical portrait of New England America that Wilder's play presents: Wilder shows us several days in the life of a town. Jenkin shows us one night in the life of a town. Wilder's characters are noble, simple, decent, respectful, and so on. Jenkin's characters are hysterical, lonely, frightened, slightly insane, and often crooks. Wilder takes us, in act 3, to a cemetery, where the dead are waiting patiently and silently for some great apotheosis to happen. A character in Jenkin's play also anticipates death, but in this manner:

> What do you think, Pauline? You think the world's gonna end tonight? Twenty ton hypernuclear bomb drops right through the

roof of the motel. We're safe in the eye, sitting here in a great crown of fire, while in the sky, all the dead from all over America, each one a thick paper of ash—and the fire dies and the wind dies and they float down from where they been spinning in heaven, drift down slow and easy, doing their last dead dance in the air. (act 2)

Another way in which writers demythify grand narratives is to mix what's called "high culture" with "low culture." We typically place a major distinction between what some would call "real art" versus "commercial." However, when Andy Warhol paints pictures of Campbell's Soup labels, or when Roy Lichtenstein paints large canvases that are parodies of comic strips, they are mixing these kinds of cultures. When Eric Overmyer writes about publishers working on a novel, we assume that to be a "real" play, while a corny detective story would be only pulp fiction—and yet he puts the two together in one work, *In Perpetuity Throughout the Universe*.

The Plays Are Often Infused with a "Carnivalesque" Feeling

One of the characteristics of postmodernism is its sense of fun and play about the work. Writers enjoy parodying previous works and will often use comedy as a weapon, as George Bernard Shaw used to do. Or the writer will pause in the action to take a character on a side journey; or she will put the character into some outrageous situation that is clearly meant to be a parody of some cultural institution or another. And when we spoke earlier about language, we made the point that some of these writers love to play with words in different ways.

Eric Overmyer's *On The Verge; or, The Geography of Yearning* is about three Victorian ladies who ostensibly are exploring some unnamed tropical jungle. Along the way, they meet a variety of zany characters: a German airman with whom they have tea, a troll who is really an actor in their play, various natives who speak English. In the second act, they suddenly find themselves traveling through time: They wind up in America in the 1950s; they meet Mr. Coffee (a plantation owner, not a kitchen appliance) and find themselves in a diner where "Rock Around the Clock" plays on the jukebox; and they run into Madame Nhu (a mysterious figure from the inscrutable East); Gus, a gas-station attendant; Nicky, a lounge entertainer in a club in Cuba; and so forth. Overmyer tosses in parodies of Victorian melodramas, Shavian comedies, 1930s Tarzan movies, 1950s beatnicks, song writers, philosophers, and even a parody of his own work. Specific cultural references leap in and out, daring the audience to recognize them: The Actor's Studio, Cool Whip deserts, the *National Review*, Velveeta Cheese, the "Hand Jive," and so forth. At one point, a lady gets a message in a fortune cookie, which another lady refers to as "fanmail from some flounder"—a direct quote from *Rocky and Bullwinkle* cartoons. The whole play is basically a tongue-in-cheek send-up of a wide variety of cultural icons and references—saying, in essence, that there are no "pure" art forms anymore, so let's just have fun with collage.

In other plays, this circuslike mood is enhanced even further: Carnivals form part of the setting itself, and characters often behave like the circus barkers, masters of ceremony, hucksters, and con-artists one might find there. Or the characters may actually be part of a sideshow. In Parks's *Venus*, the central character (an African aborigine) is hauled away to London to become part of a freak show. Mac Wellman's *Harm's Way* has its central characters spend time in a circus. And Len Jenkin's *A Dark Ride* is specifically intended to give audiences the feeling that they are on an amusement park ride; the last line, spoken by an unseen voice, says

> Those who wish to ride again, stay in your seats. A man'll be around to take your tickets. Those getting off, step lively. Exit to your left or to your right. (act 2)

How Does Postmodernism Define the World?

We've taken a rather lengthy and perhaps complicated look at postmodernism, trying to fit it into a historical tradition and to look at some of its assumptions. Contrasting it with liberal humanism, we've seen how it basically contradicts all of our previous assumptions about literature, culture, and plays. We can conclude by saying that writers who use the techniques of postmodernism depict the world as an artificial set of structures based upon the paradigm of language. Language is arbitrary; we make of it what we need. It is essentially symbolic: There exists an uneasy correspondence between signifier and signified. It is relative: Meaning always depends on the context in which a word or speech appears. However, it is through language that we define ourselves. Thus, the whole concept of what a play means is altered; it no longer "means" an idea that comes from the author to us; it means the event in which it occurs.

Questioning the Play

1. Overall, which set of assumptions do you think the play rests on, those of liberal humanism or those of postmodernism?

2. Does this play seem to be working toward an essentialist meaning? If so, how do the conventional elements of play analysis help you find it? If not, what do you think the center of interest in this play is?

3. Examine the play by its parts. What kind of fragmentation does the author use? How does each section relate to those around it? What meaning might be implied by these relationships?

4. Does anything in the play seem to reflect a grand narrative? Are these "myths" and general beliefs necessarily true?

5. Does the play tell one story, or are there multiple stories in the play? How are they related?

6. Is there a narrative at all, or is the play structured as a dance, a ritual, a celebration, or a collage?

7. If there is a narrative, what do the characters seem like? Are they behaving in psychologically realistic ways? Or are they meant to be parodies or puppetlike figures in the service of some idea or other?

8. How is language used in the play? To what extent does it seem to exist in order to make the audience clarify the play for themselves? To what extent does it seem to exist for its own sake— as puns, wordplays, elaborate riffs, and so on?

9. Does the play seem to be mixing "high culture" with "low culture" in any ways that you define those terms? If so, why?

10. How does the spirit of fun or carnival work in the play? To what extent is the performance itself the point of the piece?

Glossary

Index

Glossary

Act of Shame: one of the elements of classic tragedy, this refers to any deed that violates an important part of the universal moral code and sets the tragic pattern into motion.

Agent of Action: one of the functions a character might fulfill and often called the *protagonist*, this is the character who has a main goal in the play and whose efforts to achieve this goal drive the action forward; that is, the character who "makes things happen."

Alazon: a type of character found in classic comedy who acts as a blocking force, standing in the way of another character achieving his or her goal. Also referred to as a *blocker*, this character's ideas and attitudes are often the issues that the author disapproves of.

Alienation: a feeling of disassociation between members of the audience and the characters in the play, a sense of being apart and separate from them.

Alienation Effects: several devices used in epic theater to keep the audience from feeling empathy with the characters, to set up a feeling of disassociation between the audience and the play. Its purpose is to keep the audience from becoming so emotionally involved that they forget to think about the issues underlying the events.

Antagonist: one of the functions a character might fulfill, this is any person who stands in the way of the agent of action achieving his or her goal.

Blocker: see *Alazon*

Blockhead: one of several kinds of "fool" who appear in farce: the fool who is defeated by nature.

Buffoon: a type of character found in a classic comedy who is typically ancillary to the main action but provides a source of laughter and often serves as a foil or a confidant to a more central character.

Character-Driven: describes a play in which the interest lies more in the revelation of character than it does in the unfolding of the plot.

Characters: one of the six elements that Aristotle lists as the components of an overall dramatic action and that refers to the people who inhabit the play.

Climax: the point in a well-made play at which the story turns in a major new direction and the agent of action faces a final obstacle and often makes final choices. The climax may contain a reversal and/or a recognition.

Cognitio: a moment (typically in a classic comedy) when a secret is revealed, a discovery is made, or something unknown comes to light. This discovery is often the climax of the play.

Comic Relief: one of the functions a character might fulfill, this refers to a person who provides a temporary moment of comedy within an otherwise tense or frightful scene.

Complex Plot: an Aristotelian term that refers to a plot in which a character undergoes both a reversal and a recognition.

Confidant (or Confidante): one of the functions a character might fulfill, this is a person whom another character confides in or delivers information to.

Crisis: a moment in the play in which a character is faced with a new development or unexpected problem (an obstacle) and must undertake a new strategy.

Dotard: one of several kinds of "fool" who appear in farce: the fool who is defeated by time.

Efficient Cause: one of Aristotle's four ways of considering the perfect form of an object, this describes what went into its making. In play analysis, this includes the life and times of the author and the social/theatrical conventions of the time.

Eiron: a type of character found in a classic comedy who interacts with the *alazon*, often enlightening her, removing her objections, tricking her, or in some way removing this obstacle. Also referred to as the *teacher*.

Empathy: the feeling of association that an audience has with characters in the play, connecting them to the emotional life of these imaginary people.

Essentialism: a concept derived from liberal humanism that states that all things can be reduced to a basic, all-encompassing element that expresses that thing's core identity.

Exposition: any information that the audience is given that helps them understand the background of the play, the previous lives of the characters, or some event that has happened offstage.

Final Cause: one of Aristotle's four ways of considering the perfect form of an object, this describes its intended purpose. In play analysis, this deals with how the author wants the audience to respond.

Foil: one of the functions a character might fulfill, this is any person who in some way compares and contrasts with another, who is used to illuminate the personality of other characters, as well as to help dramatize the meaning of the play.

Formal Cause: one of Aristotle's four ways of considering the perfect form of an object, this deals with what the piece represents. In play analysis, this includes the story, or the overall dramatic action.

Hamartia: an element in classic tragedy referring to a bad decision made by the tragic hero, which often causes him to commit an act of shame.

Humours: bodily fluids that were once believed to control the emotions; hence, when any one kind of fluid was in excess, the person would become out of balance. This theory forms the basis for a source of laughter in a comedy.

Idée Fixe: a device for arousing laughter that stems from a character's fixating on some idea and maintaining a foolish attitude or belief no matter what the circumstances; often called a *comic obsession*.

Inciting Incident: the second step of a well-made play, this refers to that person or event that disturbs the state of equilibrium and forces the agent of action to begin to take steps to achieve a goal.

Incongruity: a device for arousing laughter that stems from juxtaposing things that don't normally belong together.

Inflexible: one of several kinds of "fool" who appear in farce: the fool who is defeated by himself.

Innocent Victim: an element of classic tragedy, referring to a character who suffers from the act of shame committed by a tragic hero.

Language: one of the six elements that Aristotle lists as the components of an overall dramatic action, this refers to the choice of words the characters use to communicate.

Liberal Humanism: a conventional attitude toward literature, consisting of several important tenets about authorship, meaning, and purpose.

Major Dramatic Question (MDQ): that central question that runs through the whole play, causing the audience to wonder whether or not the agent of action will achieve her goal. It appears in a well-made play as a result of the inciting incident having disturbed the state of equilibrium.

Material Cause: one of Aristotle's four ways of considering the perfect form of an object, this describes what the piece is made of. In play analysis, this would include such elements as plot, character, setting, and so on.

Metadrama: a play that makes no pretense to be reality; a play that makes reference to the fact that it's a play, such as Thornton Wilder's *Our Town*.

Music: one of the six elements that Aristotle lists as the components of an overall dramatic action, this refers to the sounds the audience hears, either as music or as the euphonics of the language.

Nemesis: an element in classic tragedy referring to a force of vengeance, punishing the tragic hero for the act of shame she has committed; this may be in the form of a character in the play or some idea (such as fate) suggested by the text.

Overall Dramatic Action: the essential thing that a play tries to show, a specific event that occurs over a limited time in which a significant change occurs.

Plot: one of the six elements that Aristotle lists as the components of an overall dramatic action, this refers to the selection and arrangement of the incidents, or how the story is told.

Plot-Driven: describes a play in which the interest lies more in the unfolding of the plot than in the revelation of character.

Presentational: describes a form of drama in which the actors break the "fourth wall" and interface directly with the audience, as does the Stage Manager in *Our Town*.

Raisonneur: one of the functions that a character might fulfill, this refers to any person who, at some point in the play, utters a line or delivers a speech that sums up or expresses the idea of the play; that is, a spokesperson for the author.

Recognition: something that a character comes to understand or learn as a result of the events of the play. Often considered part of a complex plot.

Representational: describes a form of drama in which the action takes place entirely separate from the audience; there is no interaction with the audience, and the imaginary "fourth wall" provides a psychological barrier.

Resolution: those events in a well-made play that occur after the climax and that typically show how the play now moves to a new state of equilibrium; often called the *falling action*.

Reversal: a moment in a play in which a character's fortunes shift, when something happens to change the circumstances and turn the story in a new direction. Often considered part of a complex plot.

Rising Action: the central part of a well-made play dealing with those events and strategies that occur as the agent of action tries to achieve his goal. It consists of a series of crises that gradually build tension as they move towards the climax.

Simple Plot: an Aristotelian term that refers to a story in which neither a reversal nor a recognition occurs.

Spectacle: one of the six elements that Aristotle lists as the components of an overall dramatic action, this refers to the visual impact made by the production. While it may reflect the ideas in the play, it is not necessarily part of the text.

State of Equilibrium: one of the seven steps of a well-made play, this shows us what the world is like, how it is stable, before it is interrupted by an inciting incident.

Teacher: see *Eiron*

Thought: one of the six elements that Aristotle lists as the components of an overall dramatic action, this refers to the ideas that the characters express through language.

Topsy-Turvy: a device for causing laughter that stems from turning things upside-down, reversing the usual order of expectations, as in a slave being smarter than his master.

Tragic Hero: the agent of action of a classic tragedy, characterized by the following: commits an act of shame through *hamartia*, is responsible for other people, goes from good fortune to bad (suffers), and achieves some insight that leads to redemption.

Universal Moral Code: an element of classic tragedy, this refers to that particular set of values or ideals that permeate the culture of the play. The breaking of this is what starts the tragic pattern in motion.

Utilitarian: one of the functions a character might fulfill, this refers to a person whose primary purpose is to help move the plot forward when there is no other or better way; for example, a servant who walks on to deliver a message.

Well-Made Play: originally meaning a play written according to a particular formula in the nineteenth century, it now refers to any play that is structured according to a specific pattern of events and that attempts to show a realistic world behaving in a logical cause-and-effect fashion.

Index

Aaronow *(Glengarry Glen Ross),* 149, 152
abstract terms, 81, 208, 210, 232–34
absurdist plays. *See* theater of the absurd
acting, 141, 245, 248
action: antecedent, 64; and epic theater, 248, 251, 257; and major dramatic question, 48; as part of play, 14, 15, 23–24; rising, 39, 49, 118; static, 209; three phases of, 38, 42; and Three Unities, 192. *See also* dramatic action
act of shame, 102; defiance as, 103, 108; in *Fences,* 104; and innocent victim, 109–10; in *Oedipus Rex,* 103–4, 108; relativity of, 103; in tragedy, 100, 102–3, 108; universality of, 103–4
Adding Machine, The (Rice), 188, 218, 221, 223
advance notice, 253–56
Aegeus *(Medea),* 152
agent of action, 46, 48, 50, 52; and act of shame, 102–3; as bad guy, 150; and comedy, 118; as confidant, 71; death as, 208–9; in expressionism, 222; in farce, 158–60, 167; as function of character, 71; good guy as, 149; versus main character, 71; in melodrama, 142, 145; Nora as, 48, 60; and playing a trick, 119; and recognition, 61; as revealer of information, 72; teaching as goal of, 119–20

agit-prop, 242–43
agon ("struggle"), 32
alazon ("blocker"). *See* blocker
Albee, Edward, 230. See also *Sandbox, The*
Alexandra *(Little Foxes),* 150, 151
Algernon *(Importance of Being Earnest),* 121, 129–30
alienation, 247–58
All My Sons (Miller), 201
All's Well That Ends Well (Shakespeare), 137
American Notes (Jenkin), 267, 429–30
America Play, The (Parks), 270, 274
anagnorsis ("recognition"), 59
Anatomy of Criticism (Frye), 120, 124
Anna of the Tropics (Cruz), 173
antagonist, 32, 70, 71, 109, 119, 142
Antigone (Sophocles), 104
Anya *(Cherry Orchard),* 175, 176
Aristophanes, 121, 155, 230. See also *Lysistrata*
Aristotle, 4; on comedy, 114, 172; definition of *drama* by, 12–13, 23; on *hamartia,* 107; and six elements of play, 31–33; on thought, 31–32; on tragedy, 172. See also *Poetics*
arlecchino (clever servant), 136
Arsenic and Old Lace (Kesselring), 159
aside, 202
aspects of character. *See* connotative aspect; functional aspect; literal aspect
As You Like It (Shakespeare), 164, 169
At the Hawk's Well (Yeats), 210
audience, 203, 242, 243, 248

David Rush is an associate professor and the head of playwriting in the Department of Theater at Southern Illinois University Carbondale. He was named the Association for Theatre in Higher Education's Playwriting Teacher of the Year in 2002. He has had plays produced in Los Angeles, New York, Chicago, and elsewhere. His work has received three Jeff Awards as well as the Los Angeles Dramalogue Award for Excellence and two Emmys. Named a Resident Writer of Chicago Dramatists, he is also a member of Chicago's Stage Left Theatre Company.